# MADE FROM SCRATCH

## THE LEGENDARY SUCCESS STORY OF TEXAS ROADHOUSE

### KENT TAYLOR

**SIMON & SCHUSTER**

NEW YORK    LONDON    TORONTO    SYDNEY    NEW DELHI

Simon & Schuster
1230 Avenue of the Americas
New York, NY 10020

First Simon & Schuster hardcover edition August 2021

SIMON & SCHUSTER and colophon are registered trademarks of Simon & Schuster, Inc.

For information about special discounts for bulk purchases, please contact Simon &
Schuster Special Sales at 1-866-506-1949 or business@simonandschuster.com.

The Simon & Schuster Speakers Bureau can bring authors to your live event. For
more information or to book an event, contact the Simon & Schuster Speakers
Bureau at 1-866-248-3049 or visit our website at www.simonspeakers.com.

*Interior design by Ruth Lee-Mui*

Manufactured in the United States of America

1   3   5   7   9   10   8   6   4   2

Library of Congress Cataloging-in-Publication Data has been applied for.

ISBN 978-1-9821-8570-1
ISBN 978-1-9821-8572-5 (ebook)

*To Mom and Dad—Texas Roadhouse could not have happened
without your unconditional love and endless support!*

*I also want to thank my kids for your sacrifice through the years. While
I missed many events or moments in your lives, your support and
understanding were invaluable to me and the success of Texas Roadhouse.*

*Finally, thanks to the thousands of Roadies who have made Texas Roadhouse
the success that it is today. I am proud to be your partner!*

# CONTENTS

# PREFACE

About a decade ago, we received one of those fortunate phone calls that change your life. We were invited to speak to the leadership team of a favorite restaurant chain of ours—Texas Roadhouse—and there we met the founder, Kent Taylor. As authors, we were fascinated by his rags-to-riches story; as business consultants, we were intrigued by the company's methodology, which (how to say this tactfully?) did seem a tad off plumb.

After all, isn't it a little crazy for a publicly traded restaurant chain with seventy thousand people to mostly hire folks who didn't quite fit into other places or may have messed up a few times? Is it lunacy for a huge restaurant chain to do almost no national advertising? Is it certifiable to keep prices low, even as food and labor costs continue to rise, or to avoid hiring anyone with an MBA or PhD, or to keep the menu basically the same since it opened, decades before?

Does it fly in the face of conventional sanity to not allow coats or ties in the home office (to the point of keeping scissors handy to cut neckties off visitors) or to have a founder, chairman, and CEO who dresses like he's part of the landscaping crew?

Probably. To all of the above.

Welcome to Texas Roadhouse, where crazy works. What they've cooked up is an island of misfits that's cool with being different. They

1

are wild about giving their employees love and respect, and encourage store managers to spend considerable amounts of time and money on employee fun, outings, contests, and trips (in fact, for their silver anniversary, they took three original twenty-five-year kitchen employees from the Clarksville, Indiana, store number one—dishwasher Robert, cook Mike, and hot-prep guy Dan, as well as their spouses—to San Diego, and gave them a backstage visit with rock star Steven Tyler before his show).

They're crazy about having fun, but their people are serious about following meticulous recipes, always use fresh food, and make everything from scratch every day. Each store has an in-house bakery serving up some of the world's best rolls—hot out of the oven, and sent directly to guests' tables as they sit down. Each restaurant has in-house meat cutters who spend hours each day in frigid thirty-six-degree rooms to ensure each cut is perfect.

While many of their competitors have cut back on making things from scratch, portion sizes, or the number of people helping serve or prepare food, Texas Roadhouse has added more people into their restaurants, including food runners and more hosts. They've upped the portion sizes on the free peanuts, rolls, and honey cinnamon butter.

It's a MADHOUSE!

Most of the insane ideas at Texas Roadhouse originated with some rogue store manager or Roadie, Kent told us. Roadhouse's blossom sauce was created by Jeff White, store number one's kitchen manager, who challenged the founder, in the company's first year. Jeff said he had a better recipe for a dipping sauce than the one Kent had come up with, and darn it if he wasn't right. They let employees and guests try it. Jeff's sauce sent Kent's packin' and is still being served today. As for Jeff, he's still an important player in the company twenty-seven years later.

Brian Judd, managing partner of store number one in Clarksville, Indiana, told us that Kent from day one encouraged any and every crazy idea. They tried Mexican food for a few weeks (didn't work), they had a stage for live country music bands over the bar (guests wouldn't leave, so adios bands), they delivered food in shopping carts in the mall and held crazy contests for employees.

The employee line-dancing the chain is famous for also came from rogue manager Neal Niklaus in Ashland, Kentucky, who started encouraging his Roadies in 1998 to do the boot-scootin'-boogie every hour. A home-office big shot told Kent he needed to visit that store and quick, as they were "breaking the rules." Kent drove the three hours to Ashland and fell in love with line-dancing. "Heel, toe, do-si-do, come on, baby, let's go boot-scootin'!" Doesn't it just make you wanna hook your thumbs in your belt and kick up some peanut shell dust? Kent thanked Neal (who is today one of the company's five regional partners) and spread his great idea to the rest of the stores. Kent then had a coaching session with Mr. "Don't Break the Rules," who didn't quite fit and chose to leave the company six months later. Probably ended up working at a bank.

## CRAZY-GOOD RESULTS

Sales at store number one were just over $2 million annually in the first years, with most other early stores averaging even less than that. In fact, three of Kent's first five stores would fail and close their doors, heavily in debt. By the end of 2019, Texas Roadhouse had more than six hundred stores and they were averaging more than $5.4 million annually, serving about six thousand guests seven nights a week, with lunch on Fridays in about half of the restaurants and lunch on Saturdays and Sundays system-wide with no lunch Monday through Thursday. Those kinds of numbers are pretty much unheard of for restaurants that serve three meals a day, let alone those mostly open only evenings. Same-store sales increased 4 percent annually (on average) over the last ten consecutive years.

## INSANE GROWTH

As you'll see in this wild, amazing autobiography from Kent Taylor, it only took Texas Roadhouse two decades to become an overnight success. In the early years, restaurants such as Outback, Lone Star, and Longhorn barely paid attention to this upstart steak and rib joint. Kent told us he once met Outback's founder, Chris Sullivan, at an industry conference, and was hoping for the chance to pick the great man's brain for a few minutes. What a thrill it would be, he imagined, but instead of a meeting Kent received a polite rebuff. "When he found out I only had five stores, he said, 'Well, best of luck, kid. Maybe one day you will have ten or even twenty.' " A decade after that conversation, Kent had two hundred locations, and didn't need the Outback chief's advice, but he's always been willing to pay attention to the good and bad choices other restaurant chains make.

## CUCKOO PRICING

Texas Roadhouse has purposefully trailed the industry in menu price increases. It appeals primarily to families who watch every dollar, and such being the case, the company respects their guests' pocketbooks. Each year Kent talks to more than one hundred team members—from market partners to store operators to servers—to determine what to do price-wise on every single menu item. Sometimes they do make adjustments upward, and sometimes they lower prices here and there to make things more attractive to guests. They have twenty regional menus with different prices around the country. What works in Adrian's closest location of Sandy, Utah, may not work in Chester's closest store in North Plainfield, New Jersey, so pricing decisions are made regionally—on the front lines—rather than in corporate finance or marketing departments. Such contrarianism is a consistent trait of Texas Roadhouse.

## UNHINGED PROFITABILITY

You can't buy shoes with percentages . . . you buy them with cold hard cash, Kent told us. Most companies we've studied in this space are so focused on labor-cost percentages, labor productivity, schedule models, theoretical food costs, and other ratios that they lose focus on making a buck. Tell us, what's sane about that? Texas Roadhouse has always been first and foremost about its people and guest satisfaction. They know that if they take care of their Roadies, they'll take care of guests. After that, the measure the company strives to achieve is top-line sales growth, because they know that will drive profitability. Such talk as this would drive many finance-oriented folks crazy, and it certainly goes against what's taught in many business schools. It's blasphemy to put people over profits, to ignore the percentages and focus on making employees happy. Such beliefs would probably earn you a D or an F, which are exactly the grades Kent earned in graduate business school (that's foreshadowing!). And yet this MBA-dropout's company's net income graph for the last three decades looks like a StairMaster.

## A LEVELHEADED BALANCE SHEET

We find most of the top casual-dining restaurant chains are significantly leveraged, which may not be a bad thing when interest rates are low, sales are positive, and margins are steady. But when times get rough (and they always do), it can be a recipe for disaster. Roadhouse's balance sheet is built to protect the brand over the long haul. Going into the 2020 crisis, the company had more than $100 million in cash on hand and was debt-free—giving leaders more freedom to make smart decisions for the success of the business without having to worry about short-term issues like making interest payments.

## MADCAP STOCK PERFORMANCE

TXRH is traded on the Nasdaq, and no one can argue with results for lucky stockholders. Investors over the long haul have been rewarded by the leaders' contrarian approach as the stock price has steadily increased along with the company's addition of more restaurants and increases in same-store sales. Over the ten-year period from January of 2010 to December of 2019, TXRH appreciated by more than 400 percent, crushing the increases achieved by the S&P 500 as a whole.

## OFF-THE-CHARTS GUEST SATISFACTION

Year after year, Texas Roadhouse has also led all full-service restaurant brands studied by the American Customer Satisfaction Index, which annually surveys more than twenty thousand consumers at random. Heck, the majority of reviews of Texas Roadhouse restaurants are five star. The company brass reads all public comments—good and bad—and takes any ideas to improve to heart. We thought this example from Chris in Palo Alto, California, speaks for many customers: "There are many fast-casual steaks elsewhere that are, well, mediocre. You get a better-quality steak here for the money than possibly any other steakhouse. I've had steaks that cost a hundred dollars more that weren't as good. In addition, the side dishes here—especially the complimentary hot rolls—are worth choosing this restaurant. We have to drive across the Bay to visit Texas Roadhouse. Still, it's worth the drive, the traffic, and the toll. Five stars!!!"

Customer reactions like that are why these Roadies do what they do.

## AND THEN, THE PANDEMIC

All was going great for our friends at Texas Roadhouse. The year 2020 was set to be one of the best in the company's history, and then Covid-19 arrived.

To understand how hard the pandemic hit restaurants as a whole, consider the numbers: Within two months of the first U.S. coronavirus cases, 40 percent of eateries in America had closed their doors and eight million U.S. restaurant workers were out of work. The nation's restaurants in those months lost a collective $120 billion.

Kent and his leadership team sprang into action. We were privileged to listen in on their daily Zoom calls during the crisis as they planned their strategy for each day. Their goals were to (1) keep paying their Roadies, and (2) feed America. Both noble aims.

One of Kent's top personal priorities was keeping his people and his guests safe. Since Texas Roadhouse has restaurants in other parts of the world that had already been successfully battling the disease—such as Taiwan and South Korea—Kent picked up the phone and learned what they'd done. Thus, before the rest of us knew about PPE, Kent had ordered massive amounts of gloves, masks, and temperature monitors for his people. "You'll freak out our guests if we wear gloves and masks," was an early pushback inside the company, but as usual, Kent didn't mind swimming upstream. He believed that soon they'd freak out many guests if they *weren't* wearing safety gear. And he was right.

To feed their communities, the chain had to move to one hundred percent curbside dining. The trouble is, Texas Roadhouse is designed to host a party in the dining room every night—providing Legendary Food, Legendary Service, in a sit-down environment. To-go orders, which had never been more than 7 to 8 percent of total sales, would now be everything. Doubling or even tripling the curbside business would be a monumental task. Forget that. To survive, they needed to do ten times more to-go than they'd ever done.

So Kent called his "crazies."

During crisis times, Kent often gets on the horn with his most creative (if not roguish) store managers (they call them Managing Partners), and he asks them what new and innovative ways they are serving their guests. He had little idea then how many completely mad, certifiable ideas they were going to need to survive what was to come.

One market leader had been trying something called Family Packs, a collection of four steaks/chicken/ribs, two sides, and rolls for a low price. He showed the rest of the company how it should be done. Another managing partner was moving five-dollar sliders in the parking lot; another was selling hand-cut steaks out the door. Another had tried a farmers market. Pretty soon, the entire company was implementing these crazy ideas.

You may have read that to keep paying people, Kent donated his entire 2020 salary to frontline employees, then wrote a personal check for a $5 million gift to the company's employee relief fund, called Andy's Outreach Fund, which helps hourly Roadies in need (he's also donating one hundred percent of the proceeds from this book to the fund).

Other company executives followed suit in donating parts of their salaries to workers, and Texas Roadhouse as a company dug into its coffers and sent out several stimulus packages for workers—totaling well over $15 million—also designed to benefit those in hourly roles. When tens of thousands of Roadies got these Texas Roadhouse stimulus checks and posted their thanks online, things got really crazy. Guests lined up in their vehicles for more than half a mile, with many saying they'd heard the CEO was giving up his pay and they wanted to support a company like that. That week, store sales spiked 45 percent.

Over the coming months, Kent and his team would have to negotiate everything from meat-plant closures to worker shortages to dining room reopenings (see Chapter 19 for all the details). All along, while the restaurant industry kept laying people off in droves, Texas Roadhouse was hiring. While casual-dining restaurants as a whole saw a 60 percent drop in traffic during the pandemic, Texas Roadhouse was back in the black in just a few short weeks. Near the end of the year, survey giant TOP Data found Texas Roadhouse was one of the country's most popular casual-dining restaurants in the Covid world, and claimed it was "Dominating America's return to well-known, sit-down restaurants."

Texas Roadhouse's 2020 out-of-the-ashes story puts it in rarefied company.

But we are getting ahead of ourselves.

To understand how this company turned on a dime and survived the pandemic, we need Kent Taylor to take us on a trip back in time—way back—to see the lessons learned along the way, the many missteps taken, and how our now-dear friend—a scrawny, distracted, unlikely kid from Louisville—created anything worthwhile at all.

ADRIAN GOSTICK AND CHESTER ELTON
*New York Times* bestselling authors
January 15, 2021

PART I

# THE SKINNY KID FROM LOUISVILLE

## CHAPTER 1

# BORN TO RUN

The day I set foot on Ballard High School soil in 1969, I was a five-foot-two-inch-tall, bespectacled, 110-pound freshman, barely fourteen years old (and looking all of eleven), and desperate to prove myself. I had just moved to Louisville, Kentucky, from Richmond, Virginia, and figured the fastest way to make my mark was to become a straight-up, albeit tiny, football star my sophomore year. What kid my age didn't know the names Jim Brown or Johnny Unitas? Hell, what girls my age didn't know about Broadway Joe Namath?

I didn't have any real illusions about sporting panty hose on TV commercials (à la Namath), but if I could at least get a foot on the field now and then, in my mind, I'd have it made.

I was quickly cut from the team (big surprise), but somehow I convinced the JV coach to give me a second chance, and I took the final slot on the third-string JV team, playing defensive back. The coach liked my attitude and hustle. The bigger and more athletic kids were told to "work as hard as that punk over there." Think of me as Rudy, just smaller. I then spent the entire year riding the pine at the far end of the bench. I was so far down there I made friends with the *other* team's mascots. After my sophomore season, the football coach sat me down and said, "Taylor, don't even think about coming back next year. If I ever let you get into a game, they're going to kill you. I mean you could die. *I can't have that on MY résumé, now, can I?* Why don't you go try the track team, where a skinny little kid like you can maybe do something!"

The football coach had already spoken to Dick Bealmear, the new young track and cross-country coach, and it was all arranged. I found my new mentor in his broom-closet-size office. Only a dozen years removed from high school himself, Coach Bealmear smiled and encouraged me to take a few laps around the track, away from the refrigerators on the gridiron. Then, after timing me, he confided, "I hate to say this, Kent, but you apparently have no natural speed or talent, so your only likely option is long-distance." I'm like: *Gee, Coach, don't hold back, just tell me straight.*

I finished my first race near the back of the pack, getting lapped by the better runners. And I got laughed at in the process by kids in the stands. I wouldn't say that I was embarrassed. I mean, I sure as hell wasn't afraid to show my face the next day. Quite the opposite. I wanted more than anything to prove to the other guys, my coach, and the grandstand guffawers that they were wrong. To this day, I'm not sure why I stuck it out with the other slow runners on the team, the outcasts, the never-going-to-make-the-big-league guys, but I enjoyed the camaraderie. I was part of a new group. Yeah, one of the nerdy, slow guys, but I had a place, and I was okay with it.

**DICK BEALMEAR,** track and cross-country coach, Ballard High School (1971-77)
Kent was this very awkward kid, and I think at first even half the shot-putters could have outrun him. I suggested he try the two-mile; eight laps around the track, where even the least talented runners could improve if they trained hard enough. I was thinking he could improve from awful to mediocre, which for a lot of kids is a self-esteem builder. Yes, sure the other kids laughed at him; his form was so awkward, and he was so gangly, but he always had this strange positive attitude, no matter the poor result. And, by the way, two years later no one was laughing. Most of those who had laughed at him were now eating his dust.

By my junior year I had a new problem. I had grown about eight inches but had only gained ten pounds, so I was a gangly five-ten, 120 pounds, and easily blown over by a strong wind. I was so tall and skinny I could have slipped through a grate of a storm sewer. My new track coach nicknamed me "Snake." As you are well aware, snakes slither on the ground and get stepped on. Other guys on my team got nicknames like Bull, Muskrat, Bear, Horse, but there was only one reptile—me, the Snake. Based on my lack of speed, they might as well have called me "Worm."

I ran six to eight miles a day the summer before my junior year, more than probably half of the cross-country team, and surprised quite a few people with my improvement. My form still sucked, but I was able to gut it out and slowly that season graduated from the back of the pack to the middle, now joining the average runners and finally escaping the laughter and those comments that plagued me my sophomore year.

After that junior cross-country season, a group of us traveled down to Knoxville, Tennessee, to watch the NCAA cross-country championships, featuring the trifecta of Oregon's Steve Prefontaine, Villanova's Marty Liquori, and Western Kentucky's Nick Rose. I will never forget Prefontaine powering through that tough hilly course, challenging anyone to catch him as he picked up the pace on each rise, daring all comers to endure pain only he was capable of enduring. Steve won the race, no problem, and wore about him afterward an aura of extreme confidence that captivated me. Still, to this day, I can remember that look, as if he wanted his challengers to bring on whatever they had, and he'd find a way to bring that much more.

After the race, I followed him around like a puppy dog as he was interviewed by several reporters. I finally built up the confidence to ask him to autograph one of my brand-new Nike Cortez shoes (Nike's first). Later, I asked Marty Liquori to sign the other Cortez. He was gracious and did sign but chuckled, as Nike was not his sponsor, and said to me, "I'd rather sign an Adidas next time." The following week—after I'd showed off my trophy shoes to many—someone busted into my locker and stole them.

At home, my mom tried to console me, but to no avail. To soothe my soul she clicked on our RCA stereo, which was almost always on at our house. Usually she played Ray Charles, Nat King Cole, and the Drifters, or Motown artists like the Four Tops and the Temptations. Whether doing the laundry, cleaning, or cooking, she always seemed lost in the music, singing along and dancing as she worked. I caught the music bug early, too. I had received my first clock radio in third grade, and after my parents said good night and turned off my light, I would put the radio under my pillow and listen to WAKY AM, a Top 40 channel, falling asleep to the latest hits or *The Casey Kasem Show*.

When my dad came home, the music would shift to Frank Sinatra, Dean Martin, Sammy Davis Jr., Herb Alpert, or Elvis. Music was part of my life from day one. Sometime around 1969 we were lucky enough to get our first color TV. Talk about a game changer. On Sunday nights *National Geographic* came on in full color, showing the wonders of our planet, and then *The Ed Sullivan Show*. Super cool.

That spring, in addition to my many grass-cutting gigs, I applied at the Captain's Quarters seafood restaurant in Louisville and got a job working part-time as a busser: clearing tables, filling water glasses, delivering bread and butter, all in my white busser top and dark slacks. It was my first taste of the restaurant business. The owner, Dottie Mahon, was as nice a human as ever walked the earth, yet she held everyone accountable. For some reason Dottie took a liking to this gangly kid busing her tables. So now I was getting positive vibes from my parents, my track coach, and my new employer, which was very cool.

I had a fairly decent track season—nothing outstanding—but the summer between my junior and senior year I learned what would be my greatest lesson in running, something that would eventually help me in the early days of Texas Roadhouse: that ladies dig letterman jackets. Actually not, just kidding. The lesson was: If you outwork the other guys, you will eventually get where you want to go and be somewhat luckier than others think you should be.

Case in point: One of my teammates that junior year, Steve Bullock, had just won State in the mile run and was one of Kentucky's best cross-country runners to boot, so I asked him if he'd mind me tagging along on his summer training runs. I figured if I chased him all summer I could improve vastly and pick up some of his confidence. And trust me, he wasn't just confident, he was cocky, with a badass swagger to go along with it (albeit in knee-high, white tube socks, but who knew better back then?). I wasn't signing up for full-on cocky or looking to develop said swagger, but I figured a little more confidence couldn't hurt. He said, "Sure," with a bit of a laugh, but I needed to know that his plan was to run twice a day and put in more than one thousand miles that summer, as one of our teammates' dads said he would give a one-thousand-mile T-shirt to anyone on our team who accomplished that feat.

I said, "I'm all in."

Steve said, "Rest up, hell begins tomorrow."

Bullock was a robotic runner, a machine; barrel-chested, relaxed stride, he almost flowed. He had built up his cardiovascular strength from many miles of training along with a naturally strong mental toughness. And for the first month he pretty much dusted me, but with every mile we ran, with every stride, I was reshaping my body. Over a very hot, muggy summer—when pollution levels in Louisville were off the charts thanks to leaded gasoline at twenty-two cents a gallon—I learned to endure more pain than I thought possible. I'd start the run thinking, *Today I'll gut it out and push myself and stay with Steve for three miles of our ten-mile run.* A week later I'd try to hang for four miles. And so on.

I learned to push myself through ungodly amounts of agony, picking up the pace on uphill inclines, which by midsummer would piss Steve off. For me, I was creating a mini race with each hill. I usually died at the top, but it felt good to torment my mentor.

Sometime in late July, we both passed the one-thousand-mile mark, with me cheating and running a third time a day, about three times a week, without Steve. I wanted to put in more miles than he did. At the end of the summer, when we all turned in our logs, three of us on the team had passed the fifteen-hundred-mile mark, which equated to fifteen and sometimes twenty miles a day.

I had been building up the muscles in my heart, and by cross-country season was able to pump blood farther with less exertion, increasing my lung capacity to bring more oxygen to my leg muscles. Most importantly, I was expanding my brain's ability to tolerate pain and push myself beyond what I had felt possible. I was reshaping myself and my destiny.

**DENNIS HADDAD, Ballard High School cross-country and track teammate, retired senior director of product development, running shoes, Nike**
When they started, Steve Bullock and Kent running two-a-days in the summer, it was secretive. No one knew about it. Kent was obsessed with putting the miles in, and it was one of the hottest, most humid, polluted summers I've ever experienced during my years in Kentucky. Not only were they doing two-a-days; I later found out Kent pulled some three-a-days, absolutely crazy. Pure guts and determination.

Now in training with Steve, instead of finishing a dozen *Love Boat* lengths behind him, I was usually within sight at the end of the runs. We both started to realize that with our improved running—plus a few other guys who improved while earning their one-thousand-mile shirts—we just might challenge the two Catholic-school cross-country powerhouses across town and maybe even pull an upset and earn the Kentucky cross-country championship, which would give our new high school its first-ever team state championship. All for the price of a few T-shirts. Go figure.

As that senior cross-country season started, I was approaching six-foot-one and had gained ten pounds of muscle over the summer, drinking protein shakes and adding raw eggs—"Yo, Adrian"—and basically running my ass off. As I began the season, I was finishing in the top seven to ten in the big meets, usually racing against more than a hundred other runners. Steve was typically a few spots in front of me, if he wasn't winning. Most of the elite guys thought I was a transfer in from another state. They'd never heard of me and certainly hadn't noticed me finishing well back in the pack the year before.

With each race, my confidence, speed, and endurance grew. My new strategy was to accelerate up the hills where the pain was the greatest. I found guts and endurance could help me overcome the runners with more pure speed than I had.

Then, about halfway through the season, a miracle of all miracles happened. I beat my mentor, Steve Bullock, in a race not once, but a couple of times—always on courses with the most hills.

Running in the lead pack, if not outright winning races, revealed an unexpected pleasure. Being in contention, dueling with someone to win, it was a rush. *How cool is this?* I felt good, I felt fit, and I was ready to tap into my potential. No substance on the planet can rival a rush like that.

By the end of the season, I was All-State. I had as many medals and ribbons as a Russian general, and our team pulled the ultimate upset in the state meet, despite me (and others on the team) having the flu and not running a great race. Big thanks here to my other one-thousand-mile buddies for coming through.

### DICK BEALMEAR

The morning of the state cross-country meet, over at Creason Park in Louisville, Kent was really sick and having a severe nosebleed from blowing his nose constantly. His lungs must have been full of mucus. I wasn't sure if I should run him, but he insisted. So, I'm like, okay. With the amazing season he had just had, why not? And another one of my boys, Jim Beck, was also sick, as the flu was going around. They both ran and had horrible races. As we were one of the team favorites, I'm thinking we're done—as Kent would normally be in the top five. In a big meet you enter seven runners and score your first five, and whatever position you finish, that's how many points you score for your team. It's like golf, low score wins. We did win, but it was a lot closer than it should have been if Kent had been healthy. In the Ballard High School Distance Hall of Fame, there are many sub-ten-minute two-milers, but Kent still has the fastest time on record in the two-mile category.

Honestly, I should have been home in bed that day, snug in my fifteen-hundred-mile T-shirt. But as miserable as the state final was, running with a 102-degree fever and Kleenex jammed up my nose from the gusher, I felt good that even in the worst condition of my life I was able to compete with the best in the state. It taught me that you can train your mind to overcome any obstacles. Much of my confidence was instilled by Coach Bealmear. He was the first person I'd found in sports who continually used positive, not negative, reinforcement and truly believed that anyone, through the power of thought, could achieve more than they or others believed was possible. If I had a bad race, he always found some positive words and reminded me to push forward and not dwell on the past.

Most people don't think of cross-country or track as team sports, but Coach helped us bond and ensured that even though we competed with each other individually, we truly wanted everyone to be their best, always. We were a tribe—a band of brothers.

The only time that changed was when the race started and running became an individual sport. Then it was me against the clock, me against the world, even me against my teammates, and definitely me against my competitors. For them I had no mercy. I had trained like I had never trained before; and when I lined up and waited for the gun, I was there for one thing: to be my best, endure the most pain, make sure that on every hill or on every lap I would crush my rivals. It was nothing personal.

Before a race, I would usually warm up for about a quarter mile, walk over to my cassette player and put on "Hold Your Head Up" by Argent, and get myself pumped. Just the anticipation of the starter's pistol set my heart to racing. Then off in the distance I'd usually hear my mom cheering something like, "Come on, Kent. Let's go. You can do it," even before the race started.

It was time to be "Takin' Care of Business." BTO was also on my playlist.

---

**MARILYN TAYLOR, my mom**

Do you know what they said to me after he left high school? "Marilyn, it's so much quieter now that Kent has graduated." Because he was a distance runner, he ran around the track so many times, I'd start up in the bleachers and I'd practically end up right down where he was coming in by the end. I didn't miss any meets at all. I was there every single time, cheering him on. I was so proud of him. I think he got his running ability from me. In first grade I was running second behind a boy in a race, and I wasn't about to let him win, so I sped up, grabbed his shorts to slow him down, and unfortunately I pulled too hard and his pants came down to his knees. My dad, who was watching, was not happy at all.

---

My senior year I took home a medal or ribbon in every race I ran in cross-country and track, won my regional (setting a record in the process), and finished third in the state in the two-mile race. My crap luck at state meets continued as I stepped on the yellow line near the start and a judge later disqualified me and another runner. The infraction didn't affect the race in any way. I still ran the entire distance and placed third. But those were the rules. Anyone who followed the sport knew the time I had run. The newspaper, according to my coach, had my name in there as finishing in the top three, just with a little asterisk beside it. So, don't cry for me, Texarkana, I survived.

**DENNIS HADDAD**

Kent really didn't have the speed at the end of the race to outkick somebody, so he was tough during the race and would take the lead and push the pace and wear the others out before the end. In the state meet he was running with John Wright, who set the Kentucky high school record in the two-mile, and Terrell Pendleton, who was a state champion in the two-mile a year before. Kent hung right with them and ran toe to toe with the best two-milers in the state. Kent and another person, Preston Young, got disqualified, but Kent blew it off again. It was out of his control; he had showed everybody. These geeky runners have this competitiveness inside of them. I think it goes back to not wanting to lose. There's a parallel there between running and life. There are similarities between Kent and Phil Knight [founder of Nike who ran at the University of Oregon], who was in the office just down the hall from me. Believe me, Phil Knight wants to beat the competition, all the different brands that are Nike's competitors. Kent's the same way.

Two years of hard work and dedication had paid off. I had the positive assets of a strong work ethic with side effects of increased physical strength, much lower blood pressure, a positive attitude, and a way to find a natural high.

Now I was looking forward to running in college. All I'd had to do was convince a coach at the University of North Carolina—who had never heard of me and had no funding left—to give me a scholarship. How hard could that be?

# MADE-FROM-SCRATCH SIDES
# (WHAT I LEARNED):

- There's a perception that we can't do much about our weaknesses in life, so we should focus only on our strengths. That's BS. We can often get better at something if we love it and are willing to put in the work (running, in my case). In some cases, we can even become outstanding. Weaknesses can become our strengths.
- Find yourself a good coach who will give you honest feedback. Tiger Woods has a coach, Serena Williams has a coach. If every great athlete has a coach, shouldn't every great salesperson/ businessperson/etc. have someone who will give it to them straight on how they can get better and what they can do to push themselves?
- If you outwork the other guys, you'll get where you want to go. Pain is not necessarily your enemy; it teaches you a lot about yourself and what you are capable of.
- Never underestimate the power of a simple but symbolic motivator (even a cheap T-shirt).
- If your team needs you, then show up (I had the flu at the state meet, but my team was counting on me).
- Positive reinforcement inspires much greater performance than fear ever can. Great leaders show their people a better way, i.e., what they can achieve if they strive for greatness.

## CHAPTER 2

# I'VE NEVER LET ACADEMICS INTERFERE WITH MY EDUCATION

Three months later, my legs feeling as strong as suspension-bridge cables and my feet thick with calluses from running more than one thousand miles the summer before college, I sat in the backseat of my parents' 1971 Oldsmobile as we passed through the Smoky Mountains on our way to the college town of Chapel Hill, North Carolina. *Go 'Heels!* Always in charge of music, I had my portable eight-track player beside me, and rotated through the Stones and Zeppelin, playing a few of my folks' favorites like Frank Sinatra and my mom's all-time favorite, Nat King Cole, with a couple of Hendrix tracks thrown in for good measure.

To back up, starting senior year of high school, my dream had been to run on scholarship at the University of Kentucky, both my parents' alma mater. But I'd found no love in Lexington. The Wildcats had a new track coach from Chicago who wanted the best from Illinois, not some chump Kentucky third-placer. So I had tagged along with Steve Bullock on his campus visit in the spring of our senior year to the University of North Carolina, Chapel Hill. My Ballard teammate already had a letter of commitment in his pocket from the Tarheels and was getting a full-ride scholarship. The visit was more of a formality for him; for me, it was everything.

I figured that if they had money to throw at my training buddy, I might score some scholarship cash as well; so I was full-on ready to pile on as much BS as I could imagine. Steve didn't mind me coming along on the spring recruiting trip. He figured it would be a hoot to have a buddy on the team, and we could split ride expenses when we came home for visits (ten hours in my Green Machine, a 1970 used Pontiac LeMans with eighty thousand miles on it, which only took two quarts of oil and three fill-ups to get home).

That spring we had arrived on the beautiful tree-lined campus in the dusky glow of a warm North Carolina evening. UNC was a tidy, ivy-covered institution with collegial redbrick buildings, fine-trimmed lawns, brick sidewalks, and more pretty girls in bell-bottom pants and midriffs than my teenage libido could process. Go 'Heels, *GO*! We found the track coach, Joe Hilton, in his office. He was sixty-four years old, of Native American heritage, and proud that his grandkids called him Chief (which my grandkids call me today, in honor of Coach). As for the nervous-looking, stick-figure kid Steve had brought along, Coach Joe looked me up and down like a dog-show judge might do if he was assessing a junkyard mutt. I met his gaze squarely, panted a little, stuck out my hand to shake (like a good dog), and pulled out my newspaper clippings. He cleaned some stuff from his ear with a paper clip and stared at me for a few seconds, then looked up into outer space for an awkward few more, then finally looked me straight in the eye, ready to deliver the bad news.

Before Coach could get a word out, Steve spoke up for me. He talked about our workouts, my fifteen hundred miles the past summer. "No one trains harder than Kent," he said. Then I finally was able to rapidly rattle off my well-rehearsed and confident pitch: "My best two-mile is 9:25, Coach. That's a regional record in Louisville; and I know I can get faster." I practically yelled it all into his face. The words hung in the air. I stared at the coach, waiting for a response, or possibly a call for Security.

After I made my pitch, Coach said, "Sorry, kid, all of our money is already allocated. But hey, good luck."

I made one last plea. "Look, sir, just keep my number. Y'all got a wait list?"

I can't remember if he said anything else, I was too busy thinking about Plan B—whatever that would be. Would Dottie take me back as a busser? Was the Piggly Wiggly hiring?

Well, shut the front door, will wonders never cease, a few weeks later I came home from track practice and my mom was standing by the door. She said the track coach from North Carolina had called and his phone number was in big block letters on the chalkboard by the new rotary wall phone, the one with the conveniently pre-tangled ultralong cord. I was supposed to call the coach the next day. Mom was talking a mile a minute, bouncing-off-the-walls excited. But we had to wait. I suppose I get my energy from my mom, Marilyn. My mother grew up in Mount Vernon, New York, in the 1940s and '50s, in as diverse a neighborhood as America had. Her 1952 A. B. Davis High School yearbook showed the place as the melting pot of America, and she loved everyone; apparently they loved her as well, as she was voted the Friendliest and Most Happy by her class-mates, not to mention Best-Looking at the Senior Dance. She used her energy in sports—playing everything available to young women at the time—and did well. She even majored in phys ed in college. Pretty cool.

I called Coach Joe the next day at the appointed time. He told me how some big-deal high jumper they'd recruited pulled out at the last minute. He rambled on a bit about the disloyalty of this new generation. Finally, Coach got to the offer. He said the long and the short of it was they were splitting Mr. High Jump's money—one half to me and one half to someone else. He had called Coach Bealmear, heard more of the story of this underdog kid's success so far, and thought, *What the heck; you never know.*

"Are you in, Ken?" he asked. I took a pause, thinking, *Did he just get my name wrong?* But, of course, I blurted out, "I'm in."

*Go 'Heels!*

My mom, coming in from the next room (where I guarantee she was listening the whole time), asked, "Well?"

"Wrong number," I said.

"You little rat, what did he say?"

"I'm in. Half scholarship, room and board," I told her.

She twirled around and let out an ear-busting scream. I laughed, she laughed, and she broke out a few dance moves on the linoleum floor until Dad arrived and asked, "What's for dinner?"

So my mom and dad dropped me off on campus, and Steve and I began our freshman year 1973 during a one-hundred-degree August day. Our tiny dorm room had no air-conditioning, no internet (not invented yet), no television, no beer refrigerator. We had communal phones, communal bathrooms, and communal showers. I imagine most students today would be on the next bus home pretty quickly, but to the two of us, the University of North Carolina could not have looked any better.

At track practice, I decided early on to try my hand at the steeple-chase. It's about two hundred yards shy of two miles, with three-foot barriers—about every one hundred yards—and a twenty-foot water hazard on each lap (which seems to grow taller each time you hit it). I was drawn to the event because with my height I fancied myself a decent hurdler, plus I liked the two-mile distance. In addition, the best guys on the team were running the mile or the 5,000 meters, so I had a better chance of standing out. But to be honest, I liked that it was the first race in a four-to-five-hour track meet. I got my event over and could be up in the stands working on my third beer while the rest of my teammates were still waiting on their event and typically not enjoying the oft-blistering heat of a Carolina day. Track meets can be quite boring, and after a tough race—back before Gatorade made it to Chapel Hill—an ice-cold Bud seemed the logical choice. I was eighteen (the legal drinking age in North Carolina at the time), which might explain a lot. *Hic.*

**DICK BEALMEAR**

Kent kept getting better and better in college. He got into running the steeple-chase, which in track is probably the most grueling race. It's a distance event and you've got to run hurdles and water jumps, and you have to be really mentally tough. I think that Kent's biggest asset is his mental toughness. Most of your good distance runners are generally pretty smart and dedicated and apply themselves, which you have to do to be successful on the track or in business.

Coach Bealmear is too kind, but it took me, as usual, two years to find my stride (pun intended) at UNC. I ran my miles, but I really wasn't pushing myself my freshman and sophomore years like I had my senior year in high school. So, for two years, I was a pretty mediocre college runner. Unfortunately, my training buddy Steve Bullock—probably the most naturally gifted runner I'd ever been around—was having his own issues due to injuries, and we weren't pushing each other like we'd done back in the day.

Still, there was a lot to learn and admire on the team. My freshman year I got to watch Tony Waldrop and Reggie McAfee compete for UNC. Both were sub-four-minute-milers and were two of the best in the world. Waldrop (now president of the University of South Alabama) ran eleven consecutive sub-four-minute-mile races and for a while held the world indoor mile record at 3:55. He had long blond hair like me, and also stood about six feet tall, so I looked like I could be his younger brother. When running around campus in my UNC track attire, I got quite a few "Go Tony"s, and I was good with that!

**TONY WALDROP, former UNC track teammate, now president of the University of South Alabama**

When I had the string of sub-four-minute miles going and had set the record, I never wanted to refuse anyone an autograph. But before a race, I really wanted to be left alone and do the psychology that you always do before a race. So Kent, who looked somewhat like I did at the time, would sign autographs as if he were Tony Waldrop. Let me tell you, it was extremely valuable to me.

While my teammates may have been amazing, I was distracted. I had moved from my cozy house in Louisville—complete with two parents, my younger brother Bryan, a dog, cat, and two fish—to a co-ed dorm complete with cafeteria, no curfews, and plenty of party options on seven floors and four wings. The coaches tried putting all the UNC athletes—football and Olympic sports—into a separate dorm to keep us in check. But the resident assistants went home at seven, so that didn't work very well. My decisions every night were: (a) study and get to bed early, or (b) find someone to listen to music with and have some fun until the wee hours of morning. Tough call.

I had entered UNC in the fall of 1973. The Vietnam War was ending, and I was in the last year to receive a draft number. Yes, Nixon had stopped drafting by then, but people my age were still very nervous. After dealing with draft protestors, burned cars, and building takeovers for the past decade, the UNC administration and campus and Chapel Hill police gave students a lot of leeway—as long as we were not doing any of the above. We could do pretty much anything we wanted, and we did, causing U.S. senator Jesse Helms to refer to Chapel Hill as "Hippie Hill." High noon was kicked off near the Bell Tower with open pot smoking. We held a world record for streaking (which stood for a week) before the University of Georgia broke our mark of nine hundred people running naked across campus. And there were lawn parties with bands, kegs aplenty, and free love in the dorms and local campus parks. Holy cow, did I pick the right decade to go to college, or what?

I was grooving on the scene, with my long hair, tie-dyed shirts, and bell-bottoms—though I went back to straight Levi's after two pairs of bell-bottoms got chewed up in my bike chain (we had to put on a rubber band each time we rode, and who remembers to do that?). Iconic bands came to campus to play (or nearby Duke University or NC State), so I got to see the original cast of the Rolling Stones live for $8.50 (which we thought was exorbitant), Eric Clapton (a more reasonable $5), Emerson, Lake & Palmer, Three Dog Night, Jimmy Buffett, and many others. We enjoyed either twenty-five-cent-draft nights, twenty-five-cent-dog nights, or whatever bar had the best ratios of girls to guys. Steve, still my roommate, took the preppy route, and I chose the hippie route. His side of our dorm room was clean, mine had clothes piled into a shopping cart I had borrowed. There were hippie tapestries around my bed and on the wall. For the first two years of college, I was the guy who wasn't about to let academics interfere with his education. For instance, I took French, but concentrating was tough as our class was 80 percent female (one of my early clues as to the importance of location, location, location). Freshman and sophomore years of dorm living, partying, and listening to music had yielded me a C average, barely keeping me my scholarship.

One day my dad got my grades in the mail and called me up. He was pretty ticked.

"Yes, sir, I'll refocus," I told him.

And as luck would have it, I had to.

In the summer between my sophomore and junior year, I took a job as a camp counselor at Falling Creek Camp for boys in Tuxedo, North Carolina, in the shadow of the Great Smoky Mountains. I watched over a cabinful of prepubescent boys from cities in the Southeast, and would teach them to swim, paddle a canoe, go for hikes, or fish. In my off time I rediscovered my passion for hard work. I trained like I hadn't done since before my senior year in high school. Running in the mountains was refreshing, Zen, or something cosmic—the feel of the misty mountain mornings or a twilight run (after dinner) with the sun going down. Running that summer took on a new dimension for me. That summer love affair with the Smoky Mountains is something that stays with me to this day.

I got myself into the best shape of my life, between my twice-daily mountain runs, complete with uneven trails, bears, and snakes, as well as two-a-days when I went back home to train with a group of runners from various colleges who were home for the summer. That group would normally run after dinner, in Cherokee Park, then meet up at one of Louisville's bars or discos until late.

One night after such an outing, driving home about three a.m. with my running buddies, we came to a stop at a light with no one around. I told the guy at the wheel that he had no guts unless he ran the light, which, of course, he did. Flashing lights soon followed. We quickly tried to clear the air inside by opening windows, and as the deputy strode up smoke rolled out into the night. It was like something from a bad teenage movie. The policeman, somehow, let us off with a warning. He was probably getting off in a few minutes and didn't want to bother with us. Of course, that would never happen today, but we were living in a different time and were as lucky as hell.

By the time my junior year kicked off I was a different runner. I was running stride by stride in training with our best distance guy, Ralph King, at least until he got sick of his shadow and dusted me on the last mile. My junior year in cross-country and track were much improved. I was one of our school's top five cross-country runners. When track season started, I won most of my steeplechase races, clicking off one-after-another seventy-second laps like a machine. I finished second in the ACC championships (I should have won it) and was one of only four Tarheel track athletes who that year qualified for the NCAA championships.

Off the track I was living with two teammates—Tom Ward and Dave Hamilton—away from the dorms, so my grades vastly improved. Yes, my apartment-party skills continued to get better as well, but I wasn't able to devote much time to that pursuit as I was studying more and had a few part-time jobs to pay for dating expenses.

**TOM WARD, former UNC teammate**
When Kent first got to Carolina, I don't think he had drunk a beer in his life. But once he started partying, he became the life of the party. He brought a lot of

energy and just craziness. He'd play air guitar on his leg or just act goofy. He was fun to be around. I think that's what he's done with Roadhouse. I think his idea was to replicate his track family: to get people to have fun and party together and enjoy being around each other. He's also extremely loyal. He's definitely part of the glue that's kept our group of friends together for forty years now.

Junior year I was also able to fulfill a promise. In high school, I had told Coach Bealmear that if I ever won a watch running in college, I'd give it to him. Coach had believed in me when no one else had. He taught me more about myself and the possibilities that were out there for me than anyone. I owed him.

Not only did I win one watch: I won four. One for Coach, one for my dad, one for me, and a very special one for my grandfather (my mom's dad), as he was quite proud of his eldest grandson. He wore the watch until the day he died.

### DICK BEALMEAR

I had completely forgotten about the watch promise, but Kent hadn't. It was one summer when he was at North Carolina and the doorbell rings, and there's Kent at the door with a watch he had won in a race, which just really shocked me. I gave him my very favorite watch back, a stopwatch I had framed special because I timed a lot of outstanding runners with it. And Kent was one of them.

(I still have that watch Coach gave me framed in my home office.)

And so, with things finally all going well for me in school, my senior year I decided to prove that old adage: Frat life can be detrimental to grades and athletics, and exacerbate anything out of favor with your parents. Having spent my college years focused on intense fitness and training—at least my junior year—I decided the only logical thing to do was move into the Sigma Chi house and refocus my intensity on the seven deadly sins—after I found out what the seven deadly sins were.

That was the year a small group of runners organized our first-ever two-mile beer chug for the UNC track team, which became an annual tradition for years to follow. The rules were as such: A runner had to drink six beers during the eight-lap race, but they had to be standing still when they drank each beer and they could only down one can per lap. And if they threw up, they were disqualified. Naturally. All this meant there was strategy involved. Do you get your drinking done during the first six laps and then push it for the last two (with a full belly and a little tipsy), or do you get a head start on everyone by running the first two laps beer-free and then save your drinking for the last six (but that would allow others to catch you)? The whole thing may sound insane, but we took it as seriously as we did any other big race. Winners would often cross the line in under ten minutes, though as we got older six beers became three and two miles became one.

Senior year I kept running (in non-beer races), though not as well as my junior year. I did win a few meets, finished third in the ACC in the steeple, and barely qualified for the NCAAs. Coach Joe sent me to nationals, saying I didn't deserve it, but I qualified, so off I went and had a great time.

The die was cast, however. I had started blossoming into this new social guy. Boy, did I know how to hold a bash by then. When you think about it, that is what I still do to this day. Every single day at Texas Roadhouse we throw a party. But I'm getting ahead of myself! Pass me the peanuts and listen up.

There would be no honors' tassels on my robes—hardly—but I got out of UNC with a degree and a bunch of lessons learned. Like, for example, how to hook multiple kegs together, how to market yourself to college co-eds, and that the steeplechase may have been my event but looking back it was really a metaphor for my life to come. Every lap there are plenty of obstacles. If you lose focus, and miss just one, you break a knee. In the steeplechase, every lap, there's a big water jump—one major barrier that you must deal with.

As I've now lived another forty years, I see that every five or so years of my life is another lap, with a major obstacle I have to power through.

For me, the next barrier was finding a job.

# MADE-FROM-SCRATCH SIDES
# (WHAT I LEARNED):

- Get out of your comfort zone. I was incredibly uncomfortable marketing myself to Coach Joe, but sometimes you have to try new things to get where you want to go.
- When life throws you a curveball (I didn't get an offer from Kentucky), try another avenue (UNC). Don't give up and don't be afraid of rejection.
- Never lose sight of your goal, pay the price to achieve it, and get your butt moving to do the things that will get you there (for me, running my ass off in the Great Smoky Mountains).
- With all that said, remember that sometimes goals change, and that's just fine. Be aware of your evolving passions (like my transformation from runner to entertainer), let old goals go, and embrace the new. And if you can actually make a living at what you love, then more power to you.

# CHAPTER 3

# NIGHT LIFE

With my less-than-stellar GPA, the big banks and accounting firms weren't exactly beating down my door to get to me and my newly minted bachelor's degree in business on their payroll. So the summer of 1977 I did what every ambitious, new college grad does: I took that well-deserved four-year diploma, and with a sackful of gumption and moxie I marched back to my old job working for Dottie Mahon at the Captain's Quarters restaurant in Louisville, this time as a server. A little older and wiser, I became fascinated by how the kitchen processed orders, who on the staff excelled and who sucked, and what specials garnered the most interest. And while it was not what I'd been trained to do in business school—it wasn't high finance, after all—I really did like waiting tables: rushing around, upselling items, and finding ways to entertain the various types of guests. The tips I counted at the end of each shift were a trophy of sorts, proving that I'd done some kick-ass work.

I had been accepted into the University of Kentucky's MBA program and was set to start in the fall of 1977, but I also had one semester of athletic eligibility I'd been granted by the NCAA and was going to return to UNC in the spring of 1978 for a final track season. I'd been injured my freshman year as a result of a bone bruise (inflicted by a dormmate who body-slammed me into my bed during a Friday-afternoon keg party), so I was getting a do-over.

As fall began, I moved to Lexington, went to my MBA classes at UK, and finished the semester with a B average. Not too shabby. Take that, scoffers; I could do this studying stuff.

In the afternoons I trained with the University of Kentucky track team—I knew a few of the upperclassmen from my high school running days—and in the evenings I bartended at a club called the Library Lounge, which was owned by my uncle Bill (more on him in a minute). Bill had struck gold with the lounge; it was the hottest disco in town. Working there, I got to see firsthand a lot of the crazy stuff happening with the disco craze that was sweeping the nation. I'd guess a majority of the patrons were coked up, high on Ecstasy, or blitzed on some other mystery substance. I swore to myself that I wanted no part of that scene; I was happy to take their tip money, though, being a poor grad student.

By spring, I found myself back in Chapel Hill in fair running shape and helped our four-mile relay team win the early-season Florida relays. I also added some quality steeple times to our team's scores at meets. Since I had to be enrolled in UNC, I attended grad school in the phys ed department. I did just enough in class to get by, knowing that within a few months I'd say goodbye to Chapel Hill forever and be back in Lexington working on my MBA.

As luck would have it, midway through the track season I tore my hamstring clearing a hurdle, and when I hit the ground the first stumbling step told me my college running career was done. I hobbled to the house I was living in and flopped on the couch. I was rooming with Tony Waldrop, who was working on his doctorate in physiology, and William "Rose" Roseman, another former UNC track guy. We lived in a house owned by the Chapel Hill Baptist Church rent-free if we locked up the church each night, changed the sermon title on the board out front before Sunday morning, and washed dishes after their Wednesday fellowship dinner. *Pfff, done!* On the other side of the church was the prestigious

Beta fraternity, the campus preppies (think Omega Theta Pi from *Animal House*). These guys loved to have their sorority mixers in the front yard, snapping their fingers and bobbing their heads to bouncy beach music. Just to mess with them, Rose and I would open our windows and blast out Willie Nelson, Merle Haggard, or David Allan Coe. It was me and my buddy against the world—well, against sixty preppy dudes in pastel Izod polo shirts and cardigans twisted around their shoulders.

**WILLIAM ROSEMAN, college track teammate and recent retiree from AT&T**
When I was a high school senior I got recruited to Carolina. Tony Waldrop was the world-record miler and he was showing us around. We met the team and I remember Taylor. First thing he says is, "You want to go out tonight?" That's how it started. He always was up for doing something. He'd pull up in his Pontiac close to the house and it had an *ahooga* horn. All the windows were open because we didn't have air-conditioning, so you'd hear the horn going and you'd stick your head out the window. "All right, I'll be down." Well, we used to go camping a lot in the mountains with a bunch of guys to a spot near Mount Mitchell, but one year the road was closed. It was about midnight and we left a note there saying, "Find us at the next overlook." We were sitting at the overlook, hanging out. It was just beautiful and quiet and then all of a sudden we hear, *Ahooga, ahooga*. Here was Kent coming through Blue Ridge Park blowing his horn.

After the injury, I was unable to run, and with six weeks until the end of school I had three choices: (1) studiously attend my PE grad courses, (2) move back to Lexington, get a job, and prepare for MBA summer school, or (3) blow off classes, party, go to the beach, and do some more camping in the North Carolina mountains. *Hmm, what to do, what to do?*

After I decided on option three, a couple of weeks later the head of the PE department stopped me as I strolled across campus (for the life of me I can't think why I was there), and he demanded to know why I hadn't been to his class for several weeks. "Oh, uh, I've been under the weather,"

I said, and then promised to be in class the next day. Technically, I didn't consider myself lying. I had been "under the weather" at the beach, in the hills, and in my room (hungover). True to my word, I went to his class the next day, then blew it off for the rest of the semester, had fun with Rose and Tony for another month, and finally packed up my old Pontiac and headed back to Lexington.

**TONY WALDROP**

It was my first semester of graduate school in physiology, and I was working three jobs to pay my way through school. When I would get home, I would lock myself in my room. Every so often I would come out and run my hands through my hair and frown. My roommates would meet me at the door and mimic the same actions back at me. When people [find] out that I know Kent, I tell them he would've been one of the last people I imagined going on to the success he's had. He's proved me wrong many times over. His skills are his determination and his focus on making someone happy. I think that's one really important thing he's done at Texas Roadhouse, that it should be a fun experience for everyone.

Back in Lexington, I moved in with Tom Hagan (who ran for the University of Louisville) and Jim Hilliker (who had lived in my neighborhood growing up). They didn't have a third bedroom in their funky pad, so I set up a sleeping chamber in their dining room with a tapestry for a door and a four-by-eight sheet of plywood as a wall to close me off somewhat from the kitchen.

My college diploma landed me a summer job at the Idle Hour Country Club with its forest green lawns and who's who of Lexington blueblood society. I bartended and waited on tables at the pool patio, and endured—on occasion—more than a fair share of abuse from the members' uppity offspring. Still, the pool scenery wasn't bad, and the tips were above average, so I endured.

However, what suffered was my attendance at my eight a.m. summer MBA course. What had I been thinking signing up for that? Pretty soon my other summer courses became problematic, too. It was pool/tips/girls versus managerial-accounting/homework/professors in tweed suits. It wasn't really a fair fight. At the end of that semester, I quit grad school and decided to strike out in the working world full-time. A semester of D's and F's will do that to you.

I landed a job selling industrial chemicals, traveling the byroads of south central Kentucky. By studying my road atlas as I drove, I found all sorts of out-of-the-way industrial facilities, most of which didn't want what I was selling. A few bright spots: I found a rather creepy niche selling to funeral homes, which bought chemicals for their carpet cleaners and whatever else they needed (I didn't ask). But after three months with few new contracts on the books, my career in door-to-door sales came to an end.

As 1978 clicked toward '79, I traded my jacket and tie for suspenders and "flair" as I drifted back to bartending, this time at TGI Friday's. I became proficient at making their froufrou drinks, using both hands independently, with enough talent to make Tom Cruise look like a clumsy busser. An emerging entrepreneurial bug also struck. As I tended bar, I peddled my own wares to the patrons. I would bring in something unique I'd picked up for a couple of bucks in a thrift store—a Richard Nixon or Jimmy Carter mask, for instance—and as the customers poured in from the track in Lexington and got a little tipsy, I'd bring the masks out and ham it up. With a couple of drinks in them, the patrons thought I was a hoot and would hand over twenty-five bucks for the mask as if they were getting a Mickey Mantle rookie card. After a while, I'd wander outside and grab another mask from my trunk. It may sound like small potatoes, but every night I'd add a tidy sum to my take-home tips.

All seemed pretty good to me, but after a few months of pouring mojitos and rum punches, on a visit home my dad sat me down and gave me The Talk: "Son, the friends you graduated with are getting good corporate jobs. They are building their futures. And here you are bartending."

Good thing there were no cell phones then, as such parental scolding couldn't last past the front door. I didn't even have a landline, so Dad could only tell me off if I went home again for a free meal. And I didn't for a while. Still, his words stuck, and I eventually went to see my uncle Bill, my dad's younger brother.

If I'm honest with myself, I get a lot of my risk-disposed traits from my dad *and* my Uncle Bill (not to mention a good amount of seasoning from my mom). My dad may have been more constant than me in working for a single company, putting in thirty-five years at GE, but he was an entrepreneur within the box. He served in various management positions with the company, including general manager of telecommunications, and eventually pitched Jack Welch on starting what they would call the GE Answer Center. His idea: Customers would call an 800 number with all sorts of issues about GE products—my clothes dryer isn't getting warm or how do you get a fork unstuck from the dishwasher drain—and Powell Taylor's team at the Answer Center would find a solution while they were still on the line. Picture Google before Google. The team even got a call one day from a submarine; GE had a lot of products. When Dad retired in 1990, he traveled the world to consult and make speeches on what he'd done at General Electric. He ended his working days with NBC Sports doing the setup and telecom for the Barcelona Olympics. Pretty cool stuff.

As for my uncle, Bill Taylor, he's a serial entrepreneur and always had a new idea to make a buck. He was thirty-eight years old and around Lexington was starting to become a big deal. He had a few dry cleaners, Big Daddy Liquor stores, the Library Lounge, and an after-hours joint called Circus Disco. Over the next two and half decades he would own everything from Christmas tree lots to apartment buildings. In the late eighties, he sold the whole works and moved to Puerto Vallarta, Mexico, and married a senorita many years his junior. He is our family's Papa Hemingway.

Maybe after a word from my dad, in late 1978 Uncle Bill agreed to take me on to run his after-hours club, Circus Disco, which opened

Fridays and Saturdays at one a.m. and closed at five. He paid me $300 a week, and the job allowed me time to train with the Mason-Dixon Track Club. For the first couple of hours of my shift, I worked the door, ensuring all cover-charge cash made it to the safe, then watched the floor, busted up a few fights, and made sure the DJ stayed clean—away from booze, drugs, and girls.

**UNCLE BILL TAYLOR**

There was so much volume and so many problems in the club, Kent learned he couldn't be a perfectionist. You had to swing with the flow because it was just too big of an operation and hectic as hell. On a Friday or Saturday night we had seventy-five employees and over a thousand customers, and they spent a lot of money. If you can make it in the nightclub business, and that type of high-volume club, taking a job somewhere else is lightweight because in a nightclub it's like New Year's Eve every night.

Bill was impressed enough with my work ethic to tag me to open and run another Circus Disco he wanted to put in Florence. No, not the one in Italy. If only! This Florence is in northern Kentucky.

As research, we went to a couple of disco conventions—one in Vegas and one in New York City—to look at lighting and sound systems. It was New York in 1979, so we had to visit the Copacabana and Studio 54, which set new records for me in batshit-crazy stuff going on and the number of people running around totally buzzed. We finished one night at five a.m., sitting on a pile of garbage in a back alley eating pizza and talking about what we'd learned and the wild stuff we'd witnessed.

Bill had wanted to own the rights to the biggest in the world of something, so when we got back to Kentucky he ordered a 102-foot-long copper-topped bar to be put in—because some guy in Australia had a 100-foot-long bar. I talked the handler for the Cincinnati Bengals cheerleaders into having a few of the girls bartend at the opening. They didn't need to know how to mix drinks, they were just there to smile and have fun. And so Circus Disco II opened, and for the first few months, the place was packed. Cincinnati residents made the half-hour drive over to Florence and the joint was hopping.

**UNCLE BILL TAYLOR**

Kent never stopped asking questions and worked extremely long hours. When we were about to open the Circus Disco in Florence, Kent decided we needed an employee manual. The next morning he handed me a manual that should've taken a normal person a week to write–about twenty pages, handwritten–and he'd done it overnight, he did not sleep. He also oversaw construction of the club. He was there before the contractors and after they left at night, six days a week. I knew then that he had a burning desire to become successful and it wouldn't just be working for somebody else but to own a business himself one day.

Jim Hilliker, my friend from the same neighborhood during high school, had joined me there as head bartender, and the two of us rented a house in a quiet neighborhood with our head of security, Dan Merryman. The disco wasn't an after-hours place, but still it was open until two a.m., which meant we wouldn't get home until around three. We'd sit around for a little while decompressing, then finally get to bed about five. It was an insane lifestyle. The loud music, flashing lights, and slick silk shirts of the late-1970s disco scene were not quite my cup of tea, but heck, I was managing a business at age twenty-four, meeting and dating a few ladies, and beginning to figure life out.

Then one night my DJ didn't show. I filled in and climbed up to the booth with our puppy—named Max—that Dan, Jim, and I had just adopted because I've always loved animals and, more so, because girls love puppies. And before too long a cute girl came up to request a song. She saw the puppy in the booth, squealed with delight, and stayed with me for about twenty minutes snuggling the dog and chatting me up. Her name was Laura, and eventually she admitted that she was only nineteen and had snuck in with a fake ID. Being the responsible general manager, I did what anyone in that situation would have done: I invited her to go water-skiing the next day. A few dates later I ended up with a girlfriend who later became my wife and the mother of my two daughters, neither of whom *ever* fake-ID'd her way into a nightclub (at least that's what I've chosen to believe).

**JIM HILLIKER, bar manager, Circus/Maximillian's**

Back in the day at Maximillian's, nightclub times were pretty crazy. The club would be rocking. People back then partied pretty hard, and our after-hour parties at our house would last until daylight on occasion. We had fun to the max, we had a dog named Max, and now Kent has a son named Max. Go figure.

The club's honeymoon period, however, ended before a year was up. Attendance was down and revenue below costs. Bill was freaked and tried various promotions, but to no avail. A disco joint playing Donna Summer and the Bee Gees to northern Kentucky blue-collar folks was never going to make any of us rich. In analyzing radio station data from the area, I found rock and country stations ruled in northern Kentucky— shocker. Disco stations pulled their listenership from nearby Cincinnati, and the Cinci folks were getting tired of making the commute to Florence. Since we couldn't move the club, it became obvious we had to close or reformat.

I pitched Bill on a plan to convert into a rock club.

My uncle reluctantly agreed to give me some money to let me bring in rock bands, rename the place, and make a few cosmetic changes. I suggested the name Maximillian's. I thought it was hip and, more to the point, we already had our mascot Max the dog.

As an aside, one day my son, Max, put something together. He remembered that I'd run a nightclub named Maximillian's with a dog named Max and wondered, "Was I named after the dog or the club?"

I asked, "Which one do you want me to say?" I thought that was hilarious; he, not so much.

I had worked in tandem with my uncle on launching Circus Florence, but Maximillian's was all mine to figure out. It was a crash course in designing spaces for people. For instance, I learned to design in cruise patterns that give people multiple escape routes because after a guy strikes out with a girl (which happens a lot), you don't want to have him walk past her again. Another idea: You don't put booths all on the same level or people end up staring at each other all night. A few inches' height difference here and there between booths can make a big impact on the quality of the evening's experience. Lighting is also vital in a club. With low lighting, everyone looks hot.

We relaunched—with most people thinking it was a new club— and the crowds did not disappoint. In addition to running the place, I became a band talent scout, scouring the area for the best groups. I marketed the place like a demon, realizing we were competing with other rock bars, discos, country music joints, hotel clubs, and even bowling alleys for a limited amount of entertainment dollars. So we pulled out all the stops. We would also put on fashion shows with free cheap champagne to bring in a crowd of women, then open at ten p.m. for the guys to come in. We had country nights, ladies' nights, and a mechanical bull (until it broke). Whatever it took to bring people in, we tried it.

While checking out the competition, I found myself running into Jeff Ruby here and there. He ran the Holiday Inns in Cincinnati and had opened a club in each one. Smart move; he had a captive audience every night. We developed a mutually exclusive respect for each other's talents to create and run nightclubs, and when we bumped into each other we often talked about various ideas. Then one day I got a call from Jeff, who said that he and a partner, a guy named Don, were going to open a pub in a strip mall in northern Cincinnati. Would I be interested in being a partner? I'd get a 20 percent stake for my sweat equity if I designed it, led the build, and then ran the club.

While I liked working for my uncle, a dream of doing my own thing had been brewing in me for some time. Ownership and a chance to use my design skills were too much to pass up. I thanked Bill for believing in me, turned in my notice, and took the leap. It was 1981, and I was going to finally become an entrepreneur.

Jeff and I agreed on the name Mabel Murphy's, and he and his partner let me—this twenty-six-year-old kid—do the rest. On the back of a napkin I designed the new pub. I had loved my architecture course in high school and had seriously considered becoming an architect, but the University of North Carolina didn't have an architecture major. Of course, I'd also had a brief obsession with dentistry in school, since my family dentist lived in a posh house back in Louisville. One semester of Chem 11 disavowed me of that and I said, "Screw this." Thus, business became my major and my future.

I managed the build and we opened to great acclaim. The place was packed most nights. One odd thing: Our landlord, an Italian dude with not the best reputation, began stopping by—a lot. He would pump me for information: How was the night's take or what food items weren't moving. *Strange*. He also made comments about Mabel Murphy's being "his club." While his demeanor was out of the ordinary, I didn't worry too much about the guy. I thought about bringing it up with Jeff but always forgot since we were so busy. Jeff had quit his job overseeing the Holiday Inns and was developing an upscale steakhouse called the Precinct with partners Cincinnati Reds greats Johnny Bench and Pete Rose. *Swanky*. Jeff allowed me to shadow him now and then when he picked out plates, glassware, silverware, or when he worked on menu options, restaurant layout, or decor. That was awesome.

And then a few months after launch, my cool new life got tipped head over heels. Jeff came into the pub and told me the bad news. He'd sat down with Don, who reminded him that the club's legal rights were in his (Don's) name—since he had put all the money up. Don had decided to shake things up and take over the club one hundred percent. And that meant Jeff and I were out. No hard feelings, he hoped. Oh, and by the way, Don had had a silent partner all along who was a part owner. Yep, you guessed it, our landlord.

Jeff said they wanted me to stay and run the place, but at a reduced bonus of 10 percent of profits with no ownership.

We hadn't consulted a lawyer before jumping into the venture, and like a couple of clueless chumps, Jeff and I had no rights to anything. It was like some cautionary tale I'd learned about in business school—when I had gone to class—except this was happening to me. How could I be this gullible? Another lesson learned: Get the legal stuff figured out before you go into business with anyone and spend the money to hire yourself a lawyer who knows what she/he is doing; it will pay for itself in the long run.

I was devastated. Laura and I were living together, so I didn't have much of a choice of what to do. We needed my paycheck. I reluctantly agreed to their terms, and in my spare time began looking for another way to earn a living. I couldn't wait to say adios to my so-called partner, asshole Don; and really I knew it would just be a matter of time before they found out how I was making the club successful and dumped me anyway.

**JEFF RUBY, owner, Jeff Ruby Restaurants**

A club in Fairfield, Ohio, became available. My pal Don was my partner, along with a young kid from Louisville, age twenty-six, Kent Taylor. We named it Mabel Murphy's. I trained the staff and Kent handled the remodeling and ran the club. After the club became successful, and since we had nothing in writing, Kent and I got screwed by Don and the landlord. We had done all of that for nothing.

Jeff, always a stand-up guy, found me a job managing Tomorrow's, a nightclub that filled a full city block and could pack in fifteen hundred people. It was actually too big to be profitable and, indeed, was in bankruptcy. Mike McGraw, the contractor who built the place, had taken over when the original owner had no money to pay what he owed. The club was only busy on the weekends, and then only with barely legal teens who had little money for the gas to get there, let alone to buy drinks.

This wet-behind-the-ears twenty-six-year-old convinced Mike to cut a third off the club and make that into a rock place with live music, while the larger side would remain a disco. Then I brainstormed other ways to generate revenue on the dance side. Another lesson learned: Think outside the box.

The job was fun, the money okay, but I was getting home at three or four a.m., which was not a great fit with Laura, who worked nine-to-five as a paralegal. The long and late hours definitely were wearing on me and our relationship. Then Laura announced she was four weeks late.

"*Late* late?" I asked.

"Yep. I've just taken the test. I'm pregnant. For sure."

*Gulp.*

Between my parents, her parents, our friends, and the stress of running two clubs, life was interesting, to say the least. I got down on one knee to propose. Laura said yes to that *and* to what would be next for my career, which I wasn't even sure about.

I'd had enough experience so far in food service to believe that I could make a good living as a restaurant manager and at least be home before midnight.

I started sending out résumés.

# MADE-FROM-SCRATCH SIDES
# (WHAT I LEARNED):

- Become a student of your craft—whatever it is. Read, research, and pay attention to the little details that make businesses like yours successful.
- Don't dump more money into failing concepts. Cut your losses and try something new. Every great inventor failed more times than he/she succeeded.
- In any service industry, spend time and attention on your working spaces.
- Get the legal stuff figured out before you go into business with anyone—even family—and spend the money to hire yourself a lawyer who knows what she/he is doing; it will pay for itself in the long run.
- Be creative when faced with a customer base with limited resources.

## CHAPTER 4

# A BEGINNING AT BENNIGAN'S

It was the spring of 1983, and a buddy who worked at Bennigan's, Rick Akam, set me up for a job interview. The chain was still pretty new and featured Irish-themed casual dining (as if ribs and chicken fingers are on every menu in Dublin). In its heyday it would grow to almost three hundred locations. It's down to about thirty-three now, but back in the eighties it was hip and happening, and I wanted in.

The job interview was scheduled during the National Restaurant Convention in Chicago, and I was told to fly in the day before and introduce myself to the brass at a party that Bennigan's was throwing that night. I showed up and joined the shindig. Ribs and chicken fingers abounded, as did the spirits. I mingled and chatted with as many people as I could and piled on the charm I'd honed during my college days. By the end of the night, a guy in a polo shirt from HR flagged me down and pointed to one of the many folks I'd been talking with. "That man over there. He was going to interview you tomorrow. He says never mind; the job is yours."

Me: Okay. Cool.

The guy then handed me a T-shirt with a Bennigan's logo. "By the way, he was wondering if you would . . . um . . . if you would be okay maybe running tomorrow morning as part of our 10K team. It's a team race against the other restaurant chains, so it's a matter of pride. He really doesn't want Bennigan's to be embarrassed. It would mean a lot."

Me: So I'd be a ringer?

He blushed. "Well, not really. I mean, you *will* be part of the team in a few weeks."

I thought about his offer for a moment and realized it didn't bug me at all. I'm very competitive, as you've surmised, and he was right that I'd be on their team officially when the paperwork cleared.

"Why not?" I said. "I bet I can kick some of their weekend warrior butts for you."

The next morning I clocked a subforty 10K without breaking much of a sweat and helped their team finish much better than they would have normally. I showered up at the hotel, caught a cab, and jumped on the plane back to Louisville—fired up to take no prisoners in the world of casual Irish dining.

Over the next few months, I learned the Bennigan's way as a trainee in their smaller Louisville store. Since I'd worked as a cook at various jobs in college, I wasn't intimidated pulling training shifts in the Bennigan's kitchen. About a third of their menu was made up of frozen items either grilled or fried, and heating those up didn't exactly require Gordon Ramsay–level skill. When I did a week washing dishes, I rolled up my sleeves and dug in and gained a lot of respect from the guys who worked in the back. It was a tough, wet job, and I wanted these full-time dishwashers to know I was there to learn from them, and I put in the effort to do it well. Working the front of the house was easy with my background in the club business, and I even found time as I waited tables or hosted to give some helpful suggestions on how to increase bar sales to the general manager, who told me to focus on my training and keep my opinions to myself.

Sometime that summer I got to fly to Dallas for a week of classroom instruction from their home-office training team. A highlight was a series of speeches by their founder, fifty-two-year-old Norman Brinker (who also founded Steak and Ale); their president, Chris Sullivan (who was only thirty-six at the time, a University of Kentucky graduate) and future founder of Outback Steakhouse (along with Bob Basham); and their VP of operations, Bob Basham. Bob kept things cut-and-dried in his talk, going over basic operations, but was thorough and professional. The founder, Norman, impressed me as a regular guy, very down-to-earth, and he did a superb job describing his vision for food and service quality. Chris was a different story. The young president struck me as a very cool dude. He was a rock star on the rise in food service.

At the end of his speech, Chris mentioned that he and a few of the other executives would be at a certain club later that night, and we were welcome to stop by. Are you kidding? A chance to pitch my ideas to the president of Bennigan's? I was down. I was among the trainees who hit the club that night, excited at the prospect, and we waited and waited. But no Chris. Most of the group drifted back to the hotel, but I stuck it out with a few diehards. Checking out how clubs ran was kind of my thing anyway. Finally, around eleven o'clock, Chris came in with a few friends. He greeted us like we were his long-lost buddies from 'Nam, chatted for a while, did a shot, and finally headed home (with a designated driver).

I left Dallas with some solid product knowledge but, more importantly, with an appreciation for the leadership styles I'd witnessed, especially those of Chris and Norman. While different in their approaches, they were both down-to-earth, not acting too impressed with themselves—a rarity among many successful people.

Back in Louisville, my training was wrapping up and I knew my wife and I would have to pack up our new daughter, Michelle, and move to who knows where for my first real assignment. We'd been living that summer with my parents—a trend that would be repeated several times as I worked to get my career rolling. My mom was a buyer for a women's clothing store, and she spent the months we were in Louisville trying to turn my wife into a preppy dresser, to no avail.

Finally, the call from headquarters came with my assignment. I would be working at a Bennigan's in Philadelphia and would start in two weeks. I rushed to a department store after work and bought an armful of warm winter apparel. Twenty-four hours later, I got another call and someone at corporate mumbled an apology, saying, "We've changed our minds. You are going to be working in Dallas." I rushed right back to the store and exchanged the parkas and turtlenecks for cargo shorts and T-shirts.

My first real leadership gig in the restaurant world was as bar manager at the Bennigan's in the Dallas Galleria. The store was on the lower level of the mall and overlooked an ice-skating rink. Let me unpack that for a moment: There was a big friggin' sheet of ice in the mall in Dallas! In the summer! Outside you could fry eggs on the sidewalk, yet here there were dozens of preteens holding hands and spinning around the ice to Journey's "Don't Stop Believin'." Not exactly what I was expecting in the Lone Star State.

The Galleria was also the closest store to Bennigan's home office. Big mistake by the brass putting me there. I had designs in my head for new restaurant concepts, and binders full of suggestions for new menu items. I was excited to share them with the movers and shakers at the company as they came in to grab lunch. I fully expected them to pluck me out of obscurity and make me part of the team at corporate, one of the big shots.

Yet I discovered that the term *bar manager* really was code for *closing manager*. By the time I clocked in, the company brass were packing their briefcases to head home to watch *Dynasty* or *Golden Girls*. I worked six nights a week, usually getting home by eleven. That was a cakewalk compared to the three or four a.m. closings I'd had in the nightclub business, but the late shifts did put a crimp in schmoozing with the honchos from HQ who could influence my career.

Now and then I did get to work a lunch shift, and I'd spot the execs and rush over to serve them myself, pitching my menu ideas and restaurant concepts. The reception was cool. Usually I got something like,

"Oh sure, buddy, great idea. Can I get a tea refill?" Translation: *Is there a restraining order on the menu?*

Within three months I was promoted to service manager in the restaurant, overseeing the waitstaff. My area manager, Tony Stinson, was intense and focused on food quality, but I noticed when he visited how he would take the time to speak with everyone at the restaurant—high and low—and that was impressive. I wasted no time in letting him know I wanted to get promoted. Man, was I a pest. I knew I needed to run a kitchen first, so I asked if he could make that happen. Tony told me to have patience, and eventually he would find an open kitchen position. *Good enough.* I could be somewhat patient. But I did get bored easily; I'm always thinking of creating something unique, so while I was waiting for the kitchen job I developed more restaurant ideas and sent them to people around the home office. I never heard anything back, but I didn't get a cease-and-desist letter, so every few months I'd fire off another batch of suggestions.

Finally, Tony stopped by and said that Bennigan's was planning to open a restaurant across town, on Northwest Highway in Mesquite, and they wanted me as the kitchen manager. I later discovered that some of the home-office folks were glad to put distance between them and me as my constant flow of ideas was getting old. But at first I didn't know anything about that. I was getting a shot to grow and develop. *Bingo.*

Laura and I moved into a two-bedroom apartment just eight miles from my new store, but with the brutal Dallas traffic it still took thirty minutes of gridlock to get into work many days. But being relatively close, I was able to spend more time with the family. We had Michelle in day care; a new dog, Carolina; and Laura was working at a Dallas law firm and pregnant with our second child (who was scheduled to arrive in April of the following year).

My new store manager, Tony Thill, was a revelation. A dedicated weight lifting buff, he was not only extremely organized—he had a checklist for everything—but also was super focused when he worked with me and my staff in the kitchen. Tony developed a realistic plan for my development, which I loved, and was amazing at follow-through, holding me more accountable than anyone ever had before. And, because he held me accountable, I started holding my team in the kitchen accountable: Everything was timed. Food quality was paramount. Inventory doubled, checked weekly. Workstations sparkled before every shift. Dead lifts and squats were optional.

After about six months, Tony realized he'd created this monster in the kitchen. I was a giant pain in his ass, suggesting more ideas and efficiency hacks than even he could handle; and he convinced our area manager to give me my own Bennigan's. I was grateful for everything Tony had taught me, and in late 1984, when it seemed all people could talk about was gas prices soaring to one dollar a gallon (can you imagine?), I took over as general manager of the Richardson, Texas, location, about thirty feet from I-75.

About two weeks into running my own store, while I was still a restaurant novice, in walked our founder, Norman Brinker. He was famous enough that I guess about a third of the patrons knew of him. He went from table to table, chatting with each person, and didn't move on until he'd found a way to create a smile. It was another lesson to me in charm, humility, and the power of a friendly conversation. On his way out the door, he stopped by to tell his new general manager that he was doing "a nice job, good to see you." *Wow!*

I was pumped for weeks, until we were notified that Norman was leaving Bennigan's to purchase the casual-dining chain Chili's. Not long after, Chris Sullivan and Bob Basham would follow to become Chili's franchisees in Florida. Shame. It wasn't long after that that rules and a cost focus replaced culture and a people focus at Bennigan's.

Still, life was good for me. I was finding my groove at my new store in Richardson, and my second daughter, Brittany, was born on April 20,

1985. Two kids, a wife, and a dog, with my own restaurant; I wondered how could things get any better? When you start thinking that way, that's when the universe has another hurdle for you to clear.

Richardson had never been the busiest location for dinner, as traffic in front of the store was total gridlock from about four until seven, Monday through Friday. And that was hurting our sales. The good news was that the Texas Department of Transportation was about to fix the problem. They were going to widen the road. *Hurray*. The bad news, we found, was that in order to do so they were going to bulldoze my store, which would put a slight damper on the dinner service.

I was bummed out, but eventually realized it was probably for the best. I had grown tired of the concrete jungle that was Dallas. I loved the people in Texas, but I missed trees and hills. I figured it would be great if the company had any openings somewhere like Colorado, so I asked my area manager to make a pitch for me. At the same time I figured it wouldn't hurt if I doubled down and sent a few new ideas for restaurants to the new CEO of Bennigan's, Kyle Craig. I wanted to show him I was a talent just waiting to be discovered. Maybe he'd find a place for me in corporate if the Colorado idea didn't pan out.

One idea I pitched was a casual restaurant concept with a limited menu. In brief, it would be a smaller, faster version of Bennigan's. You can read Kyle's response below. The rejection letter is now on display at Texas Roadhouse headquarters. Kyle was polite in his letter (on the next page) back but told me my concept was not unique enough to succeed. If I wanted to work on *their* new concept—the Key West Grille—I could make a pitch to join the team (but, reading between the lines, I shouldn't hold my breath).

As it happened, Bennigan's did have a plan for me. They had an opening for a store manager in one of their lowest-volume stores in Denver, on Arapahoe Road. The big shots were itchin' to send me as far away as possible from HQ so I couldn't pester them with my ideas anymore. That was okay, I could work with that.

In November of 1985, Laura and I loaded up our only car, two kids, and the dog, and headed north to the Rocky Mountains.

KYLE T. CRAIG
President

December 30, 1985

Mr. Kent Taylor
Bennigan's
9281 E. Arapahoe Rd.
Englewood, CO  80112

Dear Kent:

Many thanks for your outline of the new concept idea you sent to me. As you probably know we're already developing a potential new concept with the Key West Grill — and thus I don't want to take on any additional concepts at the present time.  I did look over your proposal, and it seemed very sound operationally. However, it didn't seem to have the truly unique look or menu that is so essential to success.

If you're interested in new concepts, I'd suggest you contact Dennis Hood who is the concept G.M. for Muggs/Key West Grill. In the meantime, congratulations on being named the new G.M. at Denver Arapahoe.

Good luck in Denver, and I hope to see great things out of your restaurant.  Have a great 1986.

Sincerely,

Kyle Craig
President

KC/vy

# MADE-FROM-SCRATCH SIDES (WHAT I LEARNED):

- Want to get the respect of your people? Then roll up your sleeves and do the most menial of tasks. When the proverbial dishes get stacked high, put in the effort and do it well and your people will follow you anywhere.
- The best leaders stay down-to-earth, approachable, and aren't afraid to have a beer (or soda) with the team after hours now and then.
- If you have a good idea, pitch it. If no one is listening, that tells you something about the culture you are in. You then have three choices: Put your head down and get along, try to change the culture, or get out of Dodge.
- When you visit a location you talk with everyone, starting with the people on the front lines. Talk to the manager last. By then you'll know the reality of the restaurant's environment.
- Great managers take the time to draw up realistic development plans, meet with their people often about those plans, and then hold them accountable for stretch goals.
- As a CEO, you never know where great ideas will come from. If you have an employee with ambition, find a way to give them some autonomy and support and see what happens.

## CHAPTER 5

# ROCKY MOUNTAIN HIGH

Denver, Colorado. I couldn't believe my luck in landing there. Talk about a place that I was born for.

We bought a split-level home in the suburbs, only five miles from my new restaurant, and just a mile from County Line Road, where nothing but open space, hills, and bike/running trails ran all the way to the Rocky Mountains. I jogged in those hills and joined a fitness club where I lifted weights. As I turned thirty, I was in my best shape since college. And I couldn't wait to try this skiing thing when the snows arrived.

Laura and I found an elementary school we liked for Michelle and a lady to watch Brittany, and Laura landed a job in a Denver law firm. We traded in the old car and got two used vehicles, a GMC Jimmy four-wheel drive for me and a used sporty Mazda RX-7 for her. We had a mortgage, two car payments, and a pile of everyday bills, so finances were tight. We had no money to furnish our living room or dining room, but we made do. We had the essentials: couch, TV, kitchen table, and beds for all, so life was good.

I arrived at my store pumped, but things weren't what I was hoping for. The facade looked relatively new, but inside everything was decaying. Morale was in the crapper; the team was understaffed (and paying a ton in overtime); and the bad apples were trying to spoil the whole barrel.

The store was doing $35,000 a week in sales, among the lowest in the Bennigan's system, and the trend was heading downward. That slump would impact me in the wallet, big-time. Any bonus money that I had been promised—a third or more of a GM's compensation—was going to be far down the road, if it came at all.

Still, I'd encountered tough situations before in clubs I had taken over, and I wasn't intimidated. I knew what to do. I spent a few days conducting one-on-ones with each staff member—from the kitchen manager to the dishwashers. By listening more than I talked, I learned a lot about each person, took note of their wants and skills, and got a pretty good sense of who was helping the cause and who was keeping us from reaching our potential.

A plan developed quickly. To turn the store around, I would need to let a group of the current folks go (about twenty who were toxic) and would have to hire thirty or forty new people. I put an ad in the paper (what I would have given for the internet then). But unfortunately, the people who answered those ads were most often not the type I was looking for. Many had been let go from other jobs or were unhappy with their current positions or bosses. A lot were miserable about life in general, and I certainly didn't want them serving my guests or cooking their food.

So, on my own dime, I would eat at other restaurants. When I spotted a talented host or server, or get a well-cooked meal, I'd introduce myself to the person responsible and give them my card. Did I get in trouble? Hell yeah. More than a few times I was asked to vacate the premises by the manager. Did I care? Not at all.

Getting creative, I also sent flowers to my unit accountant in Dallas and convinced her to allow me to hand out spot bonuses to my best employees who recruited their friends. I begged her not to bust me with the new area manager. She remembered me serving her at the Dallas Galleria and thought I was a nice guy, so she was happy to buy into my idea. I wanted high-energy, fun people on the team, and those types of folks tend to hang out with other high-energy, fun people. I didn't care what age or gender or anything else they were; the more diverse our team became the better; the only requirement was a positive attitude and high energy.

Once we'd hired about twenty new people, I was able to move on to the second part of the plan—eliminating the slackers and trouble-makers. Funny thing, as I let those people go, none of their teammates complained. If anything, with each layoff, the morale in the kitchen and dining room soared. Team members were happier, cleaned more, moved faster, and took more pride in their work.

The third part of the plan was to take back control of the bar. I had two guys who were co–head bartenders, and they gave themselves and their friends the best shifts. That meant a lot of talented people who worked for them were relegated to the service bar. If you aren't familiar with the service bar, it's behind the scenes (often in the kitchen), where bartenders make drinks for people at the tables in the dining room. It's a great place to put newbies who are perfecting their cocktail-making skills, or folks not known as people people, but many of our service bar-tenders were experienced and personable and should have been out front.

I took over making up the bar schedule and assigned the two head bartenders to work in the kitchen service bar for the foreseeable future. I was ready for a revolt from the entire staff—as the two guys had tenure and seemed quite popular—but what happened surprised me. Many of the staff told me it was about time those prima donnas got what they deserved. Huh? Another lesson I've learned: If you have big egos on your team who aren't pulling their weight, the other employees will eventually become angry at those folks. But sooner or later, if you do nothing, the team will turn their anger toward you—their boss—for keeping the jerks around and letting them run roughshod.

As you might imagine, the two bartenders revolted. They cornered me one afternoon and told me if I didn't put them back at the main bar they were going to quit. They threatened to take most of the bar and waitstaff with them. I had been having one-on-ones every week or so with the entire staff, and now knew what the other bartenders thought about them, so I knew the guys were bluffing or completely ignorant.

"Well, if you feel that way, we could make today your last day," I suggested. One agreed and walked right then and there; the other backtracked but left a week later. And, big shock, not a single soul left with them.

A little aside about bartending. It's a hard job that looks easy. It is physically demanding: You stand for ten hours or more, rarely get a break, and are doing something complex—mixing drinks—while people are talking your ear off. Bartending is a challenging, skill position, no doubt, but instead of hiring new people from the outside with experience, I replaced my two departing guys with the most personable, energetic people I had on our waitstaff, who knew little to nothing about the craft. I paired them with veteran bartenders as they got up to speed. Learn they did, and soon they were flourishing. And, best of all, bar sales kept moving north.

Thankfully, the new-hire incentive program was starting to pay off. Great staff members were recommending friends left and right, and within a few months we were approaching full staffing. And so, after about six months of incredibly hard work, I was seeing light at the end of the tunnel. We had a restaurant full of great employees, the team was happy and productive, and sales were growing. Things were great, which meant I should have expected the unexpected.

Enter Steve, my area manager, stage right.

He had been all over my ass throughout the entire rebuild, but when I hit the six-month point he focused his attention on me like a laser. He'd seen my rising expenses, what with all the new hires and the subsequent training, and he didn't like it one bit. *Did I know my labor costs were sky-high?* Yes, I told him, but we are getting fully staffed, front and back of house, so guests wouldn't have to wait forever for their dinners. *Did I know my food costs had risen at a faster pace than sales?* I took a deep breath. Yes, I said, that trend would start to improve soon, but we had hired a lot of new cooks who were still learning the ropes. They often overcooked items or didn't make things right—and I was being a stickler about the quality that left the kitchen. I also had a policy that if a guest got a meal that wasn't to their liking, we would comp the entrée. I wanted them to give us another try, and we had to build goodwill.

Well, said Steve, that wasn't how he wanted things done. Guess that wasn't the Irish way. He told me that if my profits didn't improve immediately, my job would be on the line.

How to best describe my area manager? *Hmm.*

There I was, busting my ass, working eighty-plus-hour weeks, and he was trying to get me to perform better with threats. I tried to calmly explain that I had a plan and it was going to pay big dividends. He needed to give me a little more time. He was having none of it. He said I had two months, no more.

The next couple of months slipped by in a blur and I kept our focus on what would pay off in the long term, quality and service, not the short. The entire staff held each other to high levels of accountability. With the improvements we had made, sales kept moving in a positive direction. Word was getting out and guests were coming back. The place was buzzing and the positive vibe was on the rise.

I was still training a lot of new people, but we weren't hiring much anymore. Turnover had slowed to a trickle. The only people we turned over were those who failed to show for their shifts without warning and I had to let them go. I didn't get much flak from the rest of the staff, as we all knew the rules, and everyone wanted to make the place a success.

I had started a back- and front-of-the-house employee-of-the-month program, a certified trainer program, and personally funded co-ed teams in bowling, volleyball, softball, and flag football to build camaraderie and team morale. When cooks and servers hang out together in activities like these outside the job, everyone seems to work together better in the restaurant.

I had also added an interesting twist to our group training. I would get small groups together, with front and back of the house combined, and together we would create an outline with tasks to be completed to host an apartment party. The teams would brainstorm a list including food, beverages, what people would wear, lighting, music, and so on.

We would then tie in those thoughts with what each shift at Bennigan's would look like, as we were effectively hosting a party seven nights a week in the restaurant, with each employee playing their part in making our party successful. It worked great, and my folks began to understand better the whys behind the actions we were taking each day. They could better relate to things such as music and lighting levels and restaurant temperature.

My plan was finally coming together.

Then the second month's financials came in and Steve called a meeting with me. He said he wanted to do it outside the restaurant. That's never good. For the next two days I agonized over what I'd say, eventually memorizing a bunch of BS I was going to throw at him. It was pretty clear he wanted to fire me or put me on notice.

When we finally met, Steve got to the point. It was the latter. He said if I didn't hit a 34.6 percent in total controllable income (TCI) for the month we were now in, I'd be out. As background, *TCI* is a term we use a lot in restaurants. It's where we identify the expense items that can be controlled by unit management (like labor or inventory) and subtract those expenses from revenue. So, for instance, if your controllable income for the month is $40,000 and your sales are $160,000, then 160/40 is 25 percent TCI.

It was a big ask to hit 34.6, and we'd hadn't come close yet, but Steve was fed up with me and probably wanted me gone. I was pissed, too. He had put me in a restaurant that hadn't seen any growth since the Ford administration, and I was finally increasing sales and building a kick-butt team. He didn't appreciate any of that because expenses were also rising. Any first-year business student would be happy to take sales growth in a retail location and then work on trimming expenses later. As for my boss, he couldn't spot the difference between a stud (GM) and a dud. I assumed he was getting heat from his boss who was sitting in Dallas reading reports.

I went home that night fuming. Sometimes when you're in that space you make decisions you regret later, and that's just what I was about to do.

Working myself into a lather, I called Steve's home number and his wife answered. My plan was to tell him that if I didn't hit a 34.6 TCI I would quit. Honestly, I'd done the math since our meeting, and while it was a bit of a stretch it was not unattainable for the month, so I wasn't too worried. He took the phone from his wife, and I told him in a harsh tone, "If I don't hit a 36.4 TCI, I'll quit."

Without a beat he said, "Fine with me. I'll hold you to it." And he hung up.

*Well, I told him, didn't I?* Then, almost immediately, I replayed the conversation in my mind.

"Um, I said 34.6, right?" I asked Laura, who had been listening.

"Nope, you said 36.4."

"No way."

"Yep, one hundred percent."

"Son of a bitch."

I stayed up half the night trying to figure how to add two points to our P&L. The next day I called my unit accountant and she gave me some good ideas. Then I called a store meeting with a handful of my most trusted employees and explained my dilemma. Bless their hearts, they spread out and got the entire staff to pull together and do whatever they could to save my job: They sold extra items, double-checked that every soda was rung up, managed our inventory like misers, and so on.

Four weeks later, when the monthly P&Ls were tallied, our store delivered a TCI of 36.4—no more, no less. Steve called to congratulate me. Yeah, right. Fat chance of that. True to his character, my area manager called and told me he would be going through my P&L with a fine-tooth comb because what we had done was not possible.

Thankfully, I never heard the result of his autopsy and we kept rolling. After the 36.4 month, our sales ratio kept climbing like a hiker on Pikes Peak, and my boss moved on to torment another poor GM while I, shockingly, became his prize pupil. *Look what happens when you apply a little pressure!*

During these first six months in Colorado, I attempted to learn to ski, or more accurately learn to fall down without getting hurt. I was hooked from day one. The first outing was actually with the other area manager in Denver, Steve Ortiz, and a few of his store managers, as well as our area manager and all my fellow store managers. Of course, my area manager wanted nothing to do with a rookie skier and took off, which was fine with me, and I ended up riding a ski lift for the first time with Steve Ortiz, who would eventually become my friend and work with us at Texas Roadhouse. In addition, one of his store managers, Wayne Jones, who later went to work for the Cheesecake Factory and rose through the ranks to become COO there, rode with us. Wayne then moved on to P.F. Chang's as CEO. Talented dude, no less.

When the lift got to the top, I had no idea what to do. I shuffled off the seat like the others, slid awkwardly for a few feet, windmilled my poles, then fell flat on my face into a pile of snow. Wayne helped me up and gave me some helpful hints. Steve Ortiz watched all of this for a minute, shook his head, and said, "Tough luck, kid, maybe you should get a lesson." He then skied off. Kind of reminded me of my early days running track with no talent and no form, and I was the butt of a few jokes that day.

Back in Denver, despite the early progress we had made, it took a full two years to deliver the sales results I knew we were capable of. Guests who are used to poor performance or food quality don't change their dining patterns overnight. It takes a lot to get someone to trust you again. I went out into the community, passed out my business card, and gave out coupons for free meals to convince people to come back and try us. I visited hairdressers, health clubs, and tire shops. I worked a deal with the six hotels near us and had the front desk clerks send people our way, giving out discount cards to their guests. When we got ten cards with a desk clerk's name on the back, he or she would receive a coupon for two free meals. The term to describe my approach to building sales can be called grassroots marketing. I called it survival marketing back then.

We even started delivering food right to people's rooms in the nearby hotels—that is, until one guest attempted to get freaky with one of our food runners. From then on, we delivered to the front desk and the guests had to walk down to get their grub.

It was the mideighties, the stock market was soaring, and I figured we could make a couple of bucks off the trend. I created an account for a penny-stock firm that was just a block away so their people could flood our bar a few days a week and pour down cocktails like they were free. That worked until the stock market crash of 1987 and it took me three months to collect what the firm owed us. After that, no more accounts. The Denver Broncos practice facility was just a few miles away, and I convinced a bunch of the players and staff to come in. A little-known backup quarterback named John Elway even hung out, playing our Pac-Man game while downing wings and a couple of beers. In February, when the snows were flying, we had a beach week and brought in sand and a reggae band. The bottom line: I learned to think outside the box and was bold enough to take action. That's when good stuff happens.

When I arrived in Denver in 1985, the store was doing about $35,000 a week in sales; by 1987, we were approaching $50,000 a week and leading the region in sales growth and profitability. But cashing in on that success was never easy at Bennigan's. One year, for instance, the company had a bonus plan in place that rewarded GMs financially if they increased sales and profit, which makes sense. I cleaned up. But the next year, when I again focused on topping the charts in sales growth and profit, the bonus was changed and tied to something else. It was as if they didn't want their GMs making too much money. I decided right then that if I ever owned my own restaurant, bonuses would align store managers with ownership and would never, ever change. (At Texas Roadhouse, we did just that. Our bonus system has not been changed in three decades and it's made thousands of employees a lot of money, and I'm thrilled for them.)

I was having success, and even had the guts not to wear a tie, as was required by Bennigan's rules. I kept a clip-on tie in the office in case any Dallas big shots showed up, which happened just twice. I was also getting creative. For instance, we had been scooping out potatoes for our potato skins and throwing away the good pulp. What a waste. So I created a made-from-scratch recipe for potato soup that was way better and cheaper to produce than our frozen bag soup. I even sent the recipe to Bennigan's' corporate chef. The result was a call from the regional manager, who told me to cease and desist. The chef had shut me down. A year later, said chef rolled out a new idea: made-from-scratch potato soup. Wow, what an idea! And surprise, it was my recipe.

Getting recognized was never in the cards at Bennigan's. After all the success our restaurant achieved, I was stoked to be up for general manager of the year at the national convention. As the evening banquet progressed, it was looking like a lock for me. I had already been onstage twice to receive two of the three big GM awards—best financials and best people development (quite a few Bennigan's leaders had been promoted out of my store, and I was excited for their success). The only award I didn't get was for operations. As they built up to the General Manager of the Year award, it was pretty clear to everyone in the room that my name was going to be called, as a few fellow GMs leaned over and patted me on the back or flashed me thumbs-ups from across the room. In my mind, the Denver Arapahoe store was the comeback story of the decade in our region, and I was ready to get a little love for my hard work and sacrifice.

A few seconds later, they called another guy's name as winner of the GM of the Year and I snuck out the back door and headed to my room. There, I grabbed a square ice bucket, filled it with half a bottle of bourbon, two Cokes, and a dozen ice cubes, then partied late into the night, trying to forget the jerks I was working for. My friends told me the next day I was thrown out of McDonald's at four in the morning, but I remember very little.

It might not be shocking to learn that I went back to refining new restaurant concepts so I would never have to work for someone else again. I had an idea for a Texas-style steak place (you know how that turned out), a Rocky Mountain ski lodge (that would eventually become the Buckhead Bar and Grill), a concept I called the Florida Salad Company (not too bad an idea), and last . . . and definitely least . . . the Pelican Head Seafood Company (don't ask). In my spare time I was hitting up investors to drum up money to launch one of the concepts but was turned down by everybody and anybody I could get time with in Colorado. I even made a pilgrimage to Louisville to hit up anyone who might have known my parents and had a couple of bucks. No luck.

As I was growing up in Louisville, I'd watched the career of John Y. Brown, the fifty-fifth governor of Kentucky and the man who had built Kentucky Fried Chicken into a global brand. He was at the top of my list of likely backers, and year after year I visited him to make a pitch. I hunted him down in Louisville. Swing and miss. I visited him in Florida. Again, no luck. I kept track of the great man and pitched him five years in a row.

**JOHN Y. BROWN, owner, Kentucky Fried Chicken (1964-71) and governor of Kentucky (1979-83)**
Kent's dad was a dear friend of mine growing up in Lexington. Kent chased after me for about five years, pitching various restaurant ideas. He was a big dreamer, lots of energy, very persistent. He was very curious, always asking questions, but wore me out, if I'm honest with you.

By that time, I had made sixty presentations to potential investors about my ideas and heard "no thanks" sixty-plus times. Yet I'd long been okay with rejection. My time at the University of North Carolina had taught me that getting a "no" wasn't the end of the world. A lot of the part-time jobs I applied for, it was no. When I asked a girl to dance, the usual answer was in the negative. But I found that if my goal during a dance was to get turned down ten times, usually by rejection seven or eight, a girl would say, "Okay." I could work with those odds.

In 1987, however, I was about to get a rejection that would really hurt. My wife, Laura, wanted a separation and, most likely, a divorce. We talked it out, but there wasn't much hope. I didn't blame her. Work had become an obsession for me, and relationships can suffer in those circumstances. It happens.

After that, when I wasn't at the restaurant, I put all my effort into the kids. They lived almost full-time with me in our house. Since I was responsible for the mortgage, day care, or other bills, money was tight. Still, I paid the bills and got to all the dance recitals, Halloween parties, and whatever else I had to do to keep those girls happy. After a couple of years, however, I was running on empty. I had one full-time job at the restaurant and another as a dad. Dating. What was that? I needed help. I figured it was time to move back home and be close to my parents, brother, and a network of friends. Surprisingly to me, Laura said she'd be okay with it, and if things didn't work out for her in Denver, she might head back to her hometown of Cincinnati.

I turned in my notice at Bennigan's and my daughters and I loaded up the Jimmy and headed east for the next part of this adventure. And what an interesting part of the journey it would be.

# MADE-FROM-SCRATCH SIDES
# (WHAT I LEARNED):

- Regular, consistent one-on-ones with each staff member are the best way to get to know your people, understand their frustrations, grasp any interpersonal issues on the team, and help them achieve their goals.
- Don't hold on to toxic people. Try coaching first—some people have no idea how they are coming across—but most often it's best for you and them if you move them on to new opportunities without delay.
- If at first you don't succeed (like me skiing), try, try (fall) again, and eventually you may surprise yourself (today I'm heli-skiing).
- Be creative when finding talent. You never know if your next awesome employee will be helping you at the dry cleaner, or if your team's heart and soul will be discovered rotating your tires. Positive attitude and a willingness to learn new things trumps experience.
- Don't underestimate the power of grassroots marketing and the power of personalized connections.
- Make sure bonuses are aligned with what you want to achieve as a team and then keep them consistent and achievable. Share the wealth.
- Don't be afraid of rejection. Ask for the moon, and now and then you might just get it.

## CHAPTER 6

# MY OLD KENTUCKY HOME

I landed with the girls back in Louisville in 1989, unemployed. Michelle was six and Brittany four, and with my parents' help I enrolled my oldest at Dunn Elementary and my mom watched Brittany and took her to preschool.

Rick Akam, a buddy from Bennigan's, got me a job interview with the Hooters franchise. No, not as a server. I had interviewed with a few other restaurants, but Hooters offered a semidecent salary with an area manager's title. They were also interested in my construction experience, as they were adding new stores, each with its own look.

My area at Hooters would include just two stores at the start—one in Louisville and the other in Nashville—but there was also a store under construction in Nashville and another to be completed in Knoxville, Tennessee, within the year. The stores that were already up and running were doing okay; they just needed to tighten up on food execution and profitability. I helped oversee operations while also working with their development guy, Bill Hysinger, on the design and hiring for the new store in Nashville. I found managers, got staff lined out, and disagreed quite often with Bill on restaurant layout and decor. I had a fundamental issue with the new Nashville location. I thought it was a poor choice and would be a challenging place to make a success of; I wanted to pull the plug and start over. Bill said the die was cast and we were past the point of no return. The store got built but never did very well and closed a few years later.

The group was led by a very successful apartment developer, Neal Harding, who enjoyed the perks of being associated with the Hooters brand. I did, too. Being single for a while now and finally having steady babysitters in Mom and Dad, I now had the ability to start up a social life.

As an aside, a friend from high school, Frank Buster, tried to set me up on a date with one of his wife's cousins during my time at Hooters. No luck, he reported back; she would not date a guy who worked at that particular restaurant chain. Go figure.

Always wanting to tinker, I became convinced that Hooters could use some help improving their food. They probably didn't know that their food quality and selection could have been better. Enter Kent Taylor. Knowing that the top folks from corporate were planning on visiting our market soon, I whipped up a few items to show them what I could do. My past experience with food creation at Bennigan's had gone over like a lead balloon, but obviously that didn't affect my optimism.

The big bosses made it to my area and were most certainly not impressed by my creativity. One of the execs took me aside. "Taylor, I'm sure you mean well and all, but this is Hooters, man. If you can improve the beer, the babes, or the wings, bring it on. We are all ears. If not, keep your ideas to yourself. *Capisce?*"

New faces, same attitudes. Oh well.

I was just nine months into the job, yet it was clear this was not going to be the place for me. Traveling back and forth to Nashville and Knoxville was also requiring more weeks away from my daughters than I'd imagined, putting pressure on my folks to watch them for extended periods.

I began to shop around for a new job in Louisville and was able to snag an area manager position at Kentucky Fried Chicken. PepsiCo had recently purchased KFC and the recruiter, Tim Galbreath, said they were looking for fresh faces with fresh ideas. "I'm your guy, then," I said. "And boy, do I have ideas."

As the KFC training was about to start, I was getting more excited about the opportunity. I was a Kentucky-bred boy with a degree in business and a bucketful of experience turning around restaurants. I was even willing to grow out a white goatee. What more could they want? I would write my own ticket to the top: VP in five years, on the executive team in ten. You watch.

While I wasn't sure where I'd get assigned—Louisville wasn't a lock—I was willing to take the gamble and started my training at a KFC store about two miles from my parents' house, close to where I'd graduated high school. I watched the faces of people as they recognized me when they were giving their orders. "Hey, didn't we graduate from Ballard together about seventeen years ago?" they would ask. I would smile. "Yep, good to see you again. Would that be extra crispy or original recipe?" You could see them shake their heads. They knew all along that that Taylor kid wouldn't get far.

**TIM GALBREATH, former HR director, KFC**
Back in 1990, we decided to shake up management and hire some outsiders, specifically those that would bring an entrepreneurial spirit and challenge the bureaucracy we had at the time. Kent fit that bill and he had a passion for the business. Unfortunately, we were still very bureaucratic and Kent didn't fit well with our processes and procedures and apparently had a problem staying in his lane.

Now that I was away from Hooters, Frank was finally able to set me up to have a date with his wife's cousin Leslie Dohrman at a nice place called KT's. I left my shift at KFC, ditched the clip-on tie, and pulled on my only suit in the parking lot. Over lunch, I worked hard to impress. I explained how I was a new executive at KFC, on my way up, and talked about the turnaround of my Bennigan's. I showed her a picture of Michelle and Brittany from my wallet. Either she bought into my BS or, more likely, thought my kids were cute, but in any case I got her to agree to a second date. It had to be after the Kentucky Derby, I said, as that was a busy week. I didn't tell her I'd be working dawn to dusk cooking up batches of fried chicken for the party crowd to take to the track. She didn't need to know that.

Pretty soon my training was about to end. The last week included classes at corporate headquarters. As a final project, I was assigned to think about ways to impact customer service and made up a motivational banner that read HAVE YOU MADE A DIFFERENCE TODAY? I hung it by the employee exit at the main office and leaned against a wall to listen for reactions as people left for the day. And boy, were there comments, most snidely guffawed. Morale was far from the "super-positive Pepsi culture" I'd been promised by Tim.

When the time came to assign the new area managers their territories, as usual things didn't go my way. I drew a lot for Charlotte, North Carolina, and would need to move there by the end of the summer.

Nothing against NC, I loved the state—*Go 'Heels!*—but once again I got the feeling that management thought it best for pesky Kent Taylor and his wealth of unsolicited ideas to be hundreds of miles away from headquarters. Out of state, out of mind, as the saying goes.

I packed up the kids and found a house to rent in Charlotte (complete with a nanny's apartment behind a detached garage). I hired said nanny, got Michelle and Brittany enrolled in school, and kept up my courtship of Leslie long-distance. Once a month we would meet in the North Carolina mountains and camp with my kids, us pulling up in a very used, very stinky red KFC delivery van that I used to transport raw chicken from store to store. Chicken juice inevitably would slop onto the carpet—*Who puts carpet in a delivery van?*—and when the sun heated the vehicle up you could smell it coming ten city blocks away.

In the meantime, I started to put the KT stamp on one of the local KFCs. My favorite store was run by Michael Payne. It was a newer restaurant in the south end of the city and was my laboratory (poor Michael)—the place where I liked to break the rules, putting items on the menu that KFC would have never approved of. After figuring out which dishes customers liked and which were duds, I thought it was about time to let the cat out of the bag and get some well-deserved credit for my inventiveness. We were one of the test markets for spicy wings and some of the marketing brass from Louisville were scheduled to tour our stores in a few weeks to see how the wings were selling. It was my chance to show the big shots the future of KFC, as I saw it: chicken sandwiches, chicken fingers, and the like. *Bam*, this would probably mean a promotion and a move back to Louisville. The future was bright.

I know, I never learn.

I convinced Michael Payne to add the new items to his menu. He was against it from the start. In fact, he pleaded with me to choose someone else to convince the brass; he didn't want to put his job on the line.

Me: Don't worry, I'll take you with me on the way up.

Michael rolled his eyes and said the shit was about to hit the fan.

*Bah, what do you know?*

The head marketing guy's name was McDonald, which I had a laugh about when he introduced himself (McDonald's was our main competitor). With all the enchanting levity of an IRS auditor, he ignored my quip and entered Michael's store. McDonald took three minutes to take in my improvements and let me know he was not happy with the liberties I had taken with the approved menu. I was ordered to get the store back to spec. My bosses' boss, the regional VP, would be in to visit with me the following week, I was told. What a treat that would be.

Falling on my sword, I explained that Michael Payne had nothing to do with the changes and I had forced him into agreeing. (Funny aside: When I first entered North Carolina with Texas Roadhouse, I called Michael Payne to see if he'd be interested in working with me. His answer: "Sorry, man, my wife would kill me if I got with you again.")

The next week our regional VP, Michael Howell, came to visit. He was actually very good about the whole thing but did suggest that maybe KFC wasn't the place for me. He could see I was an independent thinker, a bit of a rogue. Maybe I should try to do my own thing, he suggested. *Uh, yeah. Been trying that.* He gifted me a copy of the book *The 7 Habits of Highly Effective People* by Stephen R. Covey and I dug in. (Michael Howell later ended up becoming the CEO of Arby's. Years later, I ran into him at a restaurant conference in Dallas and we had a great time reminiscing.)

Back at KFC, I took my VP's hint and tried to get my stores running to code, but whenever I had a free second I went back to chasing down anyone with money who could fund one of my dreams.

As if things couldn't get worse, one evening not long after, while I was working in one of the KFCs in Charlotte, I got a call that my rental house was on fire. I raced home, blowing through red lights, to find fire engines surrounding our rental home and smoke billowing from the windows. My emotions were running sky-high as the police grabbed me and kept me from entering the house. I ran around yelling and searching for my daughters, relieved beyond belief to find Michelle and Brittany sitting in the kitchen of the house next door sipping hot chocolate, thinking the whole thing was kind of interesting.

Within an hour, the fire captain found me and explained that someone (my nanny) had accidentally dropped a blanket on the space heater in the garage apartment. Fire engulfed the garage, and when our nanny spotted the flames she rushed out of the house with the kids and left the back door open, so the entire place was smoke damaged. I couldn't blame her for the mistake, as we all make them. But her apartment was toast, and there wasn't room in the tiny house for her to move in. So I had no nanny, a job on the line, and a girlfriend in Louisville whom I'd been bragging to that I was about to get promoted and move back to HQ at any time. Fat chance of that.

A couple of months later, I took my kids home to Louisville for spring break, described my dilemma to Leslie, and decided to give John Y. Brown one more shot. My fifth pitch.

I had told John that someday we would be partners and was determined to prove that out. Brown agreed to meet with me—shocker—and I pitched him hard on my Colorado-themed steakhouse idea (Aspen Inn) plus a new idea I hadn't shared with him before, a blue-collar cowboy steakhouse I called Texas Roadhouse. (I had conceived the idea in Dallas in 1984 and six years later the concept was really taking shape—at least in my mind.)

He liked the Aspen Inn idea best, but not necessarily the name. He had two restaurants in Louisville with his wife, CBS sportscaster and former Miss America Phyllis George Brown, featuring rotisserie chicken, but they weren't doing well. Maybe a steak place would appeal to the Louisville locals. He said he would consider my pitch and get back to me. I promised Leslie that things were looking up and then headed back to North Carolina to wait for (a) a call from John Y, or (b) my imminent firing.

The two arrived about the same time. A few weeks passed and my boss called me in to explain that KFC was going to scale back management layers and my job would most likely be eliminated within six months. He suggested I look for other options. As luck would have it (seemingly for once in my life), just days later, John Y called and asked me to drive up to Louisville. He was intrigued and wanted to dig a little deeper on this Aspen Inn idea. I packed up the kids, drove up in the smelly chicken van, and worked John over for a few hours. Finally, he signed on. Aspen Inn as a concept was a go (the name still in debate). We'd convert one of his chicken restaurants in eastern Louisville to the new concept.

John said he would make me a 20 percent partner and give me a salary of $40,000 a year. I was okay with the equity but balked at the money. I had made more than $65,000 a year at Bennigan's and had started at $55,000 at KFC. I negotiated hard with John, but he won out and we settled on me making $40,000 a year. I could survive, and he was allowing me to move back to Louisville and be my own boss. John also agreed to fund $80,000 to convert the restaurant. I told him I'd need at least $120,000, but he again stood firm. Knowing I had no other options, I told him I'd make the $80,000 stretch.

John still didn't like the name Aspen Inn and suggested Roasters. In retrospect, Aspen Inn does sound like a roadside motel. But I wasn't a fan of Roasters, either. It didn't exactly evoke "Colorado-themed steakhouse." On the way back to Charlotte to give notice, I kept throwing out various names to Michelle and Brittany, then still grade-schoolers. Next thing I know, Michelle hands me a picture she's drawn of a deer wearing sunglasses, holding a beer bottle. Under the logo she had printed the name "Buckhead Bar and Grill," one of the names I'd mentioned along with many others. The drawing was pretty good, but I doubted John Y would like the name. *Good try, kid.* I explained that John liked the name Roasters, as he preferred chicken to steak. Michelle kept doodling her new deer with sunglasses; this time she had the deer beating up a chicken. No paternity test would ever be needed; she was definitely my kid.

Three weeks later, as I was finishing out my KFC notice, I called John Y and told him I'd polled a bunch of people and they liked the name Buckhead Bar and Grill. Shock of shocks, John did, too. "Sounds good," he said, and that was that.

In the summer of 1991, my daughters and I moved back to Louisville and I began to build a restaurant of which I'd own 20 percent. It was eerily familiar. Was this going to be Mabel Murphy's all over again? I put the doubts aside. John and I had a solid agreement reviewed by his lawyer and mine, and he was a high-integrity guy whom I trusted, but given my earlier nightclub contract mistake, my own lawyer seemed like a good idea.

It had taken seven years of rejection, more than one hundred presentations to potential investors, but finally it was about to happen, for real this time. I was going to be an owner. Life was now looking up, or so I thought. Pretty soon I'd hit another barrier (it was the steeplechase all over again).

# MADE-FROM-SCRATCH SIDES
# (WHAT I LEARNED):

- If your people have ideas, listen to them, thank them, and consider them. Then let them know what you decided—even if it's a no-go.
- Cultural fit is paramount for employers in hiring and also employees/managers in choosing a company to work for.
- Want a quick gauge of your culture? Encourage more attention on customers and see how people react behind the scenes. If you've put employees first, they'll embrace the renewed attention to guests. If you haven't, they'll most likely react with disdain.
- Don't give up on your dream. If it takes you a hundred tries, then that's what it takes.
- Don't ignore your family's input. They'll often have a fresh perspective about your work issues.

# PART II

# PERFECTING THE ROADHOUSE RECIPE

## CHAPTER 7

# DAWN OF ROADHOUSE

A single year after joining KFC, with my chicken-thigh-in-the-sky dreams of management superstardom dashed, I was back in Louisville with my daughters in tow. It was 1991, and we moved in with my family again. Good news: I was back in the same town with my girlfriend and was eager to prove I had the right stuff to create my own restaurant (well, 20 percent anyway). Needing some construction savvy, I called up the guy who had done the Hooters builds for me, Gary Newton, and asked him to bid on the project. Gary was a tough, no-nonsense Vietnam veteran who had passed on his cigar habit to me through our shared construction experiences. He also never met a burger, steak, or doughnut he would pass on. I once suggested that he might think about reducing his waistline for his own benefit. His response: "Son, this ain't no belly, this is my extra-large storage tank for my sex machine." *Okay.* With some pencil drawings that Leslie had redrawn (my girlfriend, future wife, and part-time napkin architect), I agreed on terms with Gary and began to tear John Y's chicken grill apart and build out the Buckhead Bar and Grill.

The decor included pictures of the Colorado landscape, wooden skis and snowshoes on the walls, a stuffed buffalo, a bar, and a separate dining area. The grill was located in a small strip mall, so parking was limited. And with the lack of remodeling funds, a green awning and cheap wood siding became our street frontage—laughable by the standards we use at Texas Roadhouse today.

I hired a chef, Howard Lee, who had worked at a downtown restaurant that was pretty slow and might not survive long. I liked his style and he was able to execute the menu I had planned. Howard was a hard worker, kept the line moving, and was smart enough to ask for help when necessary, i.e., me. We hired staff and added to the team a couple of managers, one with experience and one with barely any (if I had bothered to call her references, I probably would have discovered she had zero).

With all of our preparation, the minute we finished construction we would be ready to roll. That would be the case if we weren't horribly behind on the build. Between delays with the construction crew, and my questionable management and staff hires, it would have been hard to find a place that was more ready to suck when we finally opened the doors.

Decent crowds showed up, but poor execution and so-so food quality led to sales declines week by week. I was working twelve-hour days, seven days a week, trying to figure out how to get better food out quicker or who the next person was I should fire—of which I had an embarrassing wealth of choices.

Mom and Dad would kept me abreast of their friends' comments, mostly well intended but always a bit snarky. "Joyce ate at your place. She had to send her steak back twice. But it was nice that she came in, wasn't it?" I went from weighing 190 pounds (thanks to a year of Kentucky Fried Chicken original recipe twice daily) to weighing around 155 just four months later. Thirty of those pounds were lost to worry, stress, and anxiety, while five pounds, I guessed, were due to the perspiration that rolled off me every day in waves. I can relate to that old saying "I worked my ass off," and I needed my ass for those rare moments when I got to sit on it.

When people try to reminisce with me and say, "Remember the good ol' days?" I tell them, "Yes, I do, and they sucked. Please don't bring them up again!"

Just when I thought things couldn't get any bleaker, the newspaper came out with a review of our new restaurant—and it was not good. I went from worried, stressed, and anxious to distraught, depressed, and destroyed. And yet I couldn't wallow. I had to move quickly to motivate the staff, who had received the terrible review like emotional Broadway actors and were most likely firing out résumés left and right. I talked my chef out of quitting and slapped on a happy face for my employees and guests that evening.

A lot of people must have read the review because that weekend sales dive-bombed. The place was quieter than the gallery on a Tiger Woods tee shot (not counting the guy who yells "in the hole" the second he hits the ball). Me, I was freaking out. I had no idea how to cover payroll, which was due the next week. The solution: I didn't cash my own paycheck and we limped by a little longer. But the restaurant's bills kept piling up, and I had hardly any revenue coming in to fund them. I couldn't even make my car payment and took restaurant food home to the kids and my part-time nanny (whom I also couldn't pay). By now I was working more than one hundred hours a week, and we were on cash terms with many of our suppliers.

Desperate times called for, well, you know. Nanny go bye-bye, and I had to move back in with my folks. Needing to contribute to the food budget, I figured I had to cash one of the paychecks I'd been holding on to for a month or more. At the bank I handed the teller my check and asked for cash. She clicked a button or two and frowned. Out spewed a piece of paper from her dot-matrix printer that showed me the Buckhead payroll account was down to two dollars. Two. Effing. Dollars.

I was out of options. There was nothing in the cash register at the restaurant except an IOU I'd written for fifty bucks. I survived another week with food by tapping into my kids' piggy banks and stuffing in more IOUs. I might have contemplated a bank robbery but didn't have the gas money to get to a bank. When anyone says they are going through a low point in their lives, I can relate and tell them, "No problem, dude, we're cool."

**MICHELLE, my oldest daughter**
Times were definitely tough back in the early Buckhead days. We were worried about Dad's weight loss and quite frankly he looked a bit gray. He would take money from our piggy bank so we would have lunch money for school, and he'd leave various IOUs scratched on paper. Thankfully, Mimi, our grandmother, would buy us school clothes or there's no telling what we would have had to wear to school.

It didn't take long for my partner, John Y, to summon me to his house to report on our latest financials and ask me to explain why he was getting hounded by creditors for requests for payment relating to our restaurant. "We're working on it, I'm working the plan," I assured him, then asked for $10,000 to catch up somewhat on the bills as a temporary fix. But he shouldn't worry, I said, all was golden. He reluctantly handed me a check and said, "No more."

Today, when people ask me about Texas Roadhouse's local store marketing and how it got started, the answer is: desperation. Similar to my Bennigan's in Denver, I hit the streets talking up Buckhead, working deals with hotels, and handing out discount coupons here, there, and everywhere. In my final act of hopelessness, I put a discount coupon in the local paper—the same paper that had said our restaurant was a "reluctant alternative to dining at the landfill" (the reviewer didn't actually say that, but it felt like it).

The good news: Guests started coming back, coupons in hand. The bad news: They didn't come back again if they didn't have a coupon. That idea allowed us to limp through another few months, but the short-term success quickly tapered off.

Was I panicked? Hell yeah.

Bills were mounting and I had no choice but to let my assistant manager go, leaving only me and my chef, Howard, in charge. My workload soared, stress off the charts, and my dream looked like it would be over within a few months. I was barely sleeping and would sit up by myself, in my parents' house, brainstorming any new idea that might keep our ship afloat. Every Wednesday and Saturday I would run to a nearby convenience store and plunk down five dollars on the state lottery, hoping to hit the big number and save the restaurant. Like I said, I wasn't sleeping.

One of those restless nights, about three a.m., I found myself scribbling a list of all the things that had worked for me in the past in other clubs and restaurants, analyzing my strengths and weaknesses, and then doing a cost analysis of potential options to save Buckhead. By now I was pretty much sure John Y wasn't about to fund any more of my crazy ideas. I also knew my kids needed a dad who was around now and then, and who could afford to pay for their school supplies, let alone three square meals a day. I was so anxious that as a backup I called the Olive Garden to see if they had a management job in Louisville but got a "Sorry, we're not hiring right now." I also called Outback headquarters in Tampa and told the switchboard operator that I was an old Bennigan's buddy of Bob Basham, who had gone on to be one of Outback's founders. To my surprise she connected me with Bob, but after he figured out that he didn't really know me, he politely blew me off. Strike two.

I took a rare night off and went to dinner with my parents and kids, thanking my dad for covering the check, as usual. After putting the kids to bed, I started rereading highlighted portions of motivational books I had read while at Bennigan's: *The Power of Positive Thinking* and *Enthusiasm Makes the Difference*, by Norman Vincent Peale, and *The 7 Habits of Highly Effective People* by Stephen Covey. I pulled out the options I had written out a few nights before and decided. *Screw it, I'm doing option seven.*

I dropped to sleep for a few hours then called John Y and told him, "I'm coming to visit you and I'm going to explain my new plan, and you're going to have to listen, and yes, it will cost some money."

John was in Las Vegas but agreed to meet a week later when he was back in Kentucky. In the meantime, I explained my plan to my store office assistant, chef, and anyone who would listen: our cooks, dishwashers, servers, bartenders, and even the night cleaning guys who didn't really speak much English. *"Cómo?"* Unbeknownst to me, during the week of waiting, John called and asked my office assistant about my plan and if it had a snowball's chance in hell of working. Thankfully, she lied and said my plan was airtight, a surefire winner. I would have set our odds of failing in the new venture at maybe three to one. My odds of landing a job someplace like Olive Garden or Outback I put about even. Still, if I was a betting man, I wouldn't have bet on me.

Thankfully, John Y was a gambler. He might have left a dollar or two back in Vegas, or maybe he wanted to double down on his investment in Buckhead, but he said okay to my new idea and gave me a check for $20,000, half of which went to pay Sysco (food guys) and some others we owed. The remaining ten grand I put into big TVs, a used sound system, and an area for live bands at the bar. I slimmed down the menu and scouted local talent to play. The Buckhead Grill was about to get relabeled as a bar/pub/live-entertainment venue that sold ice-cold beer and delicious cocktails, and oh, by the way, also served food.

I owed most of the radio stations money, so I couldn't announce the rebrand over the air. I owed the local paper money, so no luck there, either. With no cash to promote Buckhead II (the pub), I had to think creatively.

There was a radio station DJ who brought his mom to Buckhead on Sunday nights—I'm guessing our place must have been close to her house—and I had struck up a friendship with the guy. That Sunday I cornered him. "I need your help, and in return you'll get free food, anytime." He was intrigued but with a mouthful of complimentary potato skins said he didn't know what he could do.

"I'm guessing no one who listens to your show has ever been to Buckhead, you think that's right?" I asked.

He shrugged but thought about it for a moment and agreed. "Probably. I've never seen anyone I know in here, and no one's recognized me."

Our clientele was mostly older and probably didn't listen to his drive-time (four to seven p.m.) show on a rock station. *Crank it up, Phyllis, I can't get enough AC/DC!* Probably not.

"What if you act like you've just discovered us," I suggested. "Act like we just opened. Talk about the great bands we have in here. The beer. The appetizers. Stuff like that. What do you think?"

He deliberated. "How many people can join me for free food?" he asked, picking a lodged kernel of corn from his teeth.

"Two."

"Make it four."

We agreed, and the next day Andy the DJ was talking about us on his afternoon drive-time slot like he'd just discovered a cure for baldness. I hired some bands, printed up flyers, and talked the musicians into handing them out around town (which inconvenienced their napping). I put up flyers in the area apartment buildings, started a ladies' night, and within a few weeks our sales were up 50 percent. We were selling almost as much beer as food, caught up on our bills, and I finally cashed a paycheck and repaid the petty cash I owed; more importantly, I put the money back in my kids' piggy banks with interest. Not only did I dodge a bullet, but thanks to John Y and a little creativity, I more than likely dodged a Scud missile hit.

Sales were growing and our food started getting better as well. I was able to hire another manager and take a few days off a month. The girls and I moved out of my parents' house, this time renting a place near my kids' elementary school. And I finally had time to spend with my gal, Leslie.

### JOHN Y. BROWN

Kent was an extremely hard worker, very humble, and treated everyone right. Buckhead started out slow, but he never gave up and tried many things to make the restaurant successful. I didn't realize how bad things had actually gotten until a couple of years later. He has this silent confidence and will always find a way, no matter the circumstances, to make any situation work. Quitting or giving up was never an option.

It was the perfect time to stop and smell the roses, sit back, breathe a little, and enjoy the success. *Ha!* I'm not wired that way. With the pub now profitable, I convinced John Y to allow me to look for location number two.

Knowing jack squat about real estate, I ended up drawn to the Greentree Mall in Clarksville, Indiana, across the river from Louisville. The rent was cheaper than in Louisville, and there was way less competition. This time I studied radio station demographics. Whereas around our first location, rock was king, in Clarksville it was country music that ruled the local airwaves. I went back to John Y to explain that a country steakhouse, my Texas Roadhouse idea, would be a better fit.

My initial thought regarding Texas Roadhouse was to combine a rough and somewhat rowdy live music joint with a reasonably priced restaurant featuring steaks and ribs. I wanted to have the same quality of beef that Outback and Longhorn featured at the time, but with price points more similar to Chili's and Applebee's. I wanted to target the blue-collar segment of America (my peeps) who would be comfortable with jukebox country music and a casual and lively atmosphere with energetic servers in jeans and T-shirts. In short: Baby, if you want to dress up, then visit somewhere else; but if you want to dress down, we would welcome you with open arms and a warm smile.

Draft beer and sweet tea would flow and be our drinks of choice. An impressive wine selection would be for the competitors. And I knew from my days at Bennigan's and Buckhead that guests preferred booths. So primarily booths it was.

John told me to first nail down the site with the landlord and he would ponder the idea (he was also speaking with another restaurateur about moving in another direction, so he wasn't sure). I told him that if we did the Texas Roadhouse versus Buckhead, I'd want 50 percent of the business and for us to be equal partners. Again, he'd think about it.

John quickly came back with his terms. We sat down and he told me that 20 percent was the most he'd offer me for the Clarksville location. I passed.

But John had another idea: He wanted to open a few restaurants in Florida with his new friend. John would own 80 percent, I would own 10, and the other guy 10. I wasn't about to move my girls again, certainly not for 10 percent of something that might not even work, so again I had to pass.

John went on to open his next restaurant in Florida, and I contented myself with 20 percent of Buckhead number one. Maybe it was time to chill, build Buckhead up, and see what could happen. Where were those damn roses that needed smelling? Bah, that inner peace lasted for less than a month. The drive that lives within me took over and I was back to pitching my Texas Roadhouse idea to any patron in Buckhead, or anyone else around town whom I felt might have a hidden cache of cash to invest. Every week I set a goal for how many times I would get turned down, and the list kept getting longer.

Looking back, I shouldn't have been surprised by the rejection. My proposal packet was more than lame, with the name TEXAS ROADHOUSE written in Magic Marker on the cover sheet. I was going after guys who'd had success in business, and they weren't impressed. Once, I talked my way past the assistant of the owner of Rally's (a drive-in burger chain), claiming I had a Christmas gift and only he could sign for it. She showed me in to Jim Patterson's inner sanctum, and I made my pitch. Three minutes later he walked me to the door.

After that, I turned my focus to doctors and dentists, figuring they might not be as business savvy as the restaurateurs but would still have deep pockets. I also told the regulars at Buckhead that I would pay a 3 percent finder's fee to anyone who could introduce me to an investor in my Texas Roadhouse idea and actually fund my dream.

At the same time this guy came in and said he was the general manager of a local radio station. I began my well-rehearsed Texas Roadhouse pitch, but he stopped me midsentence. He had no interest in investing and told me he was going to have his afternoon DJ stop talking about us on the air unless we started advertising with his station. *Oops, wrong guy.*

I guess it was bound to happen sooner or later, but after thirty minutes of negotiation we came to an understanding. I didn't have money to invest in radio airtime, so I would now have another person (and his guests) who would be enjoying a complimentary meal or more at Buckhead.

A few days later, a couple of my regulars came in after golf, bringing in tow their buddy John Rhodes, an Elizabethtown cardiologist. The doc had attended Ballard High, graduating a year before me. So *bingo*. Instant connection. For the 130th time, I went into my pitch about Texas Roadhouse. To keep him from leaving, I made sure his beer never ran dry. Dr. Rhodes politely heard me out. Taking my crappy Magic Marker proposal in hand, he promised to ask his partner if he'd be interested. I said I'd call him the following week.

To my shock, the good doctor took my call and said that he and two of his pals—Dr. Amar Desai and Dr. Mahendra Patel—would be open to listening to my pitch. Could I drive down to Elizabethtown? *Are you kidding, I'm already in the car.*

### DRS. JOHN RHODES AND AMAR DESAI

John: I walked into Buckhead with a few buddies of mine and sat at the bar. After a few minutes, Kent sat down and chatted for about five minutes before he, in his usual deft manor, steered the conversation to this idea he had.

Amar: Kent kept feeding him beer after beer so he would keep listening.

John: Before I knew it, Kent asked if I might be interested in investing in his idea. I told him, "You pick up the tab and I'll think about it."

Amar: The next thing I knew, he had interested John in the idea, and John set up a meeting with Kent, Mahendra, and myself in Elizabethtown a few weeks later.

I was on my game. Nolan Ryan couldn't have pitched any better. The doctors hung on every word, at least that's how I remember it, and asked some insightful questions. But they didn't need a ton of selling.

They immediately grasped the concept. God bless the learned! On the spot, the three agreed to fund the build for the first Texas Roadhouse, to be located in Clarksville, Indiana. Each would put up $100,000, with all four of us signing for a bank loan to add another $250,000. Clearly, the doctors would need to back the loan as my net worth was more than a negative $20,000, with several credit cards maxed out and two months behind on my car payment.

We would have just over half a million dollars to build and open, which might sound like a lot, but today we invest ten times that much in opening a store. I agreed to take no salary (I would work my shifts at Buckhead at night, while I oversaw construction during the day), but did negotiate earning a 1 percent royalty on all sales at stores number one, two, three, and any that might follow. The doctors could do the math. They probably figured if we, one day, had three stores doing about $2 million each in sales, it would amount to $20,000 a store or a salary of $60,000 per year. Not a biggie.

We agreed to an ownership split for store one of 70 percent to the doctors and 30 percent to me. I was ecstatic. All I had to do was convince the Greentree Mall landlord to switch out John Y on the lease for the doctors, but once he took a quick look at their financial statements, he said, "Uh, yeah, that will be no problem."

Nine years after the country steakhouse idea popped into my head, after more than one-hundred-plus rejections by potential investors, it was about to happen. The time had arrived to put a lifetime of failures to work. *YEE-HAW*.

# MADE-FROM-SCRATCH SIDES
# (WHAT I LEARNED):

- Instead of offering discounts, focus on product and service quality. If people aren't willing to pay full price for your stuff, then something is wrong with your offerings.
- When things are tough, take some time to analyze your strengths and weaknesses, what has worked in the past, and what might work in the future. Don't just rush forward. Do some analysis.
- There's a lot to learn from the right leadership books. If you think you know it, think again. Ask those you trust what books have inspired them, and dig in. Always have at least one book going.
- Get your team on board with any strategy or plan from the beginning.
- Be creative with grassroots marketing (i.e., my DJ friend). If you have a big marketing budget, great, but few of us do. So think outside the box. (Unless you're competing with Texas Roadhouse. Then stick with your marketing plans. They are working just fine for us.)

## CHAPTER 8

# GETTING THE RECIPE RIGHT

Fall of 1992, while I was working sixty hours a week at Buckhead (all nights), we broke ground on the first Texas Roadhouse. Working with me was my contractor, Gary, and a few others on the crew. I did carpentry, put up drywall, cleaned out the Porta Potty, and even ran to grab lunch (after some serious handwashing).

A lawyer buddy, Bill Strench, registered the name Texas Roadhouse—in hindsight, one of the smartest moves I made. We had no idea if someone was using the moniker anywhere, there was no Google, so you would pay an attorney to do a national search then grab a spot in the five-year registration process with the federal government. You could have sent a snail coast to coast many times over in the time it took Uncle Sam to give us our registered trademark. My plans were modest—maybe to build as many as three restaurants one day—so I wasn't that worried about someone in Texas suing us. But you never know.

The next step was to find a management team. I recalled a potential manager I'd interviewed at Buckhead. Brian Judd was an ex-GM from Chi-Chi's who was running a nightclub in Louisville called Cliffhanger's. He had turned me down on the Buckhead job after watching how hard I had to work there. No dummy, he saw how understaffed the place was when he spotted me cooking (heck, I also bartended and waited tables).

I set out to do a little undercover work on Brian. I went into Cliff-hanger's one night and watched him at work. A little like a stalker (but with better intentions), I studied the faces of his employees and patrons as they talked with him; I observed him as he moved around the club. The guy had energy, his nightclub was hopping, his people hustled, and the place seemed to run with a practiced efficiency. My entrepreneurial heart went pitter-patter. I knew his personality and front-of-the-house savvy would be a great balance to my kitchen focus. I would check every plate going out to the dining room, and since the expo area I was work-ing was on the servers' way back to the dish area, I could see which items people didn't eat completely.

After an hour of ogling, I reintroduced myself and asked Brian if he was cool grabbing lunch one day. "Sure. What was your name again?" he asked. I told him. He said, "Okay, Kent from Kent-tucky. Got it."

The next week I convinced Brian to come on board as our first gen-eral manager, a title I would soon change into Managing Partner. I even got him to pony up $30,000 to become a 10 percent owner (the docs and I would split the remaining 90). Six hundred stores later, that's still our model. Today, every managing partner puts up $25,000 and gets 10 per-cent of the store's bottom line, and it's typically the best financial deal they'll ever make. I then set Brian to finding and hiring two kitchen man-agers and a service manager (another practice that exists to this day—a new store's managing partner will find his or her own staff).

These ideas were no masterstroke on my part but had been born out of necessity. Between my evening shifts at Buckhead and my construction and design-on-the-fly duties during the day, I had no time to recruit; Brian did. Luckily, he had a pal who'd worked at Chi-Chi's, Jeff White, as well as Rod Ball, who had worked with Brian at Chi-Chi's and was now at Applebee's. They fit the bill as kitchen managers and helped refine the menu. We went back to the newspaper to find a service manager and got the usual bad luck in hiring from the classifieds. We thought we'd found someone pretty good, but she got a gig modeling camo gear at a series of gun shows and soon blew us off.

I had hoped to have my chef at Buckhead, Harold, help us with the menu, but he was undergoing chemotherapy for advanced-stage cancer and was bedridden. It was near Christmas, and Harold was too sick to get out to shop for gifts, so we agreed that I'd dress in my Santa outfit and deliver some presents to his house. I gave Harold a copy of the new Eric Clapton CD, *Unplugged*, and over the coming weeks he played the song "Tears in Heaven" often (which Clapton had written in honor of his lost son). Harold presented the gifts I had purchased to his wife—a charm bracelet with all their family members represented—and his two sons got engraved money clips. They ended up being the last mementos he would give his family, as not long after, just before Roadhouse number one opened, Harold passed. I lost a good friend, and it hurt.

We were nearing the end of construction when winter brought a major snowstorm one night as I was showing my daughters our progress. Roads were shut down and the girls and I slept on the stage I had built above the bar. I had anticipated that we would have country music groups perform every night, staying true to the image of a rowdy roadhouse out in the hill country of Texas. But after I'd dealt with bands showing up late, playing too loud, or going too long (you can't turn tables when the band won't stop jamming), store two in Gainesville, Florida, and every location thereafter, would have no stage and no bands.

**BRIAN JUDD, first Managing Partner, Clarksville**

When we opened Clarksville, we were on a shoestring budget. Pretty much all of the equipment was used. We didn't even have working bathrooms when we opened. We had opened the doors a few weeks before schedule so we could cover payroll.

We would work on training materials at Kent's rental house, where he was raising his two daughters. He had no furniture in the living room, just two old desks. It was a crazy time. We would come up with an idea or recipe on a Monday, and by Friday would be rolling with it. It was absolutely nuts but quite fun as well.

Another idea was to offer free rolls. We played around with giving out popcorn, something for people to munch on immediately, but realized we wanted the smell of rolls to hit our guests when they walked in. If we were going to offer them, though, I wanted to get the recipe perfect. I set my assistant kitchen manager, Rod, to driving all over town to buy as many types of flour and yeast as he could find. We then experimented. Rod and I would try this type of flour with this type of yeast, adding so much water, so much oil, and a dash of sugar and a few other ingredients for good measure. Then we tried again. We also experimented with dozens of variations to proof and bake the rolls. Nothing tasted right.

I wanted a fairly sweet roll, but sugar and yeast fight each other, so I needed a flour that would work with both. The process of discovering the best Roadhouse rolls consumed our waking days for three weeks. I'm pretty sure it also consumed Rod's sleep. He probably dropped off at night counting bags of flour. I was tormenting the poor guy with my relentless pursuit of the perfect roll. Finally, we hit it when we mixed a certain flour with another flour. The mix came together in no time and we created the rolls we use to this day. Our honey cinnamon butter followed a similar process, eventually finding positive results.

Before the opening, we also kept debating the menu. With their backgrounds from Chi-Chi's, Brian and Jeff were convinced we needed a Mexican section on our steakhouse menu. Always willing to give things a try, I agreed. Our kitchen wasn't set up to do Mexican food justice—it's an entirely different skill set—and it really didn't fit the theme of the place. With poor execution and almost no sales, we eliminated the Mexican items two weeks after opening.

As for our steaks, I had gone to a metal supply house and acquired an eighteen-by-twenty-four-inch stainless-steel plate to sear our steaks before moving them to the chargrill. Pretty much all our equipment was used. Instead of a professional proofer for our rolls, we put a FryDaddy in a closet, wheeled our dough in, and boiled water in the FryDaddy to create enough heat and humidity to proof the bread. Thinking back, we were not the sharpest tools in the shed, as the bread was a bit inconsistent.

As our opening date approached, Brian talked a friend of his, Karen Hill, into helping us get started. She had plenty of management experience from Chi-Chi's, and her job would be to train our servers and bartenders, and then she could walk away, no strings attached. She'd told us she wanted a break from the crazy hours and stress of restaurant work and was definitely not interested in anything steady. No problem, we assured her. Several weeks later, Karen just couldn't help herself. Maybe our energy was too damn infectious. She joined the team full-time (she retired not long ago but still owns franchise stores in Wisconsin and works part-time for me doing my personal finances). I will forever be indebted to that gal who decided to model at the hunting show because without her jumping ship we never would have had Karen! Life is like a box of chocolates, or maybe like long camo underwear and shotgun shells. Who knows?

**KAREN HILL DUNN, first service manager**

I didn't want to be in management again, I wanted to be footloose and fancy-free. I was thirty, not married. But I agreed to come in for an interview at Texas Roadhouse; who knew what that was? I didn't get the job. They hired some girl who was an aspiring model. Three weeks before they were going to start training, she got her big break in modeling [the camo-gear gig] and they called and said, "You got the job!" I didn't find out until way later that I was the second choice.

My job was to train servers, but we had no manual. We would all sit at this table in the mall and put the materials together—using forms we'd taken from other chains we'd worked at. We trained during the day and would sit down at night and make out the test for the next day. We did that for the servers and then the bussers, the hosts and the bartenders. We now have a team of thirty-five people at Texas Roadhouse who do all that. Kent said he would pay me nine dollars an hour, and he'd pay me every week. I lost count of how many nine-hundred-dollar paychecks I cashed. But in the end it all worked out, and I loved being part of the journey.

Karen is not exaggerating any of that. We had no office, so we created training materials in the mall or on Brian's kitchen table. However, I don't remember borrowing anyone else's materials, and I'm sticking to that story.

It was clear that our bathrooms wouldn't be ready by opening day, so I convinced the manager of the neighboring JCPenney to allow us to use their restrooms for a month or so. We were slated to open on February 17, 1993. We couldn't delay, as I was set to marry Leslie on March 20, and I needed the place humming by then. Leslie and I had set the date back in October and it had seemed like such a safe bet at the time. I had been sure we would open in early January. Yeah, right.

That February day we opened to decent crowds and the food was good; not the quality that we would eventually develop, but definitely better than Buckhead's. The bands, true to form, were a pain, but our service was solid thanks to my plan of having servers work only three tables (what the industry calls three-table stations). The norm in the industry is a server working four to six tables, which means it takes longer to get in your order, get your food, and get out.

With upbeat country music (either from the band or jukebox), the concrete floor, and wood and tin in the building, we were definitely a bit loud. I made sure the CDs in the jukebox were country and in general high-energy songs. I like to call it a countrified cool vibe.

We had the chargrills visible to the guests, a meat display case to view our freshly butchered steaks, and you could smell the steaks cooking and the freshly baked bread coming out of the oven. The six senses would come alive for our guests—sight, smell, taste, hearing, and touch. The sixth sense was a feeling of a warm and friendly vibe.

It didn't take too long for the JCPenney manager to come in fuming. He asked me to follow him to his store, and there pointed out a trail of peanut shells on his nice shiny floor that led all the way to their restrooms. It was pretty funny, but I kept a straight face and nodded thoughtfully. He wanted to know what I was going to do about it.

I still had two weeks before our bathrooms would finally be finished, so I couldn't really say what I was thinking, but still, was this all he had to get worked up over?

"Actually," I told him, "I think you have a very positive situation here. Number one, your people don't have to give our patrons directions to the restroom, they'll just follow the peanut trail."

He was not amused.

"Number two," I added quickly, "I bet if you check the departments along the trail, you are going to see their sales are up."

He harrumphed, gave me his best stern expression, shook his finger, and vowed, "Two weeks, Taylor, and we're done. And it's going to cost you more free dinners."

I nodded.

A few days later, the manager came back into our store sheepishly and recanted. He said it would be no problem if our bathrooms took longer and our guests needed to use his facilities. *Take as long as you need.* He'd looked at the numbers, and believe it or not, sales along the path to the bathroom were up. *Really? You don't say.*

We got our bathrooms open, the store running fairly smoothly, and I was able to marry Leslie. We drove four hours into the Smoky Mountains, near where we would meet when I lived in Charlotte, and we spent three days before heading back to resume work. Every day I had at least one shift at either Buckhead (paid) or Roadhouse (unpaid). Three to four days a week I'd double up and work at Roadhouse during the day and then head over to Buckhead to pull another full shift late into the night. I was putting in more one-hundred-hour weeks, which is not sustainable. Finally, we were able to hire another manager at Buckhead, and I was able to cut back my work schedule to around eighty hours a week.

Pretty quickly after we opened, we realized we needed a signature drink, so Brian—with his Chi-Chi's background—suggested we have a signature margarita. I was like, *Whatever.* I was still dealing with construction issues, like getting our bathrooms operational, as well as continuing to run Buckhead.

Brian met with a small manufacturing company, American Beverage

Marketers, that was selling various puree flavorings. He asked them to work with him on a sweet-and-sour concentrate that we could add to water and mix with tequila and triple sec. We had quite a good time testing and retesting various batches until we all agreed on one. To this day, American Beverages' Finest Call is in our more than six hundred restaurants, and Finest Call is now one of the top three bar-mix brands in the world. Our early partnership evolved quite well for both of us; in fact, in 2021 together we rolled out the Texas Roadhouse Margarita Mixer to retail outlets around the country, and hopefully the world.

More good news: Roadhouse made money from day one, and I was able to convince the docs to break ground on Texas Roadhouse number two. Thankfully, my busy cardiologist partners weren't sticklers for details about all the business stuff, so when I told them the next location would be in Gainesville, Florida, they raised no red flags. Most savvy business folks would have realized it was cuckoo putting a second location 750 miles away from the first. I thought my reasoning was pretty sound: My best mile time (4:09) came on the campus of the University of Florida in Gainesville, back in college, and I had liked the town. Solid business logic, right?

Anyway, a buddy I knew from my days at the Denver Bennigan's wanted to move to Florida to run the store, so that would be a huge burden off me. The buddy had found a spot for the restaurant already, and all I needed to do was to run down and convince the owner to lease me the property and we'd be on our way.

Since we were Sysco customers, we had put the Roadhouse name in a hat with all the other Kentucky and Indiana Sysco customers for a weekly drawing for a three-day cruise out of Fort Lauderdale. I thought it would be perfect if we could win that, as it would give Leslie and me an excuse to head to Florida. I told her that if the Roadhouse name was drawn, we could go on a real honeymoon.

"Sure, Kent," she said. "What are the odds? One in a hundred?" She wasn't holding her breath.

I followed the weekly drawings with piqued interest, but our name was never called. Finally, during the last week of the contest, Texas Roadhouse was called. No way? I timed my meeting with the Gainesville landlord for the day after the cruise docked. We drove the five hours to Gainesville and Clark Butler granted me a forty-five-minute meeting over lunch at an Olive Garden. Mr. Butler was seventy-four and the largest landowner in Gainesville, not to mention sharp as a tack. He sized me up quickly. When I told him we only had one Texas Roadhouse, and it had opened only six months prior, he laughed and explained that I had quite the nerve to think I could successfully open a second restaurant so far from the first and actually make it work. He appreciated me stopping by, but he had an offer on the property from Lone Star Steaks and would probably take it. Buh-bye.

I had fifteen minutes left of lunch to win him over and I started wooing. Those hundred-plus rejections had taught me a thing or two, and I made my most impassioned pitch. I'm not sure what I said that won him over, but he saw something in this upstart from Kentucky. Maybe he recalled a young Clark Butler fighting to make his mark in life. The next thing I knew we were driving around Gainesville and he was showing me his shopping centers, apartment buildings, and empty tracts of developable land. Finally, he drove me to his office building for more conversation. Leslie had been surreptitiously trailing us in our rental car.

We sat down in his office and I finally got up the nerve to admit my new wife was down in the car, in the Florida heat, and would it be possible for her to wait in the air-conditioned lobby? It would be fine for her to come in, he said, and asked Leslie to join us. Soon, he was quizzing her about her entrepreneur of a husband. She was a real trouper and backed me to the nines. Clark said how nice it was that I had a wife's support (he was divorced), and a couple of hours later we were finalizing terms on the lease. I asked for ten years with four five-year options. He countered that he never gave out more than one ten-year lease with two five-year options. I did quick math in my head. After his deal, he'd be ninety-four. What was ten more years at that point?

Out of my mouth popped: "What do you care? You'll probably be dead anyway."

That hung in the air for six long seconds, which felt more like six minutes, until Clark burst out guffawing and let out a huge belly laugh. He caught his breath, looked at Leslie (who I think had just shat in her britches), then back at me. "Well, kid, you've got some balls. Sure, why not? It's a deal."

Needless to say, I've never used that particular negotiation tactic again.

My buddy from Bennigan's bailed on me before we put a shovel in the ground, but he connected me with three other guys who wanted the opportunity. They all pitched in to open the store, two of them sharing a single-bed room in a Super 8 motel for $29 a night during the build, rotating, which meant one of them slept on the floor. I shared a room at Knights Inn, for $19.99 a night, across the street with the other guy.

Our landlord, Mr. Butler, was very particular about two things: landscaping and towers. He required us to have a tower on the building—which I liked, and we still have them on our buildings—and he said that he would be responsible for installing and maintaining the landscaping. Sure, knock yourself out. Most landlords nickel-and-dime tenants and wouldn't care if you put a carnival Ferris wheel on the property as long as you paid your rent. Still, as I toured his various developments around town, it struck me how much better they looked compared to his competitors'. That lesson of keeping up landscaping has stuck with me ever since. Matter of fact, ask my people. I'm a royal pain in the ass when it comes to landscaping.

We worked through the challenges of the opening, and there were many, yet the store kicked off with even better sales than Clarksville. Interestingly enough, all three of those original Gainesville managers had long careers with Roadhouse. Two have retired, after doing well and watching their net worth grow with our stock price, and Greg Jasinski is still the managing partner of the Gainesville location. Several other original employees also have had long careers with us, with one server from that second store, Laura Cobos, now serving as our senior director of training.

It was taking a lot of my time to launch the store, and I was in Florida almost full-time while my new wife was back in Louisville with my daughters. I needed to get home, so I hired an area manager I'd known from Bennigan's to grow Florida, and I headed back to put my hand to growing Indiana and Kentucky. My docs were eager to keep rolling, so we opened three stores in 1994: in Cincinnati, Ohio; Sarasota, Florida; and Clearwater, Florida.

As usual, after a life filled with ups and downs, I stumbled into another trough. Those stores opened to extremely poor sales. I broke my rule with Cincinnati and didn't do my homework, ending up with a lousy location. I had taken my real estate broker's word about how busy the two restaurants nearby were. After we opened, I discovered both were about to close. I tried adding live bands to Cincinnati, but that confused guests and sales dropped even lower.

That summer, since we were between openings, I was able to breathe a little and made a few lake trips with my buddy Tom Kochera. He had lived in northern Kentucky when I was up there running nightclubs and had been a regular at Maximillian's, where he had met and then married his wife. Whenever he got in trouble with the missus, he would find a way to blame me, and of course, I did the same with him. We got a kick out of the fact that our wives weren't keen on our best buds.

On occasion we would play hooky and hit the lake. Tom was super fun, quick with a joke, and always relaxed. I, on the other hand during these years, was usually stressed, working way too hard, and not having anywhere near as much fun as I should have. So on a Thursday in August we skipped work again (I actually took off a second day within a week) and we had a blast at the lake. The following Monday I got a call from Dr. Steve Demunbrun letting me know the devastating news that Tom had a blood clot move from his leg to his brain and he had died. I abruptly left the office, jumped on my bike, and rode for about two hours. It was a shock to have my thirty-eight-year-old buddy gone. I had been in his wedding party and he'd been in mine.

Standing over his grave a few days later, I vowed to get back to being my old crazy, loose, fun self from then on (as much as possible) to honor him. I also found that from then on I was a better person to work for and be with. Sometimes you can get a bit of tunnel vision when you are moving fast, and many of the best parts of life seem to pass by unnoticed. Stress can usually be managed, but for some people, stress can often manage their lives, with friends, family, business, and health paying the ultimate price.

**JOE DULWORTH, longtime friend**
I had gone to high school with my good friend Tom Kochera, who was buddies with Kent up in Cincinnati. When Kent ran the club Maximillian's, both guys were full of life, very energetic, passionate, and frankly quite crazy. One night out with both would be really fun, but would require one or two days of bed rest to recover [from].

The two new Florida locations, Clearwater and Sarasota, did very well during the winter months, but sales plummeted when the snowbirds left, and they wouldn't be back for eight months. My two profitable stores were barely covering the losses at the other three. I had overextended and my three doctors said they were done. My area manager in Florida ended up misbehaving with the help and I, of course, had to say adios to him. I was forced to sell 10 percent of my ownership in Gainesville to keep the new company afloat. With a revived sense of purpose, instead of wallowing in my recent failures, I pulled up my big-boy britches and dug into all the business books I could find. They confirmed my many mistakes: bad real estate decisions, bad people decisions, inconsistent food quality, and poor training.

My doctors were history, bills were mounting. I was in survival mode once again.

Ever the optimist, I figured if I could find a couple of new investors we could right the ship. Sooner or later, I would have to make the hard

call to close the three underperforming restaurants. It was incredibly demoralizing. I have mementos on the wall of my office from each of those
three stores, reminding me of the people affected by their failure, the
money lost, and the lessons learned. With two restaurants still successful,
I somehow kept the faith.

This time, in order to grow, I had to have a better plan. After reading
some real estate books, I knew we'd need to locate any new stores near
twelve-month-a-year families and not in tourist markets. We were ap-
pealing to blue-collar folks who lived on a budget, and we needed to find
places that fit the mold, places where we could thrive.

I also needed a great chef before we would open any future locations,
as our recipes could use some work. My attorney, Bill Strench, had an
interest in a restaurant that was about to close because the location was
poor. He said they had a strong chef in Jim Broyles and he might be interested. I asked for his number, and Jim, an Austin, Texas, native, showed
up for his interview with me in the bar in the Clarksville store. Maybe he
felt he was back in his Texas roots amid the noise and commotion of the
place. We ended up shouting at each other for an hour over the sound of
the band blasting out above us, yet somehow he decided to give us a shot.
I couldn't pay him much, but promised a bright future with the potential
for ownership down the road. My new chef had quit at Buckhead after
a year, so I asked Jim to work there until I could I find a replacement. It
took us six months to finally get Jim freed up to run the kitchen in a new
Roadhouse.

Through a friend of my dad's I also met a guy in Lexington who had
a Sizzler restaurant that was failing. He was willing to throw some money
our way to try something new. As luck would have it, here was my opportunity with new investors and my new secret weapon, Jim Broyles, a
true food guru.

I knew this would be my last shot. The training and design of any
future restaurants had to be a home run or we were most likely going to
run out of money.

**JIM BROYLES, legendary chef (1994–2010)**

I had received several calls from Kent to set up an interview. We met at Road-house and talked. I could barely hear him when the band fired up, but when he mentioned $25,000 plus bonus, I heard that loud and clear. No way would I work for that. We finally agreed on just north of $40,000 a year to start.

I had to prove myself to Kent, but when I did, he gave me ownership in the company. Man, you wouldn't believe what that turned into. That changed my and my wife's lives forever. I was able to retire at age fifty-five, and now, looking back, it was one of the best decisions in my life. Amazing.

# MADE-FROM-SCRATCH SIDES
# (WHAT I LEARNED):

- Register your trademarks. It's worth the time and effort.
- Want to know how your new management works? Check them out in their current jobs, ask their people about them.
- Get the recipes right, even if it takes a thousand tries.
- Stick to what you do best. In our case it's steaks, ribs, chicken, and other roadhouse fare (Mexican food wasn't a hit and we moved on).
- Appearances matter in a retail location. Pay attention to the little stuff like landscaping and outside decor.
- From my friend Tom Kochera I learned to be myself again. You can get tunnel vision when you are moving fast, and many of the best parts of life may pass by unnoticed. Stress should not manage you, and friends, family, business, and health should not pay the ultimate price.
- Everyone fails. It's okay. But learn from mistakes. After I failed with my third, fourth, and fifth Roadhouses, I dug into all the business books I could find and did an analysis of what went wrong.
- Do things better the next time. Find the right people to ensure success, and investors who believe in your vision.

## CHAPTER 9

# CHANGES

Store number six, the conversion of a Sizzler steakhouse, was set to open in Lexington in January 1995. One afternoon after we had finished construction for the day, I was having a beer with the crew out in the parking lot. As I sat on the ground sipping my brew, an idea popped into my head. The building should have two towers. Why? Fairly complicated business formula really: The Gainesville location had one tower, but so did the last three restaurants that were losing money. Logical conclusion: Add a second tower.

I asked the guys to set up two ladders in my view of the building and a pair of them scrambled onto the ladders and held their hands above their heads in a peak. I stood back and imagined the workers were towers rising into the Kentucky sky. *Bam!* I liked it.

The next morning I was on the roof with my tape measure and duct tape mapping out the twin peaks. Benny Davidson and his crew finished them within the week, and two towers have been a fixture on our buildings ever since.

The Lexington store also featured the introduction of our murals. During construction, an artist rep stopped by and said he represented a group of local artists. He asked me to take a look at his binder, as he imagined we could use a piece or two of art in our western-themed restaurant.

I talked him into leaving his binder and returning the next day. After construction was done for the day, I stayed late in the building, downed a few beverages, turned on my music, and flipped through his book in order to feel the vibe and make a decision. He made the sale and then some. The next day, by the time my crew arrived, I'd marked on the walls where I wanted two murals to go and how I wanted to redesign the bar to accommodate four more of the murals. One of the pictures in the book was a large Native American mural, painted by an artist named Dave Carter. I liked it and asked that the rep have Dave send me some Indian chief options and I would pick one.

As an aside, a few store openings later, the artist rep called and said they were booked solid with other clients and could no longer paint for me. I'm guessing it was because I was taking sixty days to pay them, who knows, but I was pissed. I really liked the two murals Dave had already painted for us. Not to be deterred, I called every Dave Carter in the Lexington phone book (it took about thirty to find the right one) and asked if I could come and meet him in his studio. He agreed, without knowing who I was; my communication had always been through the artist rep. When I showed up, Dave agreed on the spot to keep painting for me on the side. I was paying more than the rep (who took a 30 percent commission). Inevitably, a few weeks later, the sales rep saw a mural destined for Texas Roadhouse in Dave's studio. He gave Dave an ultimatum: Paint for him or Texas Roadhouse. One or the other. Dave chose us. Eventually, he took on the role of finding other artists to paint for us as well. For several decades now, Dave has painted exclusively for Roadhouse. He and his crew have created more than thirty-five hundred murals for us.

**DAVID CARTER, fine artist**

Kent discovered my work when the guy I was working for sold a couple of my murals to Texas Roadhouse. Kent offered to commission more murals directly from me. The guy gave me an ultimatum: him or Texas Roadhouse, and he was paying me basically peanuts for my work. Thankfully, I chose Roadhouse. I've had consistent, challenging work for the past twenty-five years, and the only peanuts I've needed to be concerned with have been served with my dinner at the restaurants.

The Native American culture has fascinated me for many reasons. As a people, Native Americans share a love of and appreciation for nature and conservation. But most importantly, I admire their attitude toward their elders. A tribe is a family and there is immense respect for elder members.

My first experience with this viewpoint was at North Carolina under the tutelage of Coach Joe Hilton, who was part Native American. Coach made it a point to infuse our team with a culture of family and respect. He saw himself as the wise elder and we were his tribe, whom he coached and cared for, just as he did his own family. Just like his grandkids did, we called him Chief as a term of respect.

After college, I realized the value that older people have in life and business. It started to make sense to me that we value those who have gone before us and blazed trails. It just makes sense that they'll know more than those of us who have yet to set out. In fact, when I look back, I realize that some of my most valuable pieces of business advice and lessons have come from conversations with people older and more experienced than myself. John Y. Brown, Uncle Bill, Jeff Ruby, as well as original Texas Roadhouse board members Martin Hart and Jim Parker, Truett Cathy (founder of Chick-fil-A), Herb Kelleher (founder of Southwest Airlines), current TXRH board members Greg Moore and Jim Zarley, and of course my parents have all offered constructive praise rather than destructive criticism. My peers would usually be hung up on small things or threatened by big ideas, while the older, more experienced folks I knew were more often supportive and encouraged me to dream big.

This is one of the reasons why, as I have gotten older, if time allows,

I enjoy speaking with entrepreneurs or folks within the company who are seeking advice. While none of us want to be an "elder," we should all embrace the role because it means you have something of value to offer. Think of it as an honor to impact the lives and careers of others. If you get the opportunity, seize it.

As the business grew, our very first Roadhouse chef, Jim Broyles, continued to tweak our food and improve each recipe. Clarksville, our first store, had already won a couple of rib competitions, but Jim wasn't satisfied and kept tinkering with the formula. I told him to quit messing with perfection, that *if it ain't broke, don't go trying to fix our rib recipe.* Jim either didn't listen or didn't care, and made up five new sauces for us all to try, as well as a new slow-smoked procedure he swore was better than the one we were currently using. Our staff tried his new rib recipes and agreed that they were much improved. I still wasn't convinced, so I told Jim to cook up batches of ribs with his five sauces and our current sauce and we would set up a table in the mall and let the public decide. By the end of the day, the sauce Jim had felt was his second-best creation was voted the overwhelming favorite. Our don't-fix-what-ain't-broke award-winning sauce came in dead last. Damn him if he wasn't right. The sauce and rib recipes chosen in 1995 continue to this day.

We opened Lexington on January 10, 1995, to very nice crowds. It was our first store with two towers, a Native American mural, and much-improved food quality. If this store failed, the new company was basically toast, but if early sales were an indication, it looked like we might finally make it. And we weren't done yet.

One of my partners in the Lexington location, Robert Langley, had a failing Sizzler in Ashland, Kentucky, and asked if I would be interested in franchising him the Roadhouse concept. My manager in Gainesville, Alex Quintard, had been asking to open a franchise as well. He wanted to open a store in Lake City, Florida. I figured if I could pay for the legal work with one franchise, then with the money from the second I could start paying old bills. *Hot damn*, I thought. It wasn't in my plan, but I was down with that, dog.

There was a law firm in Dallas that had done franchising for Outback and they put together the paperwork. I'm pretty sure they used mostly the same format they'd used for our competitor—just swapping our name for theirs—but it worked. All of a sudden we were growing again. A couple of months later, another Sizzler operator visited from Muncie, Indiana, and within a year another Roadhouse was under construction in Muncie.

With the opening of Ashland in July and Lake City in August 1995, we now had eight Roadhouses, with five making money. During that summer, a restaurant equipment salesman who sold to us called a friend of his, George Lask, to let him know about this new Roadhouse concept. George had worked for Chi-Chi's designing restaurants and spec'ing equipment. He had just left Chi-Chi's, as they were closing restaurants. The equipment salesman confided to George that this Kent Taylor guy knew how to design the front of a house all right but needed some help with kitchen design and equipment needs.

George called me and asked for a meeting. I had him meet me at my house—as the janitor's closet we were using as a corporate office did not instill much confidence in our future. He showed up at my place in a coat and tie only to find me in my usual summer attire of shorts, T-shirt, and sandals.

**GEORGE LASK, former director of design and development**

I expected an older guy in a suit, not some young dude who looked like he was about to go throw a Frisbee with his dog. We talked and he said he didn't have enough money to pay me a regular salary but could use me as a consultant. I told him that if we teamed up, one day he would be rich and fly privately. He said, "Yeah, whatever. I'll be happy when I can cash my paycheck regularly." I should have caught on then that my consulting bill would not be paid quickly. But something inside told me that this guy, as quirky as he was, was not going to lose, no matter the odds. I was all in.

George and I visited stores in Lexington, Clarksville, and Ashland to see what was working and what wasn't in the kitchen. We would watch how the orders moved, often sitting five feet off the ground on the top of boxes of potatoes we'd piled up to give us a bird's-eye view of the action. After the kitchen closed for the night we'd climb down from our cardboard perches and walk through the flow of each menu item, sometimes reworking things well into the early hours of the morning until we got it right.

As for the rest of the building, I wasn't done fiddling, either. I hired an architect to design a potential prototype facade, but after many drawings back and forth, George and I decided to do it ourselves. (The architect's renderings resembled the Alamo more than a friendly steakhouse on a Texas country road. I wanted potential customers to feel warmth and welcome, not concern about being ambushed inside by Santa Anna's army.) We incorporated the roofline of Clarksville, the two towers with flags from the Lexington store, and the signage from Gainesville. As for the three failing stores we'd opened in 1994, we decided there was nothing worth taking.

For the interior, we chose to keep the bar area from Lexington, with dining rooms on three sides around. We liked certain elements of Clarksville but rearranged their location in future restaurants. Many of the design ideas and measurements were the same ones that I had used in designing nightclubs years before. Every time I visited another restaurant, I'd pull out my tape measure and measure booths, tables, plates. It was crazy.

The kitchen was pretty much George's baby, except for my insistence on display cooking that we'd had in our first store in Clarksville.

I had picked a new location in Louisville to be our prototype. It was an old gas station that shared a parking lot with a day care. Since the day care closed at six p.m., and was only open Monday to Friday, we basically got twice the parking. My original investors, after seeing the success of Lexington, Ashland, and Lake City, were now ready to get back in the game and were excited after seeing the prototype drawings as well as glancing over the last three stores' opening profit numbers. We also qualified for an SBA loan, provided by Liberty Bank, and were off to the races.

The team kept getting stronger as well. A new manager, Gina Tobin, had been lured by Al Ales, our new head of operations, from her job as an area manager for Chi-Chi's in Michigan. She was to relocate to Louisville to open and run the new prototype store. Gina paid for her flight to Louisville out of her own pocket, not sure if she'd ever get reimbursed. She traveled up to Lexington to visit our newest location, tried the food, loved the food, and then drove back to Louisville for her interview with me.

As usual, I was running late. Even though it was December and freezing outside, I apparently showed up in shorts, a sweatshirt, and hiking boots. We only had about fifteen minutes together, and I was mostly concerned with how many people from Chi-Chi's she could bring with her. Between the Sizzler remodels and attracting many Chi-Chi's folks, I was well on my way to systematically eliminating crappy food from the American palate.

I kept the meeting with Gina brief because my wife, Leslie, had just gone into labor with our soon-to-be son, Max. I had decided on the date of December 19, 1995, for our Clarkesville party because it was the exact day our baby was due to be born and what baby *ever* comes on its due date, right? I'm always late, so I was certain little Max would be, too. Boy, was I ever wrong. I'd forgotten that Leslie was always on time.

I said goodbye to Gina, raced to the restaurant for the party, said "Merry Christmas," gave a quick toast, handed my credit card to Karen Hill, and bailed just in time to welcome Max Taylor to the world several hours later. I imagined that Max the dog and the spirit of Maximillian's the disco were looking down with pride on their namesake.

Gina somehow agreed to join our ragtag team and trained in Lexington with Mark Thornburg, the managing partner. She assisted in opening Myrtle Beach and then headed to Louisville to hire a staff and open our new flagship. Cash was still tight and bills in arrears, so a month before opening I drove over to give Gina an inspirational pep talk.

---

**GINA TOBIN, VP of training**

Pep talk, my butt. Kent told me if my store didn't open strong, Texas Roadhouse wouldn't make it. There I was, I'd just quit my job with Chi-Chi's and moved to Kentucky. I'd already had one payroll check bounce and he was telling me if I didn't deliver, the entire company would be done.

I pulled up my big-girl pants and went to work. I joined the business chamber and delivered notes personally to all the members. I visited businesses with 10-percent-off meal cards. I went down to the local auto speedway and fed the guys in the announcer booth so they would promote the new opening. I went into local churches to deliver rolls and ask to cater their picnics. In one case I entered a church and looked behind me in total shock. I had just left the work site [of the restaurant] and was leaving a trail of muddy footprints on their new, white carpet.

---

A few months earlier, the word must have been getting around the Sizzler world, and I had received interest from a couple other of their operators who wanted to do conversions to our format. One operator, however, was cool about starting from scratch and building a prototype in his town of Myrtle Beach, South Carolina. In a perfect world we would have finished our first prototype in Louisville, tweaked it, and then moved on to the next. As usual, we weren't going to follow any traditional formula. We agreed to a deal with our new partner in Myrtle Beach and he put shovel to ground a full two months before we were set to start with Louisville. George and I jumped on a regional prop carrier and flew down to the Palmetto State to get things organized.

George and I spent a couple of days going through the Myrtle Beach plans on-site, changing measurements here and there by a few inches. We finished one night after midnight, flew back to Louisville at six the next morning, drove to the Louisville construction site, and made changes there until midnight. The next day we showed up at the architect's to have him make permanent changes on the prototype blueprints. We were back at the site that afternoon with Magic Markers in hand, tape measures, tape, etc., and got the crews started on the changes.

George bragged that I could never wear him out with such long hours. If I was going to run that hard, he planned to keep up, right by my side. I knew I'd found a kindred spirit. If only he'd run track at Ballard High, we'd have been unstoppable.

Our final Texas Roadhouse logo was designed around this time. A few months before Louisville was to open, I found myself out one night at Gerstle's Place, a local bar, and being "overserved," I ended up sleeping on the couch of a buddy, Joe Dulworth. I woke up the next day and drove home. I was going to change into my running shorts to hit the road and run off my hangover, but as I pulled out my money clip, change, and pen from my jean's pocket, a cocktail napkin tumbled out as well. I must have stuffed it in my pocket sometime during the previous night, and as I unfolded it, I found I'd doodled a new logo design sometime the night before in my merry reverie.

Up to this point, our logo had been a large image of the state of Texas wearing a cowboy hat and the words TEXAS ROADHOUSE emblazed across the state. The new logo I'd drawn was a variation on that theme but way cooler. It retained the state of Texas with the cowboy hat perched upon the Panhandle, but in a smaller format, at the top. The new logo had more of the ambience of a roadhouse from the fifties, with a rounded black background image that reinforced vintage neon lettering. I admit I was suffering from pride of ownership, but I thought it was on target. Everything about it spoke to comfort food and old-fashioned fun. Plus, it had the added dramatic value of being drafted on a friggin' cocktail napkin late one night in a bar where nobody knows your name.

I shared the new logo with a few of our folks and most really dug it, so I had our sign company make up a six-foot-long version and we put it over the door of the Louisville prototype. The exterior of the new building would feature both the old and new logos, which would drive my marketing folks crazy today, but back then we were still trying things. My guys wanted to slap the new logo on our employees' gray shirts, but I still didn't know if it would last. We were reworking everything. I said no at first but relented a few years later because it was obvious this would be the logo that would stand the test of time.

The Louisville prototype also featured Native American mural number four, as we'd had three successful openings in a row, each celebrating a famous Indian chief. Usually, the chief was from a nation that had been located in the area where the restaurant was located. So from that point forward, we would have all our restaurants feature great chiefs from the past, which honors their spirits in our stores.

On July 10, 1996, we opened our first Louisville restaurant. Gina had convinced a few local stock-car drivers into displaying their vehicles in the parking lot, and she had a cowboy riding his horse up and down the road carrying a Texas Roadhouse flag and waving people in. The building looked great, the crowds were strong, and the food was spectacular from the start thanks to Jim Broyles's perfectionism. I stood out front with George Lask in awe of our shared creation.

### GEORGE LASK

That opening night the building was all lit up and the American and Texas flags were waving in the wind. It was a great feeling. We had an amazing-looking building, the food was terrific, and there were so many people waiting to get in that they were hanging around outside. I sensed that from that point forward, things were going to change. I said to Kent, "You're not going to believe the possibilities ahead for us." He didn't say anything, he was in the zone, so who knows what he was thinking.

We wrapped up that year opening three more joint-venture restaurants with investors in New Philly, Ohio; Melbourne, Florida; and Clarksburg, West Virginia, in addition to Myrtle Beach. We also had franchise openings in Muncie and Terre Haute, Indiana, in addition to the Louisville store.

Brian Judd, our first managing partner in Clarksville, was responsible for finding some of the spots for his soon-to-be-opened restaurants.

I loved Brian's moxie, but told him I still wanted to approve all sites (as I have done for our first six hundred stores). I had driven over to Terre Haute to check out a location he was proposing but didn't think it was right. As we were heading out of town, I spotted a restaurant close to the interstate and told Brian that we should check it out. He said there was no FOR SALE sign out front and told me that there must be other sites. I flipped the car around, and we pulled up to the place. There were only half a dozen cars outside. We went in and asked for the owner. Brian chatted the guy up briefly then we headed back to Louisville. Within a month Brian had cut a deal to buy the restaurant. The moral: If a full-service restaurant has only six cars in the parking lot in the middle of the dinner rush, it is most likely for sale.

That fall, we filmed our first and last TV commercial, which was shown on local cable. The thirty-second spot was filmed in El Paso, Texas, at the same real roadhouse that sits out in the desert and was used for the exterior scenes in the Patrick Swayze movie *Road House*. Other than that cool bit of trivia, we didn't get much from the ad and have committed since then to do no national TV or major media advertising.

That fall we finally closed the underperforming Sarasota location, with me in charge of shutting things down. We had recently put a new air conditioner on the roof and wanted it back. We were in dire need of a new cooling unit for our kitchen in Gainesville. But our landlord had a guard there during the day watching what we were taking out of the building. I had paid for the air conditioner—to be more accurate, I was still paying for it—and I wanted it back. But the security guard wasn't about to let us pull the unit off the roof. I waited until two a.m. and brought in a crane and a crew and we lifted the entire unit off. By four a.m., the AC was on a truck to Gainesville, a sheet of plywood had patched the hole in the roof, while guard Paul Blart was cuddled up with his nightstick somewhere in the Florida night, none the wiser.

It took the landlord six months to discover we'd taken the unit. He threatened to sue, but he had carted off a lot of my TVs, so after some angry back-and-forth (with plenty of expletives), he gave up, probably figuring he was more than even.

As another plus, at the end of 1996, we were able to move from ninety days late to a mere sixty days late on payments to suppliers—a nice 33 percent improvement. Things appeared to be looking up.

My last project before the year ended was to try to convince my old Denver acquaintance Steve Ortiz to join the company. He was now a regional manager for Bennigan's in Dallas. I knew that since he was a rogue like me, he'd eventually get in trouble; it was just a matter of time. He'd blown me off two years in a row, so I decided this time to send him a plane ticket. I promised that if he'd fly to Louisville and give me just twenty-four hours, I would quit bothering him if he wasn't interested.

Steve acquiesced. He flew in, visited Gina Tobin's new prototype, but seemed very chill about the whole operation. Still, I could tell by the time he left he was considering it. I called him later and offered him the number two role in the company, heading up operations. I'd realized my current operations guy wasn't the answer. Steve said no.

We now had fifteen stores. But if Steve wasn't interested, I had to find someone to take over operations and fast.

# MADE-FROM-SCRATCH SIDES (WHAT I LEARNED):

- Your suppliers are your partners. Value them and work with them. But it's a partnership. If they don't live up to their promises, find creative ways to achieve the same goals through new avenues.
- Great inventors keep tinkering. Never be satisfied with good enough results. Encourage your people to push you to continue improving.
- Your competitors probably have amazing talent who don't feel appreciated or valued. Don't fall for the not-invented-here syndrome. Be willing to bring in good people from anywhere, and listen to their ideas.
- Don't get so hung up on following a correct formula to success that you miss out on opportunities (we opened the second prototype before the first).
- Be creative with your store openings. Think outside the box and don't be afraid to go big.

## CHAPTER 10

# STAYIN' ALIVE

The year 1997 began on a down note. We had to close our store in Clearwater, Florida. I had proved with the location just how little I'd known in the early days about selecting a site. Guests not only had to make a U-turn on a busy road to get to us, but they had to cross multiple lanes of oncoming traffic. Then, even if you were willing to take your life in your hands to get some ribs, there was a chance you might not find a parking spot. The lot only had one hundred spaces, nowhere near enough for a busy weekend at Texas Roadhouse.

Since I had had the experience of closing our Sarasota store, and remembered how much that sucked, I sent Al to close Clearwater. I wanted to focus on moving forward and didn't need the buzzkill.

Some good news—long predicted and hoped for—was that Steve Ortiz had finally gotten into trouble at Bennigan's. Hurrah! Steve told me he was fed up with fighting the bureaucracy and wanted in with me. The bad news: He'd accepted $57,000 in severance money and had agreed to a nonsolicitation clause for two years (stating that he wouldn't poach their employees). He would of course quickly violate the agreement, but more on that later.

Steve had no interest in running operations for us. Instead he wanted to do a twelve-store joint venture with stores in Texas. I agreed to that as

I knew he would attract and bring many talented people with him. We still didn't have a single location in our namesake state of Texas, though most people thought we did. I did little in the early years to dissuade them. Heck, I even had our store comment cards (located on the tables for feedback) addressed to a PO box in Dallas to make people believe we were located in the Lone Star State. It wasn't Milli Vanilli–level deception, but it had a certain charm. Our mail would arrive at a copy shop in Dallas and the staff knew to forward everything to our new three-office headquarters in Louisville (which we shared with our accountant). We used two of the three rooms. One was for Karen Hill, since she handled the money, and the other was a conference room where five or six of us at a time would cram in and jockey to use one of the two phones. I realized then I needed to invest in one of those newfangled "cellular telephones," and found a used one the size of my mailbox. The antenna alone could have herded cattle.

Steve had hired his first management team for his initial store, which he was planning to open by midyear, and may have accidentally invited a few folks from Bennigan's to come with him. His new team consisted of Jerry Morgan, Paul Marshall, Bruce Hornbuckle, and Bill Munson. Steve started a ritual at his house with the team that consisted of a run, a dip in his cold pool (it was January), and a shot of tequila. The new managers were well worth the hassle we'd get from Bennigan's. Three would become market partners (area managers) themselves, and one, Jerry, would become a regional for us and eventually president. Eight additional market partners would eventually be promoted from the twenty or so people Steve brought on in 1997, proving that he has a gift for finding and attracting talent.

Steve, in fact, has many talents. He reminds me of Vince Lombardi, the legendary Green Bay Packers coach. He's aggressive, demanding, and a solid team builder. Winning is the only option when you work for Steve, and accountability rules. What Steve didn't plan on was an additional delay of six months before his first store could open. So, with him being a partner and not an employee (drawing no salary), his savings dwindled fast. His wife had to go back to work to pay the family bills. Then, to add insult to injury, Bennigan's—not happy with multiple deserters—served papers to sue both Steve and me, draining all of Steve's remaining severance as well as what little money I had on hand to fight the challenge. Evidently, hell hath no fury like a Bennigan's scorned.

Steve finally brought on John Beck, who had been his HR guy at Bennigan's (John smartly took no severance), who took over recruiting. We knew that when we finally settled with Bennigan's, the pipeline of talent would most likely dry up, so John made hay while the sun was shining. It was a productive year for leadership hires (and grand theft of personnel). By the time we went public six years later, ten of the twelve folks Steve hired had become market partners, and all but two are with us as of 2020. One of my favorites, Greg Beckel, operates our restaurants in North Carolina and is still helping me think of crazy, out-of-the-box ideas that we eventually make mainstream.

**STEVE ORTIZ, Franchise/JV partner (1998–present); Chief Operating Officer (2001–15)**

I met Kent in Denver back in 1985. I was a Bennigan's area manager and he ran the Arapahoe Road restaurant. He was a renegade back then and seemed to get in trouble a lot. When he left Denver to go back to Louisville to take care of his two daughters, he told me that one day we would be partners in one of his concept ideas. I thought, *Yeah, good luck. Fat chance of that.* A few years later, when he opened his first Roadhouse prototype, I came to Louisville to check it out; listened to him share his excitement, enthusiasm, and knowledge of details; and apparently, after six years of him chasing me, I took the bait. His unique passion and persistence, as always, were unwavering.

With the success of our prototype location, I was sure we had something we could grow upon. The problem was funding. We were still just barely getting by, paying our bills month to month. We needed capital to expand, but I had no idea who would lend us money. I visited a few banks, but with our balance sheet in the red—due to me hiring so many people from Bennigan's—the bankers pretty much laughed or wished me good luck.

As always, I wanted to put the pedal to the metal and race to a better future but didn't have the gas money to get there. I hear that's a common flaw with entrepreneurs with a vision. As you know, some make it, and some don't.

I started getting creative in looking for money. My first mark: the country singer Garth Brooks. Random, I know, but the reality was the dude was rolling in dough and he admittedly had "friends in low places," so I figured why the hell not? I put together a financial proposal, got in my car, and drove to Nashville to find the superstar. I made some inquiries and found that he had offices. Really? A country singer with offices. I know, right?

With no appointment, naturally, I barged in like I owned the joint to find the place deserted. I peeked into offices. Not a soul in sight. I waited for an hour in the waiting room until a receptionist finally appeared— maybe coming back from lunch—who looked at me like I had just stepped off the moon. She said there was no one there for me to meet with, especially not Garth Brooks. I handed over my proposal and drove back home. But I didn't give up. After a few days I called his offices, left a message, but still no response. I called again, then again, and again. Finally, I got a callback! After a hectic evening in one of our stores, I found a message waiting on my cell phone: "Mr. Kent Taylor, this is so-and-so from Mr. Brooks's office." Holy crap! I inhaled deeply, a smile forming. Then I heard: "Could you please stop calling? We aren't interested." *Click*. Oh.

Such a shame. Looking back, I know that I could have made Garth slightly richer. Although, when I think about it, in our hundreds of locations over the years we've played enough of his music to put more than enough ASCAP/BMI money in his pockets. But hey, no big deal, just another fun name to add to the long list of people who rejected me in the early days. Just like that girl in the eleventh grade whose name I can't remember now. *Oh well.*

Another potential mark was basketball legend Larry Bird. Even more randomly selected than the others I hassled. I noticed the former Celtics great sitting in first class as I boarded a flight heading back home from Florida. I was in coach. Well, to be fair, I was in what they called economy coach, an even crappier class than coach, which were the last three rows by the restrooms. It was steerage on the *Titanic*, essentially.

I stuffed myself into my seat and pulled out one of my proposals and then waited for Larry to come back to fold his six-foot-eight-inch frame into the pisser. Halfway through the flight I realized that first class likely had its own lavatory complete with heated toilet seats and aromatherapy mists, so I extricated myself from my chair and headed up to the first-class curtain. I was on the move, an unstoppable force heading for my destiny with a legend. But when I swished open the curtain there was a much larger, opposing force in a skirt entrenched there with arms folded. The first-class flight attendant blocked the aisle and didn't care about my proposal. She told me to get back to my seat. I made an impassioned plea. *Zilch*. Listen, she said. If I behaved like a good boy and sat my ass back down, she would deliver my proposal to Mr. Bird before we landed. Fair enough.

I stayed planted in 36E until we landed, then had to wait for the slowest people in the universe to depart the plane. The. Plane. Ugh! People! After Madge and Otis finally shuffled onto the jet bridge, I made it to the front. I must admit I was half expecting to find Larry waiting for me, proposal in hand, bobbing his head knowingly (think Miss Shields's rapturous reaction to Ralphie's essay in *A Christmas Story*). But there was no Larry waiting there. The flight attendant handed me my proposal and said that Larry had been asleep the whole flight and she hadn't wanted to bother him.

"Couldn't you have given it to him after we landed?" I asked, flabbergasted.

"I do have a job, you know," she replied.

I snatched up the proposal and hauled ass through the airport, even tossing my bag behind a pillar on the way so I could run faster. Outside, on the curb, I looked right and then left and spotted Bird's lanky frame about half a football field away. I started screaming, "Mr. Bird, Mr. Bird!" and began running toward him. Just before I got there, a car pulled up and Larry jumped into the passenger seat. I distinctly heard him say, "Step on it, there's a lunatic out here," and the car door slammed shut, tires screeched, and I was left alone to catch my breath.

Another rejection down, I headed back into the airport to retrieve my bag.

Still, I wasn't deterred. I had to find some money to keep us afloat.

Somehow, by that summer of 1997, Leslie and I saved enough to take a trip for a few days to Bermuda. We checked into a modest hotel near the beach and hung out on the sand. One night, at a local restaurant, fate intervened again. Our server told us that the evening before he had served billionaire (and former presidential candidate) Ross Perot. It seemed the business magnate owned a home a short distance from the hotel in a gated community.

The next day, as we lay on the beach, my mind began swirling. I told Leslie I was going for a run, went back to the room, grabbed a proposal from my travel bag, and took off on a scooter I'd rented from the front desk. Hell or high water I was going to get my proposal into the hands of H. Friggin' Ross Perot.

Perhaps you can picture how the scene unfolded. All six-feet-two-inches of me rode the world's tiniest scooter up to the guard shack of a beautiful Bermuda gated community. I was wearing swim trunks and a tank top (what I call business formal), and I brandished the envelope containing my proposal. I claimed to be a delivery guy and used, I kid you not, a terrible British accent (not easy for a guy from Kentucky). When the guard said I could leave the package with him, I claimed, "Oh, no, there's cash inside, and I'll need a signature at his house."

I'd scribbled an address on the outside of the envelope (I'd taken a guess, of course) and the guard looked at it suspiciously. "Well," he said, "that's not right." I was caught. The guard reached over and snatched the envelope from my sweaty grip, and then proceeded to write down the right address.

Holy crap. Thank the good Lord above for this inept security dude. He then waved me up the road.

My heart racing, I puttered the scooter toward his imposing home, knocked several times at the front door, but got no answer. I leaned the package against the front door and then headed back to the hotel, where I proudly confessed what I'd done to Leslie.

"No doubt I'll hear from him soon," I said.

"Yeah, right." She laughed. "I'm sure."

We bet a dollar on it.

The next week passed and a call finally did come. Ross Perot's finance manager was on the line and said he would be calling the following week to set up a meeting with Mr. Perot, but he wanted me to know that he'd received the proposal and they were very interested. I hung up, let out a whoop, and hopped up and down. I yelled to Leslie in the other room, "I told you so!"

My daughter came running to see what was happening, and I lectured her about the power of positive thinking. Leslie handed me a buck, to pay off the bet, but as the evening progressed she seemed more and more out of sorts. I wasn't sure what was bothering her about the deal, but I couldn't worry about it. It was the best news I'd had in a long time, and I went to bed excited to tell my Roadies the great news the next day. I had the best night's sleep I'd had in years.

The next morning Leslie was waiting for me at the breakfast table. She said she had some tough news to share.

"First of all," she said, "you have to know I feel really bad." My heart sank. I asked if something was wrong with her or the kids or my parents.

"No. We're all fine. But the call you got from Ross Perot's guy, um, that was a prank."

"What? No it wasn't."

"It was. I'm sorry, Kent. I feel terrible. It was one of my friends. I got him to call you. I thought it would be funny." She backed away.

It took a few seconds to register. She had been BS-ing me. She had faked the call. I went from sky-high to dismay to homicidal maniac then back to dismay. I begrudgingly accepted her apology, told her there was no way I was giving the dollar back, and headed to the office.

Okay, so no Ross Perot, no Larry Bird, no Garth Brooks or any of the other several dozen celebrities I'd pitched was going to save us. Go figure. I had to think of my next move. By this point, the company was getting desperately low on funds, and I was less worried about funding future growth and more concerned with keeping my loved ones fed.

I had met a guy named George Rich back in 1996, just before we opened our Louisville prototype store. He was a finance guy from Baltimore. He visited the prototype, seemed intrigued, and said he could be of benefit to me. He had consulted with Outback Steakhouse a few years before and had been part of the team that took them public. Hey, if Chris Sullivan believed in him, then by golly so could I (since I didn't really have any options anyway). He said he had a special interest in retail investment, and that he could help me put together a board of advisers. We did that. It included my attorney, Bill Strench, original investor John Rhodes, and a couple of others. We then put together, with Bill and George, a private-placement offering of $5 million, money we desperately needed to pay bills and help us add more locations.

The first thing we had to do was to turn Texas Roadhouse into a real company, with bylaws and incorporation documents. At that time, Roadhouse consisted of myself; my creation; a few stores owned by my docs; some other individual store investors; as well as quite a few franchisees. The docs and I struggled to find common ground on how to incorporate, but as part of the agreement we finally decided to roll up our four jointly owned stores (Clarksville, Gainesville, Louisville, and the newly opened Elizabethtown, Kentucky, store). Since I owned the concept rights, I was able to retain more than 50 percent of the company, including the 1 percent royalty that in 1997 would pay me $120,000 in lieu of a salary (less than an average Texas Roadhouse managing partner makes today).

We carved out 15 percent of the company for the $5 million, effectively valuing the company at around $33 million at the close of 1997, even though our cash flow was negative. The doctors each put in an extra

$500,000, and I borrowed a half million from George Rich to fund my part of the private placement. I had just finally paid off my credit cards and debt, which had kept us afloat the previous five years, and maybe had $5,000 in the bank.

**GEORGE RICH, investor, member of Andy's Outreach board**

I met Kent through a friend in 1996. When I visited his first prototype in Louisville and tasted the food, I was sold. I invested in a few stores and then helped Kent with his private placement. Texas Roadhouse, for sure, has been one of my best investments ever, but more than that, I've enjoyed the people and their fun culture. In addition, I am very proud of the work their employee giving fund, Andy's Outreach, has accomplished for their employees in time of need.

And Kent, that man's smart, very forward-thinking, and mostly never serious, quite fun, and somewhat crazy. Quite the odd combination for a successful CEO.

Since I was both overseeing operations and construction, along with shouldering many other responsibilities, I decided that it was time to find someone to oversee construction. Being an entrepreneur at heart, I thought what the heck, I'll just start a construction company, find a partner, keep costs low, and build Roadhouses. We'd keep profit low on our jobs while building projects for others at a bigger percentage. And that's what happened. I found that partner in Scott Gregor, whom I met at the Charlotte, North Carolina, airport in early 1997. Since I was into buffalo, the West, and the mountains, we chose the name Buffalo Construction. We ended up saving the company quite a bit of money up to 2004 when I had to sell my 80 percent share before Roadhouse went public.

Another great hire in 1997 was Dee Shaughnessy, another Chi-Chi's alumna, who came on board to run our HR department. She partnered with John Beck and found a lot of people who helped us grow the company in the early days. She would let me know if someone was messing with our culture and attempt to coach me often on my misuse of the English language, usually to no avail.

Near the end of the year, we opened our first store west of the Mississippi, in Grand Junction, Colorado. It was a joint venture and my parents invested part of their retirement savings. My dad had just retired from GE after thirty-plus years, and told me that while he'd grown more confident in his son's business acumen, if I lost his money I was sure to earn his wrath. No pressure there.

So we closed out 1997 with a newly formed company and twenty-five stores in nine states—from the Florida coast to the Rocky Mountains. We also had developed a new "zapp" philosophy, based on the book *Zapp!* by William Byham, PhD, which embraced giving power to the people, focusing on zapping people rather than sapping them. Zapp, which we still talk about, is about creating a positive vibe with your people as opposed to sucking their energy and drive. Since I had worked for companies that did a good job at sapping their folks, I vowed to never let that happen at Texas Roadhouse. And, I promised that if our leaders ever adopted the sapp management philosophy, they would earn my wrath (a loving homage to my pop).

I also ended the year accepting an award as Kentucky and southern Indiana's Emerging Entrepreneur of the Year. It was a nice honor, and it did give me a chuckle as my "emerging" so far had taken thirteen effing years from idea to rejection, from success to failure, and finally from failure to a glimmer of success.

As 1998 dawned, shock of shocks, we were approaching the full $5 million target for our private placement. After the money the docs and I had put in ($2 million), the other money was contributed by franchisees and private investors. One of my buddies, Joe Dulworth, had purchased shares with most of the money he'd made selling his business. I tried to convince him to reduce his investment, but he said he was "all in." In the end, when we went public, Joe and everyone else made a nice multiple on their investment. But those kinds of returns were no sure thing in '98.

Early in the year, Steve Ortiz was finally able to open his first restaurant in Texas (in Grand Prairie, to be exact) and his wife no longer had to win all the bread. We also made Jim Broyles our first vice president, appointing him as VP of food and beverage. That meant that I could assume the role of president instead of founder or proprietor—not that titles have ever impressed me, especially ones you can give yourself.

We celebrated our five-year anniversary at store number one in Clarksville with the same country band that had played at our opening, Dishman & Ballard, which performed on the long-abandoned stage above the bar. Knowing that I had bailed on our Christmas party with the birth of Max back in 1995, and wanting to really celebrate our half decade in business, I threw another party in the basement of my new house and invited the doctors, the original Clarksville team, my accountant Pat, lawyer Bill, and a handful of other key players (not surprisingly, neither Garth Brooks nor Ross Perot showed). I dressed in my nasty Bad Santa outfit, complete with lit cigar, and passed out a few surprise gifts and bottles of Dom Pérignon to each attendee. We made a pact that no one would open their bottle until the day we went public. Not being one for sentiment, and having a short memory when booze is involved, I cracked my bottle and downed it within a week. Hey, it was just sitting there! Thankfully, Karen Hill and a couple of others honored the pledge and six years later we reconvened just after our IPO was issued, again in my basement, and opened the remaining bottles. A member of the team gifted me back a bottle and it sits proudly today on my bookshelf. Empty of course.

Midyear we held our first official company gathering in the garden spot of America: French Lick, Indiana. Yes, *that* French Lick, the hometown of our buddy Larry Bird, whom I didn't *bother* inviting. He had his chance. In short, French Lick may not have been Maui, but it was cheap. We finally had a little money in the bank to grow the business, but not enough for junkets to Hawaii, not yet. It was more important to invest in our quality.

As we had grown, I was noticing that the consistency of our food was starting to slip. Our food quality guy, Jim, was only one man and couldn't be everywhere at once. Between training food prep, line execution, new store openings, and meat cutting quality, I had to come up with a solution or we would slip backward, and guests would not be as loyal. So we hired our first food tech, Buddy Walker, to assist in ensuring our quality objectives. I knew that if Buddy made a positive difference, we could expand the program.

We found that if Buddy monitored somewhere between ten to fifteen stores, he could maintain his effectiveness (after we screwed up by giving him more than fifty stores). Beyond that, he didn't have enough time to make a difference. But what an impact he made. Thanks to Buddy's good work, we decided to expand the program. We later changed the name of the food techs to Product Coaches, and we promoted some of our top kitchen managers to the position. Since then, we've limited their store count to between twelve to fourteen.

I'm proud to say Buddy is still with us, protecting our food standards, and we now have more than seventy product coaches ensuring that our food is recipe right and that our in-store meat cutters maintain our strict standards.

---

**BUDDY WALKER, product coach**

I started as a kitchen manager in 1996. In 1997, Jim Broyles asked me to be our first food tech [along] with a guy named Kevin. We were to visit stores and score their food recipe adherence [and] study their food execution, cleanliness, and sanitation. In addition, we would spend time watching and teaching the restaurants' meat cutters. Jim said that Kent wanted the stores to be more consistent with our food, and was adamant about taste, flavor . . . the temperature of our offerings became legendary.

---

That spring, on my daughter Brittany's birthday, April 20 (4/20 for Willie fans), I had the additional pleasure of hiring Debbie Hayden, who had been purchasing director for Chi-Chi's, another restaurant company that by that point was not long for this world (at least this continent). She brought some great vendor relationships with her, and we quickly discovered she had an uncanny ability to earn loyalty among vendor partners. Debbie's skills would not only net us the best pricing and service over the next two decades, but when the pandemic of 2020 hit she would help save our bacon, as we were taken care of first while other restaurant chains were struggling to find supplies (more on that in Chapter 19).

Debbie took over purchasing duties from me and Jim and began immediately sourcing the best midwestern choice steaks to enhance the Legendary Food part of our mission statement. Legendary Service, the second part of our mission, was still not up to snuff, in my opinion, so I started a search for a new head of training. Just like with Debbie, Juanita Coleman arrived and quickly made a significant contribution.

**DEBBIE HAYDEN, VP of purchasing (1998–present)**
I remember first interviewing with Kent sometime in the late winter of 1998. I sat in the area by the receptionist waiting for a while and listening to the receptionist take several calls from what appeared to be either creditors or collection agencies. I was dressed in typical interview clothes, a suit, stockings, and so on. Kent finally showed up in shorts, hiking boots, and a sweatshirt. Mind you, it's probably thirty degrees out, but hey, that's Kent.

Steve Ortiz continued to bring on board quite a few Bennigan's folks, and by year's end they had opened stores for us in Iowa, Texas, Tennessee, Ohio, Pennsylvania, Utah, and North Carolina. As 1998 turned to 1999, we had forty-five locations in fourteen states and were cooking with gas.

# MADE-FROM-SCRATCH SIDES (WHAT I LEARNED):

- Acquiring great talent is worth the fight. A truly talented leader is not just worth a little more than an average hire; they can be worth up to ten times more.

- When raising money after a start-up phase, have people who know what they're doing help you. Current partners and employees are the first place to start looking for that additional capital.

- Focus on "zapping" people rather than sapping them. Zapp is about creating a positive vibe with your team members instead of sucking their energy and drive. If a leader ever adopts the sapp management philosophy, send them packing.

- Consistency and quality are paramount as you grow. Accept lower profits if you can ensure your product is always going to be as good as the original.

- Develop a simple, memorable mission statement and live it (ours is Legendary Food, Legendary Service). Invest what is necessary to live up to your mission. Hire the right people in training and quality.

CHAPTER 11

# LIFE'S BEEN GOOD

Since Steve Ortiz hadn't accepted my offer to run operations—he was happily opening stores in our namesake state of Texas—I went with his suggestion and hired a guy named Mike who took command of ops in early 1999. That spring, we also had our first official Managing Partner Conference, and we held it in Orlando. We couldn't afford to invite spouses, everyone slept two to a room, we only had one big dinner, and we had no entertainment (unless you count me at midnight after a few too many bourbons). Once again, I was asked to leave a hotel bar when, lacking patience, I had gone behind the counter to pour a few drinks for my Roadies. Seemed like a good idea at the time.

I had been wearing a newly acquired BUBBA belt buckle, which, along with whatever wild stuff I did (that is admittedly pretty fuzzy in my memory), earned me the nickname "Bubba." It has stuck to this day.

Before my high jinks in the bar, I handed out awards in a rental tux that I had purchased for sixty dollars and had worn at my wedding six years earlier. Gina Tobin became our third winner of the Managing Partner of the Year award, joining Brian Judd (Clarksville) and Jeff Read (Gainesville), who were also awarded their rings in Orlando. I figured that if we had given out those awards those two years (1997 and 1998),

143

they would have won. Neal Niklaus (Ashland, Kentucky) came in second with Dave Palazzo (Columbus, Indiana) rounding out third for 1999.

I had also created a Legends of Texas Roadhouse award, naming Brian Judd, Jeff Read, Jim Broyles, Karen Hill, and John Rhodes (original investor) as winners.

With every up comes a down, and we had one in 1999. In October we closed our third store, which had been in Cincinnati, the last we would close for more than ten years. We also opened twenty-three (like Jordan's jersey number, *Go 'Heels!*) new stores, including our first ones in Idaho and Michigan.

That year I also attended a restaurant leadership conference in Napa Valley, California, hoping to learn a few things from others in the industry, plus maybe find me a president who could enhance our support functions. At the time I was focused on growing the company, while still staying clued in on operations and food quality. In addition, I was our only real estate person, so I needed help.

At the conference I met a guy from New Orleans named G. J. Hart. He was running Al Copeland's restaurants and, in particular, a food production facility that supplied spice packages to Popeyes restaurants. G.J. was fancy dressing and fancy talking, and it seemed like he might be the well-heeled yin to my redneck yang. Weeks passed and I kept pressing him to consider being our president, figuring he would run our support functions while I drove growth and ensured my new ops guy didn't screw things up.

I had been growing worried about my new operations director. It didn't seem like he was the best fit with our culture. He had already tried to change our Roadie store uniform from T-shirt and jeans to polo shirt and khakis. You can just picture Patrick Swayze donning a pair of crisp, ironed khakis and an alligator polo in the movie *Road House*, right? When my operations director made the attempt, thankfully our supplier, Printex—run by Greg Dutton—told him there was no way under the sun that Kent would approve it. Our T-shirt vendor knew our culture better than our own ops guy.

In addition, he was more of a top-down guy rather than a bottom-up dude. What do I mean by that? To envision a bottom-up organization, think of an upside-down pyramid.

In this type of company, the leader is at the bottom and learns from the frontline people at the top. The leader's job is to support, encourage, and finally celebrate his/her people's successes and sometimes even failures. Success is so often built on attempts that don't always get results but have powerful lessons that eventually lead to kick-ass ideas.

Too many companies, small businesses, and even the government either punish risk takers or punish the manager for allowing their people to go rogue. In those cultures, failures get hidden out of fear of scorn or even job loss.

Prominently displayed on the wall of my office are artifacts from each of the three stores I opened in 1994 and eventually had to close. There's a fish from Sarasota, a cow skull from Clearwater, and a fish from Cincinnati. Under each is a plaque showing their open and close dates

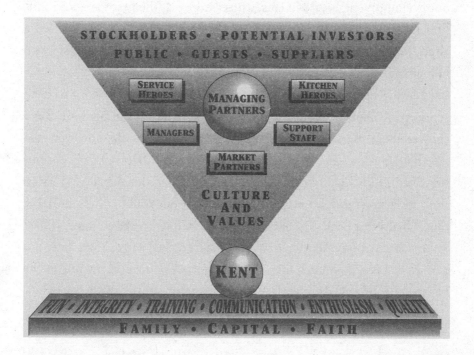

and how much money each lost. I'm proud of those failures because of the lessons learned. Since 1994, we've only had to close three of the next six hundred stores, a 99.5 percent success rate. I can live with that.

As the twentieth century came to a close, we took a deep breath. While some poor saps were pumping money into their computer systems to keep them from crashing—what a scam Y2K was—we were just happy that our paychecks were no longer bouncing.

Indeed, January 1, 2000, came without a hitch. We barely noticed. Our computer systems continued to hum along just fine without a minute of programming invested, and we turned our attention to getting to one hundred stores.

Since we were finally profitable (knock wood, spin three times, and kiss a frog), we held our second annual Managing Partner Conference, this time in San Diego, and for the first time invited spouses. We couldn't afford big-time entertainment like Shamu or the San Diego Chargers cheerleaders, but we did visit the zoo and had a nice cover band play at our evening event. Neal Niklaus, whose store was the first to pass $5 million in annual sales, won Managing Partner of the Year. He earned a check for $10,000, a cool ring, and an eagle sculpture. George Lask (who helped create our first prototype) won our Legends award.

During the awards ceremony, people thought it was a hoot to keep sending me shots of tequila and beers while I was at the podium. But I showed them! By downing every. Last. One. Doing so did, however, create an urgent, pressing, even painful need for relief. Before I gave out our big award, I just had to excuse myself and dashed out the stage door to find the nearest toilet. I returned a new man but couldn't help noticing that when I got back onstage the room was filled with laughter. *What? What'd I miss?* I figured someone must have cracked a joke. Only later did I find out I was the punch line. I had forgotten to turn off my mic in the bathroom. Oh well. At least they could hear that I always wash my hands.

As a leader, you have to accept that stuff happens.

This was the year that I also took the plunge and signed up for Flight Options, which sells flight time in small private airplanes. As we had ramped up expansion beyond Louisville, it was getting more difficult to visit potential real estate sites flying commercial. Also, most of our stores were located in smaller cities, and they often had no direct flights from Louisville. I am like a retired doctor—no "patience"—so having flights canceled, missing connections, or sitting in an airport for hours on layovers was not only annoying but a huge waste of time and money. So I visited Flight Options in Cleveland and met a salesman named Mike Silvestro. He was laser-focused on helping me out, and later I found out why. I'd be his first sale! The guy knew more than I did about private flight time, and he knew enough to get me signed up. The sale gave Mike the start he needed, and he kept selling. Today, he is the CEO of the seven-hundred-person company, which merged with Flexjet in 2013. As for me, I am still flying around the country on Flexjet planes.

In 2000, my pursuit of G.J. also gained traction. I had done a lousy job of checking out my three previous heads of operations, so I damn sure wasn't going to screw up this time. I went down to New Orleans to G.J.'s offices at Copeland's to get a feel for his management style, the type of people he surrounded himself with, how they viewed their jobs, and if they liked working for the guy. I posed as an old buddy visiting from out of town.

I particularly liked his HR guy, Mark Simpson, whom I soon targeted as well and who today is our vice president of Legendary People.

**MARK SIMPSON, VP of Legendary People (2000–present)**
I first met Kent when he visited G.J. at Copeland's headquarters, where G.J. and I worked back in 2000. I believe he claimed to be a college buddy of G.J.'s but was definitely quite inquisitive, which seemed a bit odd. When G.J. took the job at Roadhouse, he set me up to interview with Kent in his basement bar in Louisville. I'm not sure if I would actually call it an interview. [It was] more like a couple of buddies having a few Buds. Definitely not like any interview I had ever experienced.

By midyear 2000, I finally hired me a president. There had been (on purpose) an empty office next to mine for the previous six months with a sign on the door: OFFICE OF THE PRESIDENT. No one could figure it out since my title was president, but they finally clued in when G.J. arrived. I moved my title to founder and CEO.

G.J. spent three months training all positions in the restaurant, including dish machine operator, and then showed up and took over the office next to mine. I handed him the keys to our support center and said, "This is your playground." G.J. would be in charge of HR, training, finance, IT, accounting, purchasing, and legal. As for me, I'd keep restaurant ops, real estate, and food and service operations as my playground. Dig it?

I had forgotten about marketing. We really didn't do much there other than support local store efforts and make up a few print ads. I wasn't too focused on marketing, per se. G.J. then proceeded to hire his wife to run marketing. I'm like, *WTF*. I plopped myself down in his office and asked what experience she brought to the role. G.J. said she had been a TV reporter in New Orleans. Then he added that if his wife was happy, he'd be happy, and he could focus more on what he needed to do.

Knowing I had a full plate, and I needed him focused on fixing or improving a bunch of stuff, I said that his wife had one year and then we would revisit the situation. He asked about the marketing budget. I had been charging our franchisees three-tenths of 1 percent for marketing, which basically paid for menus, a few billboards here and there, charity events, our annual conference (we'd done two so far), and a few salaries. Not much else. G.J. said that would be fine.

I told him I'd see him in a month, and I hit the road. Why a month? Because for anyone in our support center who had issues—not liking someone else, for example—now G.J.'s door was open and my car door was closed as I headed down the highway, a couple hundred miles away. That's called instant change, deal with it. We were moving fast, moving forward, and it was G.J.'s job to deal with whatever came up in Louisville.

That year I also attended a big real estate convention in Las Vegas. With me was our head legal person, Sheila Brown, who was actually a paralegal and was doing all our real estate contracts. She was attending law school, so I figured that was close enough to a bar-certified lawyer for our fly-by-night operation. I was thrilled I didn't have to deal with real estate contracts anymore. I never got better than a C in English, 'cause maybe I not such a good speler or sumthin. Anyway, I was there primarily to find a real estate guy. Scouting out twenty-five sites a year (more than one hundred cumulative) for a guy who was still running ops and other stuff was getting old.

I didn't want to spend a bunch of money advertising the job in some magazine no one reads, and didn't want to use an agency, so I printed up

a black silk jacket with the words WANTED REAL ESTATE DIRECTOR, CALL 1-800-TEX-ROAD on the back. I was sure that I would be beating off potential suitors with a stick.

Proudly, I wore the jacket around the convention, waiting for a tap on the shoulder and an enthusiastic "Hey, man!" And poof, I would have my real estate dude. Didn't happen. Shocker, I know. The only tap on the shoulder I did get was from a surly maintenance guy who asked me to get my ass out of the way so he could wheel the trash out.

Sheila Brown, being smarter than me, had set up three interviews with potential hires through a headhunter without my knowledge. We borrowed meeting space from a developer we knew, and I interviewed the trio. One was a big shot, another a crazy shot, and the third had no shot. I decided to have drinks with Mr. Big Shot and then, for some reason, Crazy Shot. Well, Big Shot wanted to hire a bunch of people including two assistants. I'd been doing the job myself along with my other duties. Seriously, he needed a team of helpers? I asked him why he was interviewing with me since we could pay him only a fraction of what he was currently making, and I caught on that he was about to be canned, fired, set free to screw up someone else's world. No thanks.

Guy number two, Mike "Crazy Ass" Keaton, showed up for my next beverage session. We shared some beers and started to click. As I've been told by more than a few people, I'm definitely not wired right myself, so we were a perfect fit. Long story short, Mike and I have since done more than five hundred deals together, downed more than a few beers, and are like brothers from a different mother/neighborhood/planet.

**MIKE KEATON, VP of real estate**

In May of 2020, I was in Vegas for the real estate convention. I was working for Hollywood Video at the time, but they were slowing their growth. I could see that video stores would soon be a thing of the past, along with my job. Somehow, among the thirty thousand people there I noticed a guy walking the floor, wearing a silk jacket that advertised for a real estate director. I had set up three interviews and just hoped the strange guy wasn't one of them. He was. We ended up at a hotel bar that same night. My choice of beer apparently factored into my hiring.

I showed up at the office in Louisville a few weeks later . . . and walked around and introduced myself to the twenty or so home-office people, including one guy who said he was the director of real estate. I ran down to Kent's office and asked what the deal was. I had just met the guy I was supposed to replace. Kent said he had wanted to travel with me first, pick a few sites, and see if all was good before he let the other guy go. He could see I was not cool with that, so he said, "No worries. I'll be back in a few." Twenty minutes later, Kent came back and said he'd just let the other guy know this would be his last day, then he calmly asked if there was anything else I wanted to discuss. "Nope, all good." I was thinking maybe I need a backup plan, too.

Kent later gave me the jacket. I had it framed and it hangs on the wall in my office. Twenty years later, I'm still here.

That summer we also decided to hold our first charity golf tournament (which has since become an annual event) as a fun way to give back. Our small group of company leaders met to decide on the charity they wanted to receive the proceeds and whether or not we'd have a different charity each year. Being an old track guy, I thought that Special Olympics would be the perfect choice. Who was going to say no to Special Olympics? Since then, we've held nineteen more golf tourneys and to date have raised more than $2 million for that amazing cause.

# MADE-FROM-SCRATCH SIDES
# (WHAT I LEARNED):

- Never underestimate the power of an award when done right: when presented for the achievement of something meaningful, in front of peers, and with a commensurate level of reward.
- In a bottom-up company, the leader learns from frontline people who are at the top. The leader supports, encourages, and celebrates his/her people's successes and sometimes failures.
- Too many executives punish risk takers or a manager for allowing his/her people to go rogue. In those cultures, failures get hidden out of fear of scorn or even job loss.
- If possible, check out your key hires in their habitat. Get a feel for their management style, the type of people they surround themselves with, and if people like working for them.
- Be willing to laugh at yourself.
- As soon as you make a profit, find a way to give back. Cast your bread upon the waters.

Although my given name is Wayne Kent
Taylor, the nurses in the hospital said I looked
more like a Kent, and the name stuck.

My parents, Powell and Marilyn, and my younger brother, Bryan.

Coach Dick Bealmear created more than a track team at Ballard High School: we were a tribe, a band of brothers, and 1972 state champions.

Jumping one of the many hurdles I would face in track (a metaphor for later in business).

North Carolina track coach Joe Hilton presenting me with the MVP watch my senior year.

I hated the car but loved the puppy, especially once I realized girls loved puppies!

I stayed up all night writing the first employee manual for the nightclub Mabel Murphy's, which my uncle Bill helped me start.

As GM at Bennigan's in Denver, I learned many lessons. One such lesson: if you want the respect of your team, roll up your sleeves and put in the work.

John Y. Brown, former Kentucky governor and the man who built Kentucky Fried Chicken into a global brand, was my business partner at the Buckhead Bar and Grill, my first restaurant venture. My eight-year-old daughter Michelle created the name.

Kent and John Y. Brown (2000)
Buckhead Bar and Grill

Hard to believe that what would become Texas Roadhouse and the first location in Clarksville, Indiana, started from this sketch on a napkin!

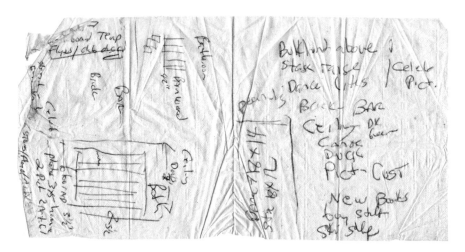

Kent's original napkin idea

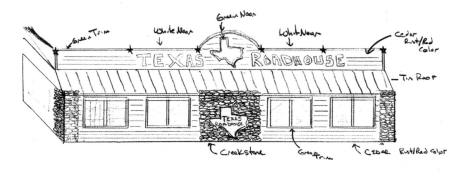

Drawing

The restaurant in Lexington, Kentucky, the first to feature two towers, opened in 1995.

The first Texas Roadhouse to open in my hometown of Louisville, Kentucky, was also our first prototype, and the design is still going strong more than twenty years later.

With my wife, Leslie, after being named Emerging Entrepreneur of the Year in Kentucky/Southern Indiana in 1997.

We held our first Managing Partner Conference in 1999 in Orlando. Gina Tobin was named MP of the Year and the team gave me a cool belt buckle and nickname, Bubba, which would later become the name of one of our concepts: Bubba's 33. *Inset:* Bubba, created in 1999.

I have always been blessed to be surrounded by a supportive family.

Favorite family photo (1998)

Family (2003)

In skiing, if you don't succeed, try (fall), try (fall), again
and eventually you may surprise yourself.

During the Texas Roadhouse IPO roadshow, Steve Ortiz, G. J. Hart, Scott Colosi, and I stopped by the Bennigan's I managed in Denver in the '80s to have a shot of tequila before meeting more bankers.

Andy Armadillo and I celebrated going public at the Nasdaq.

While I did not land Southwest Founder Herb Kelleher on our board, we were blessed to have former CEO Jim Parker join as a director in 2004. Both Herb and Jim had a great impact on Texas Roadhouse.

I have always valued and sought advice and wisdom from successful people, such as Truett Cathy, the founder of Chick-fil-A.

My friend and favorite poker player, Willie Nelson.

I learned many great lessons from former UCLA coach John Wooden.

My father and former GE CEO Jack Welch.

Being named Operator of the Year by Nation's Restaurant News in 2014 was a great honor.

The Texas Roadhouse Support Center in Louisville, Kentucky.

Bubba's 33 is known for its pizza, burgers, and wings.

If Five Guys and Chick-fil-A got married and had a hip kid it would be Jaggers.

It all starts with made-from-scratch food,
which we call Legendary Food.

Our first Louisville location opened to large crowds in 1996 and
has been one of our top-performing restaurants ever since.

Snoop Dogg and I
at our San Diego
Conference in 2018.

My son Max and I with
Glenn Frey and
Joe Walsh in Hawaii.

Darius Rucker performed
at our conference
in 2014.

In Miami with Kenny Chesney and my longtime assistant,
Shelly McGowen, who is a rock star!

Grandkids
(Halloween)

Max and I went fishing for halibut
and he caught a 406-pounder,
which was a record at the time.

## CHAPTER 12

# THE REDHEADED STRANGER

The year 2001 started rolling along pretty fast. We were on pace to open twenty-eight stores, and we were still private and had a ton of debt and promises galore. Yes, the promises would one day not only be met but well exceeded, but it would be some time before that happened, and no one could bank on our potential.

While I was busy hiring new ops people, G.J. and his wife got rolling in the new world of marketing by sponsoring a race team for the American Speed Association stock-car racing (farm team for NASCAR). They also bought a used RV for races. I met the news with zero enthusiasm. We were a company loaded with debt, and the RV was nothing but a lawsuit waiting to happen. What happened to hitting budgets? I nixed the idea after year one, and somehow ended up with the RV, nicknamed the Contessa, at my farm. It sat there collecting dust for a decade before I sold it for parts.

I will give G.J. and his wife, Juli, credit for throwing an amazing annual conference in New Orleans later that year, where our first MP in Texas, Jerry Morgan, took home the honors as Managing Partner of the Year. We enjoyed the R&B sounds of the Coasters, and one of my mom's all-time favorites: the Drifters.

In March, I went on a ski trip with Steve Ortiz to Colorado. He positioned it as a great time to blow off some steam and do some serious deep-powder turns, but he secretly wanted to sell me on the notion of doing more joint ventures with the company—as our twelve-store deal was a just a couple of locations short of being done. His plan was to take me out the first night, get an excess of tequila down my gullet, and then hit me up the next day when my hangover was raging, and I would agree to anything to shut him up. He was convinced I would say yes.

I actually had a similar secret plan; the only difference was that mine included convincing Steve to assume command of day-to-day restaurant ops. Only if he agreed to that would I allow him a few more JV stores.

Part A of both of our plans worked beautifully and we emerged from our rooms the morning of day two extremely hungover. I levered up an eyelid and we began to barter. Somehow, I had dragged myself out for an early-morning run down the slopes (a bit wobbly, admittedly) and fared somewhat better than Steve did in our negotiations. By day's end, he finally agreed to step up and take the role as leader of ops. He realized there was no way he was getting another joint-venture restaurant unless he relented.

**STEVE ORTIZ**

Back in 2000 to 2001, Kent kept pressuring me to take over as the head of field operations. I was like, "No way." I was running Texas, I was among friends and family, and home most nights. Kent was relentless.

We decided to take a three-day ski trip to Vail to discuss a few things and maybe party a little bit. I was also pressing Kent for a few more JV stores as well. After a late night with maybe too much tequila, I finally broke down and accepted the role. Note to self: Don't try to hang with Kent late-night, it's a losing proposition.

In April, we reached a significant milestone. We opened our one hundredth Texas Roadhouse in Brooklyn, Ohio, a suburb of Cleveland,

and as usual, a little partying ensued. We actually drove the race team RV up from Louisville, behaved, and did all the press requirements. Well, in truth, no press showed up. But we did take some pics, grabbed a guest for pics, and pretended he was the mayor. What the heck.

That same year, our Ashland, Kentucky, store with Neal Niklaus at the helm hit $6 million in sales. To put that in perspective, Ashland is a town of about thirty-five thousand people. By our rudimentary ciphering, about 15 percent of the population ate with us every week. Not bad. Of course, Neal likely knew most of them by name, an amazing skill I wish I possessed but don't.

I visited Ashland every now and then during the early years to see what Neal was doing to make the place rock. As I checked into the hotel, often I would ask the desk clerks where I might find a good steak dinner. Since my credit card had just my name on it, and no company listed, the clerks didn't know me from Adam. They most often told me about Texas Roadhouse, and said that I was to ask for Neal by name and say that so-and-so had sent me. Talk about an MP dialed into the community. No wonder Neal was crushing it.

The year 2002 would bring more growth as we opened twenty-two additional restaurants. For the first time we cracked Nation's Restaurant News's Top 100 Restaurants, ranking eighty-first in the country. Who would have thunk that?

We held our annual conference in Napa Valley, California—because we all felt it was high time to enjoy some good wine for a change. Dee Shaughnessy won our Legends award. She had transferred from our head of HR to our director of care and concern, and her first order of business had been creating Andy's Outreach, a fund where Roadies donate part of their paychecks to help frontline employees in times of need (funerals, floods, surgeries, fires, and yes, even pandemics). Roadies might donate anything from ten cents to a few dollars a paycheck. Thanks to Dee, I believe we were one of the first companies anywhere to establish such a fund, and it is has helped out thousands of our people over the years.

**DEE SHAUGHNESSY, director, HR and care and concern (1998-2010)**
I had been passing the hat around for years whenever one of our employ-ees had a heartbreaking story and was in need of money for an operation, funeral, or any tough situation. I approached Kent about starting a fund to help Roadies in need. To my surprise, he said it was a great idea, whipped out his personal checkbook, and wrote an astonishingly large check. He said to "go for it." G.J., our original investors, and others contributed, and the rest is history.

Steve Ortiz, with field participation, began leaving his mark in a good way as well. He established the first three of our operational goals: (1) Manager in the Window, (2) Alley Rallies, and (3) First-Time Guest Program.

By having a manager in the window (the last checkpoint before our food goes out to the table), we help ensure that each and every one of our guests receives Legendary Food.

Alley rallies are held at the beginning of each shift, before we open, when we gather all the front-of-house staff (and often back as well). Generally, these are held at 3:45 p.m. (we aren't exactly morning peo-ple) and communicate a few service points for the day, announce sales or cleanliness contests, and then possibly finish with some fun: a crazy chant or a song one of our people may have made up. The whole idea is about jacking your people up, energizing them, and teaching at the same time.

First-time guest is when our host or hostess will, on the way to seat-ing them, find out if it's a person's first-ever visit to a Texas Roadhouse. If it is, we have a manager stop by to chat and give them a special welcome. Each manager does something unique, and it varies by location, but if you really want to know what they do, you'll have to stop in and proclaim yourself as a Roadhouse newbie.

On the financial side, some of our investors were getting a little froggy. We completed our private placement in 1998, and were now five years in. Many felt we should consider going public. It wasn't a bad idea. We were piling up debt, and our investors and banks thought the solution might be a flood of capital from the IPO market. G. J. Hart as well as our CFO, Bill Rea, were pushing me internally.

I reached out to several people whom I trusted, including Martin Hart, one of our early investors and a future board member. He had taken Pizza Hut public years before. He wasn't sold on the timing, however. He recommended we build up a stronger profit line and add more finance talent to the company. Don Tyson (Tyson Foods), David Grissom (Humana), and a few others also offered advice. After several days of mulling over the information I had received, it became clear (a) we weren't ready, (b) I probably needed a new CFO with IPO and Wall Street experience, and (c) those pressuring me could kiss my grits.

We turned our attention to finding a new financial leader. We got down to a handful of candidates including a big shot from Orlando and a relatively unknown guy who was local and worked at Tricon Global (which would later become Yum! Brands). When I brought the big shot in from Orlando, I had a local real estate person show him and his wife around town, and then just the wife, as I had her husband in interviews at HQ. The real estate person gave me a call on a break, and I found out the wife was definitely not happy about moving to Louisville. Mr. Big Shot was out. I've learned over the years that if a spouse or teenage kids are unhappy about moves, then usually that person will catch a lot of grief at home and become unhappy and usually unproductive. Yes, Forrest, life *can* be like a box of chocolates, and other times it can be like a box of doggy doo.

You guessed it. We ended up hiring the unknown, Scott Colosi. I liked his spunk. He hadn't been afraid to challenge the great David Novak at Tricon. G.J. liked him as well, as did Steve Ortiz. We still made him pledge—if you will—for about a year before he attained full status with our leadership group.

**SCOTT COLOSI, Chief Financial Officer (2002-11); president (2011-19); as quoted in the company's fifteen-year anniversary video**
I was first contacted by a recruiter about the CFO position at Texas Roadhouse. Apparently they were looking for someone with Wall Street experience who could go from black tie (Yum! Brands) to Budweiser (TXRH). My wife and I showed up for what I would call a dinner interview with Kent and his wife. Of course, we were somewhat dressed up and here comes Kent dressed in jeans and beach sandals. My wife, on the ride home, said, "I think this is definitely the place for you."

The year 2003 would be a big one for Texas Roadhouse. We would celebrate ten years in business and add another twenty stores. We also cranked up a bunch more debt and started getting proposals from various banks for a 2004 IPO.

Most importantly, however, we added to our operational goals (4) Host Focus, and (5) Training Focus. As we were getting busier, we needed more front-door leadership. Think manager in the window and then add a manager or key person at the front door. Also, we wanted to dial in our training in a more effective way, providing more consistency from store to store. Juanita Coleman, who had been heading our training, was not getting along with G.J., her boss, and I knew she would not survive. I had two choices: Allow it to happen or move her to work for someone else and let the dice roll. I decided on the latter, and under Steve Ortiz's guidance Juanita blossomed, and life at HQ moved on. Funny how stuff works like that. I had made such transfers before, usually a couple of times every year or two, sometimes with success and sometimes not. Meshing various personalities requires many conversations with bosses, peers, and folks who work for others. There's never a completely perfect fix, but options emerge if you get enough people talking and brainstorming. But as always: Two ears, one mouth, speak less, listen more, always raises your score.

We celebrated our ten-year anniversary at our original location, complete with the first band that played on day one, and everyone had a big time as usual. Clarksville MP Dave Palazzo asked me that night—since we now only used the stage every five years—if he could take it down and put up some flat-screen TVs. I can't actually recall the conversation, but the stage was torn down before they opened the next day in case I changed my mind. *Speed, baby.*

That year, G.J. was approached by the bourbon company that made Old Whiskey River, Willie Nelson's brand. They wanted us to carry the spirit in our restaurants and we thought that sounded just fine. Willie was coming into town to play a private gig and G.J. set up a meeting on Willie's bus for earlier that day. When I asked G.J. about the meeting the next day and if they'd cut a deal, his response was priceless: "Well, Kent, I think so. I really can't remember much."

On a related note, "I'll never smoke weed with Willie again" became a song by Toby Keith, who admitted falling under a smoky haze in the tour bus of the Redheaded Stranger and forgetting much more about that night. Interesting, seems familiar to me somehow.

That year we achieved some notoriety in the industry when *Restaurants & Institutions* magazine voted us America's Best Steakhouse. That was pretty cool, as most of our locations were in what they call "secondary markets" (not big cities) and we did zero advertising, so maybe we weren't as far under the radar as I had believed (it was well before social media).

Venturing away from the continental forty-eight for the first time, our ten-year conference would be in Hawaii. Besides, since we were still private, we thought what the heck, let's blow the wad. Willie Nelson and Hootie & the Blowfish were our headliners, and Davey Jones of the Monkees also performed (anyone over sixty will think that's cool). Our speakers included legendary football players Joe Theismann and Marcus Allen. Not precisely a "budget-conscious event."

We even had a touch-football game with our folks playing. They were coached by Joe and Marcus, and as you might imagine, both were so competitive that they finally subbed themselves into the game. I joined the cheerleading squad in a grass skirt. Partying with Willie that night, I do still remember what happened. He might have been a little impressed that there was at least one CEO who could hang with his posse.

> **WILLIE NELSON, award-winning country music star**
> Kent was easy to be around and became a great friend. I felt we could work together because the company held the values I believe in . . . and the food was great!"

That year we also hired a big-gun marketing guy away from Papa John's named Chris Jacobsen. He had learned a ton about local store marketing when he'd worked at Waffle House. If you've ever stepped foot inside a Waffle House, you've probably noticed how friendly their people are. Their mission even talks about creating a "welcoming presence and attentive service," and they try to deliver on the promise. Pretty cool.

First thing Chris, our new marketing guy, and Juli Hart tried to do was to convince me to change our logo, the one I'd doodled on a napkin and that appeared mysteriously in my pocket back in 1996 after a rough night of partying. They worked on various versions of the logo for about six months, changing this and that. They became quite irritated and finally Chris came to my office and asked why I was constantly unhappy about their various attempts. I kindly told him that I was in no way, shape, or form going to change the logo, and was just waiting to see how long it would take them to work it out of their system and get over it. All new dogs, cats, or whatever have to mark their territory. Just one of those strange things about nature.

**CHRIS JACOBSEN, chief marketing officer (2003–present)**
I was hired from Papa John's in 2003. The odd thing was that for a couple of years, I shared the role with our president G. J. Hart's wife. The first item that we tackled was coming up with a change to the company's logo. Interestingly, we were both played for about six months by Kent, who had no intention of changing the logo and thought the whole process was quite amusing.

We ended up hiring quite a few people either as managing partners or kitchen/service managers in the early years of our first decade. A new managing partner would have to deposit $25,000 with us to run a store, then get 10 percent of the store profits and private company stock that was pretty much worthless unless we went public one day. Many of our company leaders today joined our company in those years of 2000 to 2003, and their stock awards would eventually be valued at a million to a few million dollars for those running just one store. That's what I refer to as VERY COOL, BABY!

One guy from Outback, Rex Boatright, came on board, dove in head-first, and has been one of our best financial performers, and definitely validated the worth of those early hires.

**REX BOATRIGHT, market partner**
Texas Roadhouse was very different from my many years at Outback. Outback started as an awesome company with a great culture and then for some reason moved to quite the opposite. The founders unfortunately let outside corporate manager types either complicate things or find ways to screw their people. At Roadhouse, that has never happened over the twenty years I've worked here.

# MADE-FROM-SCRATCH SIDES
## (WHAT I LEARNED):

- Our best managing partners are dialed into their communities; many consider themselves the ad hoc mayors of their towns.
- Clear operational goals help you deliver on the unique recipe that differentiates your brand. Ours are (1) Manager in the Window, (2) Alley Rallies, (3) First-Time Guest Program, (4) Host Focus, and (5) Training Focus, and each was carefully considered and helps deliver consistently in each restaurant each day.
- If they are passionate and want to contribute, talented people who are not thriving in one role might thrive under a different manager. It's worth a leader's time to see what juggling a person's direct report may look like.
- Give your managers a vested interest in their business and amazing things can happen.
- Don't smoke weed with Willie (well, maybe just a little).

## CHAPTER 13

# LESSONS FROM AN IPO

The year 2004 looked to be a big one for Texas Roadhouse. We would launch our most aggressive spurt of restaurant growth with thirty-one openings, and we held our company conference for the first and only time outside the United States, in Cabo San Lucas, Mexico. The coolest thing about the trip was holding our first of many to come humanitarian days, with seven hundred people assisting in various projects to help the underprivileged. We renovated an orphanage and made improvements to a rehabilitation center. Our people loved giving back, even in a place where we had no restaurants. Our spirits were high, and naturally some got high off spirits, but what happens in Mexico stays . . .

Many who had been too busy to do much charitable work before would be so inspired they'd return to their home markets and have their store employees and friends tackle projects to help in their communities. I wish I could take credit, but some of our folks, including Juli Hart, thought up and implemented the idea.

We had a basketball theme at the conference (*Vamos 'Heels!*) and brought in some legendary coaches to speak and coach our folks in a fun basketball tournament. The coaches included LSU's Dale Brown, Kentucky's Joe B. Hall and Tubby Smith, Arkansas coach and stand-up comedian Nolan Richardson, and University of Louisville's Denny Crum. In his earlier years, Denny was an assistant at UCLA under the legendary John Wooden. Thanks to Denny's influence, ninety-four-year-old Wooden agreed to serve as our featured speaker. He rarely spoke anymore but had been deeply moved when he heard about our planned humanitarian efforts.

---

**NOLAN RICHARDSON, Hall of Fame basketball coach, Arkansas**

Kent and the Texas Roadhouse team are special people, for sure. As the coach of the Roadhouse team at the conference, I have to admit, they were one of the worst teams I have ever coached! But what they lacked on the court, they made up for with their passion for fun and their big hearts! By big hearts, I am referring to more than one thousand Roadies spending time to build an orphanage in [a] community in which they did not even have a restaurant! Their commitment to serving others had a huge impact on me and even more on those kids and that community for many, many years.

---

**DALE BROWN, Hall of Fame basketball coach, LSU**

I have spoken at conferences in ninety countries, but the Texas Roadhouse event had the greatest entertainment, food, charitable aspect, and people I have ever seen. There was nothing phony about that conference.

I coached one of the Roadhouse basketball teams. None of the teams were any good, but boy, did they really want to win! They got injured easily, but they played hard.

---

A leadership junky myself, I stuck to Mr. Wooden like gum on his shoe, trying to glean any advice I could use to help our growing company. And I did, in fact, gain some valuable wisdom that has stayed with me to this day. After watching me almost get gored by a bull in the La Sanluqueña bullring, John patted my back and presented me with one of his famous Timeless Wisdom laminated cards that included insights from his father, Joshua Wooden.

I especially liked his seven-point creed:

1. Be true to yourself.
2. Help others.
3. Make each day your masterpiece.
4. Drink deeply from good books.
5. Make friendship a fine art.
6. Build a shelter against a rainy day.
7. Give thanks for your blessings every day.

I realized that I had put each of the seven into practice already that day. Doing humanitarian work with about one thousand Roadies, I had *helped others* and *made the day a masterpiece*. I then had *drunk deeply from a good book* (*The Wooden Way* by John Wooden) while drinking deeply from a beer on the beach. And that very evening I had tried to *make friends* with an enraged bull and narrowly avoided *seeking shelter* at a Mexican hospital. I was certainly *giving thanks and counting my blessings* that the bull's horns weren't an inch longer or I would have been singing in a much higher octave.

Another highlight of that year was opening two restaurants in Austin,

Texas, with our new friend Willie Nelson. The portion of the restaurants that he owned may have increased by as much as 5 percent as a result of some really bad poker playing by yours truly. Somehow, after a couple of hours playing with Willie, you tend to forget that a full house beats a flush. Why didn't I listen to Toby Keith?

Willie became much more than a silent partner. He wanted to be a genuine part of Texas Roadhouse, and we couldn't have been more thrilled. In each of our stores we created what we call Willie's Corner, a booth featuring memorabilia and pictures of the American legend. That was when we hired Travis Doster to head up our PR and roll out (no pun intended!) our program with Willie and many other crazy, out-of-the-box ideas over the years. We also began handing out faux Willie Braids to VIPs. The braids were red bandannas with two hairlike plaits hanging down along with a none-too-subtle Texas Roadhouse logo on the front. We made up one million thinking they would last us until the cows came home, but the braids were such a hit that they were gone in a couple of years. Our team members handed them out to anyone and everyone they came in contact with—and we have a Who's Who of patrons who sported them, from Senator John McCain to rapper Snoop Dogg.

Willie was gracious enough to agree to do meet and greets with fans at our restaurants as he toured the country, and we would partner with local radio and TV stations to give away free tickets to the events. He did fifty signings for us before his shows, and he would never say no to an autograph. He was so kind that pretty soon we insisted that he do photo ops rather than signatures as he worried that he'd get carpal tunnel. Pretty soon our PR team came up with a new idea that became a huge publicity winner. They started something called "Willieaoke" on radio and TV stations leading up to an appearance. Callers all day would compete to see who could sing the most like Willie, and the winner would get a chance to meet the great man.

Willie remains a core partner of our company today and has become my favorite poker buddy. A typical game he puts together consists of an eclectic collection of Hollywood and country music stars, farmers and ranchers who live nearby, and the guy who owns the feedlot or garage down the street. Doesn't matter who we are, we are all equal in Willie's eyes.

With everything going well, we were finally ready to test the waters on going public. Our numbers in 2003 were much improved; we had a new CFO in Scott Colosi, who knew most of the Wall Street cats who followed restaurant companies; our president, G.J., had a closet full of fancy-ass clothes, cuff links, and watches for their visual entertainment— along with a serious gift for smooth talking and Steve Ortiz had the fire and brimstone of a successful locker room coach. All that was left was me, who pretty much didn't have any of the stuff the other guys had but was the only one who knew where we'd been, where we were then, and where we needed to go next (our vision), and precisely how we'd get there. With a bucketload of debt to get rid of and some early investors to repay, it was time. Anyway, we had a bunch of Roadhouse folks who had bought into my dream years earlier whom I wanted to reward. *Why not, let's give it a go.*

First step was interviewing a bunch of bankers. I used my buddy George Rich, who had taken Outback Steakhouse public with a bank named Alex. Brown & Sons years earlier. I quickly found out George would be my main BS detector. Since he had been a Wall Street dude and had played the same game, he could sniff out any crap.

By early summer we had settled on Bank of America in New York as our lead, which meant they were basically the captain in charge of raising the $183 million we were looking for. Their guy Joe Kennedy would be in charge; Wachovia Bank from Charlotte, North Carolina, would be in second position with a guy named Jim Walsh as first lieutenant and John Tibe as second; Royal Bank of Canada (RBC) would be in third; and SG Cowen would round out the fourth and final slot.

We also needed a law firm to create the documents and an accounting firm to run and validate our numbers. Scott Colosi, Tonya Robinson (our controller and later CFO), and Sheila Brown, our new general counsel (fresh out of law school), would oversee the legal and accounting parts and G.J. would oversee the bankers.

We began endless meetings in New York and Louisville, putting documents together, crunching numbers, and spending hours and hours debating if we should use this word or that, which basically didn't mean anything at the end of the day. I say this hoping I don't offend one or two of the participants of these meetings but a lot of them. Okay, there you go; said it, done.

Since the world was only three years post-9/11, the Bank of America guys were worried about the upcoming Democratic and Republican conventions in July, with the possibility of a terrorist threat being a huge distraction, so they wanted to schedule our IPO for August. Okay. But then they started to worry about the Summer Olympics in Athens and recommended waiting until the fall.

I conferred with my team, many of whom were buying into this BS. I asked George Rich his thoughts as well as my future board member Martin Hart, former owner of Steamboat ski resort. George agreed with the bankers on this one, but Martin in his Irish brogue—chewing on a cigar, scotch in hand—said, "Well, kid, they may have a point, but from my experience go with your gut and tell them to kiss off."

There were other concerns in addition to timing. I was pushing to give myself ten votes for each of my shares (called super-voting rights) so I could still control the direction of the company after the IPO, and especially make sure no Wall Street types could force us to change the compensation model for our store operators. Many of our people had skin in the game. They had hefty stock options that would allow store operators to win big and become millionaires. I figured that if they had believed in the dream in the early years, they deserved to own a piece of that dream and I wasn't going to be pressured into screwing our folks over. Martin was very cool with the idea. I called Don Tyson, CEO of Tyson Foods, and he said, "You started the company, right? And you've stayed true to your vision and your people, right?"

I said, "Yes, sir."

He concluded with, "Well, damn it, son; stay with it and to hell with them."

"Yes, sir."

My stand on the super-voting rights didn't go over too well with the bankers, who threatened to bail. They thought it was too much for potential investors. I got pressure from G.J. as well. George Rich, to my surprise, was in their corner, too. Scott Colosi, who was still relatively new and knew whose name was on his paycheck, said, "Whatever you say, boss."

I confided with Steve Ortiz, who gave some levelheaded advice: "If you plan on sticking around, and if you want our people who believe in you to stick around, then follow your gut. There's plenty of bankers out there that tried to get on the team. Screw these guys. Let's grab other bankers and roll."

Ortiz's wisdom hit home. I told the bankers my decision and that they could hit the road if they wanted. Not one bailed. They were too invested. We were on the twenty-yard line, it was first and ten with five minutes to play. The bankers had been bluffing, some of our guys had bought into their crap, but my concern was based on treating people like partners, and that was unwavering.

With that behind, both political conventions over, and the Olympics still a few weeks away, I was ready to roll. No more bullshit, no more excuses. Right?

Wrong. A few days later, my guy from B of A called to say that the big shots at his bank were concerned with the upcoming presidential election, and thought it was bad luck to go public in October (as many of the market's worst days, historically, had come during the tenth month). They wanted to launch in mid-November. This was getting ridiculous. Next they'd be worried about Christmas.

I hung up and called Jim Walsh at Wachovia. I told him if he wanted to be lead banker, all he had to do was agree to take us public in October and Bank of America would be out. He would be promoted from lieutenant to captain. A few hours later Jim called back and said they were in. I called Joe Kennedy and told him the deal. He was out, Wachovia was in, and we were moving forward with three banks, not four.

The next day Joe Kennedy got in touch to say there must have been some internal bank misunderstanding, and they were more than ready to lead the charge for an October IPO. Being a man of my word, I told him I'd already moved Wachovia into the lead position. I'm not sure what happened behind the scenes over the next few days, but when it all got sorted out, I had two co-leads: Wachovia and Bank of America. I've always liked working in an environment with a degree of uncertainty, an uneasiness and productive tension with my executive team. It keeps everyone on their toes, and with a little internal competition, performance seems to get stronger with the pace being a bit quicker. In my mind, two leads sounded just fine.

**JIM WALSH, vice-chairman, Jeffries (formerly with Wachovia Bank)**
In 2004, I was at Wachovia and we pitched Texas Roadhouse about being part of their IPO. I think Kent liked us, as we were a bit edgy, like they were. At first, we were not in the lead position, but as B of A kept stalling the road show date, Kent moved us into the lead manager position. The Roadhouse team was very tight, a lot of fun to be with, quite frankly delivered way beyond what we expected. As a matter of fact, they are probably one of the most successful IPOs ever in the restaurant space and sixteen years later are still delivering solid results.

As if enough weird stuff hadn't happened already with this IPO, a couple of weeks before we hit the road for our dog-and-pony show with Wall Street, one of the bankers asked me how many suits I owned, what colors they were, and if they were wool or a polyblend. That was easy: I owned zero suits in zero colors with zero fabric. I did, however, own a couple of sport coats, three to be exact: one for summer, one for winter, and one wild plaid number that would have been obnoxious even in the seventies (I wore it to the Kentucky Derby the year before). Next thing I know, two bankers, G.J., and my mom (G.J. must have called her) were telling me what I needed to buy. Hey, when your mom is telling you to spiff up, you at least give it a try. Who knew a tie could cost a hundred bucks?!

The first week of the road show we were set to have presentations in Baltimore, Philly, and then fly to San Francisco, before moving on to Denver, Kansas City, Dallas, and Houston. There would be six to eight meetings a day with various investment firms, hedge funds, and other well-funded interested parties, with each meeting lasting thirty to forty-five minutes.

The morning of our first meeting, I opened my suitcase and pulled out a new suit, tie, and fancy shoes. I pulled them on, looked in the mirror, and asked, "Who is this joker? No way I'm buying into his action." So off it all came, and I put on the only pair of jeans I'd brought as well as my cowboy boots, the only sport coat I'd brought, and my Stetson hat. I intentionally showed up to our first presentation at the last second so that no one could coach me out of my attire. When I opened the door, our bankers' jaws dropped as one. G.J. glared, Colosi was not surprised, and Ortiz was stifling a chuckle. It was game on, and I went into my pitch.

Around meeting number three, I told Ortiz to lose his tie, which created quite the crew: fancy-dressing G.J., complete with flamboyant hanky poking from his Armani suit pocket; conservative-suit-wearing Colosi, our CFO; sharply dressed but with no tie Ortiz, our COO; and a straight-off-his-horse, direct-from-the-ranch Kent Taylor, our head honcho.

When it was all said and done, I actually think it worked just fine. Yet by week's end I could have stood my jeans up in a corner. Luckily I had enough clean underwear (though you probably don't need to know that).

One of the cool things about the grueling travel schedule was that the banks had rented a Gulfstream private jet to ferry us around, as we were usually wheels-up at least a couple of times a day. There would be the four of us from Roadhouse along with a handful of bankers on the flights, and we would get to enjoy the bankers criticizing and coaching us concerning our presentations. They'd keep that up during dinner, until we finally were able to escape for a few hours of sleep.

And yet they soon realized our group was going to be very different from any they'd worked with before. During our first long flight, while eating dinner, G.J. and Jim Walsh apparently had a contest to see who could drink the most wine, which ended up in a wrestling match around midnight at forty-five thousand feet. I didn't get a picture of it but did snap a photo of the two sumo wannabees resting after the match. By the end of the week, the flight crew had had more than enough of us and canceled the following week's flights. B of A scrambled and found a company that was known for moving around rock bands, and thankfully they were more relaxed about our antics.

The second week we started in Denver, visited the Bennigan's location I had run for four years back in the mideighties, and even did a shot of tequila for old times' sake. Then we moved on to Minneapolis, Chicago, and finished in Boston and New York, where the big-dog investors were located.

As we flew around early that second week, things were looking up—way up. Orders had already started pouring in from our first week of visits and we were over a billion dollars in demand—all for a $183 million stock offering. With that early success, knowing that so far our batting average was forty-four of forty-five groups we'd presented to wanting in, we may have gotten a little overconfident. When we landed in several cities, Ortiz and I sometimes went out until late and enjoyed the nightlife.

A first meeting one day was at eight a.m., and I watched our COO struggle through his presentation, sweat pouring down his forehead. It dawned on me that I might have to give my wingman a night off before I put a hurt on him. We behaved, mostly, for the rest of the week, as the bankers added even more meetings, probably trying to wear us down to keep us in check. They decided one night to throw in an evening cocktail investors' meeting in New York City, where maybe I got a little creative. The next day I had to visit the principal's office.

**JIM WALSH**

One early morning in either Minneapolis or Chicago, leaving the gym to go up to my room, I ran into Steve Ortiz and Kent, who were apparently just getting back to the hotel from a late night of revelry. The B of A guys and us had a serious discussion with G.J. about Kent's influence on Steve. Three hours after getting back to the hotel, the investor meetings were under way. Kent looked like he had slept eight hours. Steve, however, looked like he had just come down with the flu.

With week two complete, we returned to Louisville with more than $2 billion in orders (more than ten times oversubscribed). Guess my super-voting rights were safe.

We celebrated my forty-ninth birthday at G.J.'s home that weekend and then returned to the B of A offices the following Monday to price the deal and determine allocations (which investment houses would get what percent).

But we weren't done messing with our bankers. We made all of them wear Willie Braids (a red bandanna with fake ponytails) as we negotiated the pricing. That took the formal edge off the meeting. The banks attempted to reduce the share price a bit—so their big clients could take a quick profit and bail—but we held tight and made sure long-term investment firms got more of the deal and short-term houses less. When discussions got heavy, I'd click one of two hidden buttons. One was to a fart machine I'd hidden behind their seats, and the other was a "bullshit" recording positioned under the table. These serious banker types obviously had lost control. They pretty much caved to our proposed price in the onslaught of "bullshit" and "pwaaaaaf." The negotiating tactics of a seven-year-old, I know, but hey, it worked.

**GEORGE RICH**

I was traveling with the Texas Roadhouse management team on the last week of the IPO roadshow. The whole team was meeting with Fidelity Investments in Boston. I visited a magic shop at Kent's request and picked up a fart machine and a bullshit meter. The next day, when myself and the team were negotiating with the Bank of America syndicate team, Kent had a bit of fun with them, as he had put the machines under the table–setting them off at the appropriate moments when the discussions got serious. As we all know, he's a bit of a wild man.

Their IPO was quite successful, as obviously the Wall Street investors understood their focus on people, food quality, and service. I enjoyed assisting them on investor allocations, letting them know who the long-term investors were versus the flippers and short-term traders.

We went to Nasdaq the next day, pushed the make-believe button (no bell, that's the New York Stock Exchange), and started trading TXRH, beginning life as a public company. Over the next few hours we watched our stock shoot up 28 percent. It was a special day spent reminiscing about where I had come from, our early years of struggles, and chasing a dream that so many times seemed doomed to fail. Here we were, in year eleven, with 183 restaurants and an infusion of $183 million in capital.

At this point, I recognize that for most founders, the story would end here. They'd take their share and retire to a nice cabin in the Poconos or an island off Key West. I enjoyed the moment, no doubt, but the next week I was back in my office moving full speed ahead.

There would be more growth, more people, and more lessons to learn.

# MADE-FROM-SCRATCH SIDES
## (WHAT I LEARNED):

- The best business owners and executives I've ever met are voracious readers and students of leadership. Every year at our convention we bring in gurus—like John Wooden—to learn and stretch ourselves.
- When planning any public offering, assemble the right team, get advice, but don't forget it was your gut that got you to this point. Trust your instincts and push for what you know is right.
- As an owner, share the wealth with those who've helped you along the way. You stand on the shoulders of so many great people—reward them. Make them rich if you can.
- Be yourself when presenting your story to potential investors; most can smell a fake. For me, when I see someone in a business suit, I think, *That person has lost control of his/her life.* That's why I had to present myself in a genuine way.
- Resist the allure of short-term gains and focus on building partnerships with investors who want to see you grow a legacy business.

## CHAPTER 14

# WE'RE DANCING NOW

The year 2005 would bring another twenty-eight restaurants into the Texas Roadhouse family, with the two hundredth opening in April in Omaha, Nebraska.

That winter, wanting to develop a set of company core values with input from people on the front lines, we held twenty meetings around the country and picked the brains of small groups of our managing partners and kitchen and service managers. Since our mission statement was already set in stone—Legendary Food, Legendary Service—and was just four words long, I wanted our values to be boiled down to the same. Just. Four.

The concepts that emerged from the meetings were:

- Passion
- Partnership
- Integrity
- Fun . . . with Purpose

Actually, six words had been the most mentioned and believed in by our store leaders, and so we only had to eliminate the two least popular ideas. You are of course wondering what we got rid of, and for the life of me I can't remember. Blame that on one too many poker nights with Willie.

I was amazed by how open the process was, how much discussion ensued, and how pretty much no one held back or cared what they said in front of each other or me. I moderated the discussions and never gave my opinion or led a group in a specific direction. We gathered the data in each meeting, captured the reasoning behind them, and moved on to the next item. It was clear after just a handful of the twenty gatherings that *Fun* would be the most frequently chosen value, hands down. *Partnership* and *Integrity* would flip between the second and third most commonly agreed-upon values, and *Passion* would eventually edge out the rest. Sure, there are other important ideas we believe in—clear communication, local marketing, etc., and I could go on—but you have to take a stand and keep things simple and meaningful.

I viewed myself as the Keeper of the Mission, and just as importantly the Keeper of the Flag called Fun. Keepin' it light, upbeat, energetic with music, craziness, and fun was my personal mission. Conference calls, group meetings, speeches, or store visits required me to create a separate closet for my sometimes controversial collection of hats, funky shorts, or anything else I relied on to assist with my malfunctional wardrobe options. As to my executive team, I saw Ortiz as our partnership guy, who often traveled the country with various managers in tow, visiting stores that led the chase in quality, people, and operational excellence. He fostered an atmosphere of sharing, where our big dogs would dig helping the new puppies (managers) figure various ways to jump off the porch and improve their game. Colosi, our CFO, had to be the integrity guy, because if he fudged the numbers the rest of us would take the fall, too. We also made sure the folks we paid to audit our books were of high integrity and knew what they were doing. And G.J., our CEO and president, carried the passion flag. He could give one hell of a speech. He reminded me of a fancy-dressing President Clinton. Both G.J. and Bill could give a terrific fire-and-brimstone address, getting rave reviews and big applause. And yet when you would ask folks clapping with great enthusiasm which point of the speech moved them the most, the response might be, "No idea, man. Don't actually recall what he was talking about, but boy, it was awesome." Meaning not so much, but passion in spades: motivational and inspiring.

Back to our mission statement—Legendary Food, Legendary Service—which was my focus. I've worked for companies where, even though they may have had a mission statement, employees and managers either didn't know it existed or, if they had read the thing, would need to be a trained Shakespearean actor to memorize it.

One of my favorite examples occurred when Steve Ortiz and I visited Steak and Ale (Bennigan's) headquarters. They were suing the two of us for poaching their employees, and we went there to be deposed/stood in a corner/generally scolded. As we approached the receptionist, I couldn't help but notice their mission and values statements were hanging on the wall behind her desk. The Gettysburg Address was shorter, and way better written.

I asked the receptionist if she could recall, by chance, the company's mission statement. She looked at me as if I had two heads. She had no idea what I was talking about. When I suggested—with a twist of my fingers—that she might want to spin around and read what was up on the wall behind her, she admitted, "Huh. You know, I've never really paid much attention to that."

"Who do you think wrote it?" I asked.

Her response was priceless: "Oh, they probably hired some outside consultants, paid them too much money, and checked the box."

We were still laughing about that on our trip home.

In today's world, missions and values too often become as clichéd as motherhood and apple pie. They might be voted on through a Survey-Monkey with the notion that this would be inclusive enough; or maybe they are put together by a mysterious committee of the chosen ones; or worst, they are written by an outside firm paid to wordsmith. No matter how they are arrived upon, the results most likely suck. Lots of words, no real meaning, and no one really cares.

In 2005 we added a second floor to our support center in Louisville and a workout center. We began offering twelve-week transformational fitness programs, complete with contests to see who lost the most weight or walked the most steps. Today we have on staff many graduates of those various fitness programs and the results have been nothing short of amazing. A couple of our folks have lost as much as one hundred pounds, and the new attitude, energy level, and productivity of many of these newly minted health nuts have been inspiring.

We held that year's conference in Hawaii, with one of the strongest entertainment groupings to date, including Willie Nelson (who couldn't bring his bus, thank goodness); the Doobie Brothers (no bus, either); Counting Crows; and Earth, Wind & Fire. You may be asking, "Kent, do you *remembah* the twenty-first night of *Septembah*?" Or more aptly, critics asked, "Being a public company, Kent, how can you justify such expenditures?" Well, I paid for two of the bands myself. That's how. So kiss my grits.

Steve Ortiz and Neal Niklaus were co-winners of the Legends award. Neal really helped take local store marketing to a higher level, teaching many really effective classes for our new trainees. He also started our infamous line-dancing, which alone was deserving of a lifetime achievement award. As for Steve, he not only helped take our store ops to a truly professional level but successfully convinced a ton of people from other restaurants to take a chance and run a business they had a piece of, and with it the freedom to reach for the stars in their own way.

Our concerts were held at the Ihilani resort and took place outside. We had one stage on the field and one on the beach. Counting Crows and Earth, Wind & Fire on the beach, and Willie and the Doobies on grass (insert joke here). Since we were outside with a ten p.m. sound curfew, I realized our party folks would need a late-night option. Since we pretty much filled up the whole hotel, I was able to take over their boutique lounge and convert it to our first of many to come Late Nite Bars. Since I had just been to a Rolling Stones concert, I chose the name Voodoo Lounge, had a neon sign created to hang over the door, and then covered all the fancy artwork in the joint with beach towels, concert posters, beer lights, and whatever tacky stuff I could find. The extra stuff went to my suite and created the first of many after-after bars.

The Voodoo Lounge—completed at a cost of about eight hundred bucks—was a big hit out of the gate. We packed three hundred people into the place (50 percent over posted occupancy). Since then, we have enlarged late nights to accommodate at least eight hundred.

Many stories, extreme hangovers, and—since we also invite spouses—a few "conference babies" have come as a result of our late-night parties over the years. So yes, I got the fun box checked.

That year we also created the role of Culture Coaches, those Roadies who assist new hires in understanding our culture, guiding them through their early months, and showing them the special Roadhouse way. To keep new employees engaged, we've found it's best to offer a lot of TLC—helping them understand our standards of excellence, as well as how to process this often unpredictable, crazy, relaxed, and fun workplace they've landed in.

Every year must have its share of challenges, and 2005 was no exception. In August and September, Hurricanes Katrina and Rita dev-astated much of the Gulf coast. Thankfully, Andy's Outreach came to the rescue financially for many of our folks impacted by the storms.

At Texas Roadhouse, pretty much since our first group humanitar-ian project in 2004 in Cabo, our people have never turned away from problems, natural disasters, or the needs of our local communities. We turn toward them, run at them, and find a way to lift up our neighbors and communities. Whether it's floods, fires, hurricanes, or tornadoes, our people are often the first to provide food to first responders, emergency workers, or emergency shelters. In addition, our people don't have to call the support center for permission to spend the money or donate the food; they know that they are the boss. They are empowered and they just act. Giving is infectious and I'm proud that our people dig doing it.

**JULI MILLER HART, former marketing director, Texas Roadhouse**
When Hurricanes Katrina and Rita ravaged the Gulf coast, leaving New Orleans covered in water and hundreds of thousands of people without power, homes, and [hope], Texas Roadhouse mobilized. We put together a team, partnering with our still-operating restaurants, to feed and serve first responders. In ad-dition, for almost three years posthurricane, our teams of operators and their staffs from around the nation stepped up to lend a helping hand in the rebuild-ing process.

Partnering with Jim Pate (executive director of the New Orleans area Habi-tat for Humanity), Roadhouse volunteers under the direction of Bill Coleman donated more than five thousand hours in assisting to rebuild New Orleans. They framed more than forty homes, most of which ended up in the Upper Ninth Ward—a project led by Harry Connick Jr. and Branford Marsalis. In addi-tion, a big shout-out needs to go to Willie Nelson, a Roadhouse partner, who donated three eighteen-wheelers filled with his brand of bottled water, provid-ing fresh $H_2O$ to the area's residents.

We began 2006 working on various humanitarian projects in our spare time to help those impacted by the storms. We built "homes in a box" to be sent to New Orleans as part of Operation Home Delivery through Habitat for Humanity. Our Roadie volunteers built dozens of home panels to accelerate the rebuilding of already started houses in Louisiana for local musicians (who usually never make much money); they were a perfect fit for our tune-loving, boot-scootin' Roadhouse culture.

Early stores leading the charge in those efforts included Wilmington, North Carolina; Tulsa, Oklahoma; and Indianapolis, Indiana. President George W. Bush (who was in office at the time) happened by while we had a crew in New Orleans assembling the homes, led by my late father-in-law, Howard Dohrman, and "W" pounded a few nails, posed for a picture, and was the highlight of the experience for many.

The year 2006 was certainly a good one financially, as we added thirty restaurants, passing 250 total, and approached $1 billion in sales. We'd come a mile or two since three of our first five stores failed.

Banff, Canada, hosted us for our conference, where, as usual, we

provided more than seven hundred volunteers to work on local projects. We also built more homes in a box to ship to New Orleans. Pretty cool that a group of houses now standing in the Deep South were framed by Texas Roadhouse employees in the ski town of Banff using Canadian Rockies timber while we responsibly quaffed more Molson beer than the McKenzie brothers.

Our late-night bar in Banff was named the Loose Moose Saloon, and once again we may have exceeded the room's capacity. People danced until two a.m., with the room temperature rising so much that the windows steamed up; bodies rubbed up against each other, clothes were completely sweated through, and big smiles were in abundance.

That next morning I woke up with a really horrible hangover. The inside of my mouth felt as if someone had poured a bag of chalk dust in it. My brain was part fog, part pain. I attempted to cut through the haze, and with that stale smell of alcohol streaming from my pores, I looked at my watch. It was 8:50 a.m. Holy crap. I was scheduled onstage, across the courtyard in the convention center, in just ten minutes. I had slept in my party attire from our late-night bar: shorts and tie-dyed T-shirt. My cowboy hat and sunglasses were on the night table. I pulled on a robe from the closet, grabbed a Red Bull, and ran across the freshly snow-covered courtyard just in time for my speech to the assembled seven hundred people. What had I been thinking about letting my folks schedule me to do a nine a.m. speech? Now older and wiser, I only give dinner speeches. A man's gotta know his limitations.

In October of 2006, *Forbes* honored us as one of America's Best Small Companies. We were the only casual-dining chain on the list. I wondered how a billion-dollar business with almost twenty thousand employees could be considered small, but hey, what do I know?

Also that year, I ended the three-year celebration of my fiftieth birthday. My goal over that period (from ages forty-nine to fifty-one) was to ski 150 times, see fifty concerts, and get in five poker games with Willie. I scored on two of the three goals, falling about fifteen concerts short. But I did manage to see the Stones five times. Not bad, eh?

The year 2007 saw more growth, with thirty-four restaurants coming on board, possibly straining our management talent pool and definitely overworking our new restaurant-opening training teams. We topped $1 billion in sales for the first time.

I realized with our excessive growth that year that—screw the Wall Street crowd—from that point forward we would only grow at a pace that could be justified by our development of people and not by the availability of funds. We surely could use our cash flow and borrowed funds to grow at up to forty or fifty restaurants per year, but execution, culture, and not stretching people too far must rule the day. Our training, along with front- and back-of-the-house assimilation, should take a minimum of twelve to fourteen months, with eighteen to twenty-four months the best amount of time to set our people up for success and full participation in our unique culture.

Our conference was held in Southern California, where our humanitarian project was focused on Marine Corps Base Camp Pendleton. Doing cool things for the military has always been part of my wheelhouse, perhaps because I was born—all of four pounds soaking wet in combat boots—at Fort Leonard Wood, Missouri, where my dad, Lieutenant Powell Taylor, was stationed.

My dad (pictured on the next page) began his army experience in Fort Benning, Georgia, where he worked on the gun range, teaching new recruits. He claims I was conceived in the back of a '54 Chevy (today I own a '54 Chevy; odd, I know). He then went on to Fort Leonard Wood, where he ran the officers' club. Obviously, food and beverage come naturally to me.

The entertainment lineup at the conference included Collective Soul, Five for Fighting (which is one guy), and KC and the Sunshine Band. We officially violated the Laguna Beach noise ordinance when the Sunshine Band hit the stage. They blew through the opening refrain of

"(Shake, Shake, Shake) Shake Your Booty" and the roof was raised. The horns and sax were blaring, the backup singers were swaying, and our people decked out in eighties disco attire got so loud the band had to turn up their gear. So, in a way, the violation was more of a team effort. I was so proud I almost shed a tear when the local constables showed up.

Partying done for a while, that year we began a capital campaign to raise enough money to build a store where almost all (95 percent) profits would go directly to our employee assistance fund, Andy's Outreach. Our committee chose Logan, Utah, as the site. The locals were so excited to get a Texas Roadhouse that about 10 percent of the entire population of Logan applied for jobs. Unemployment was below 5 percent, and most of Utah State University's students turned out to apply as they embraced the giving concept of the store. Today, the restaurant generates more than half a million dollars annually for Andy's and has assisted thousands of our frontline folks around the world in times of need, and that brings a genuine tear to my eye.

The Roadie culture kept rolling—literally—as Steve Ortiz celebrated the fifth year of his motorcycle ride, at which a large group of our folks meet up for three days in the summer. They usually ride anywhere from one hundred to two hundred miles a day on their hogs, bonding with each other in their leather biker outfits while pretending to be a badass motorcycle gang. *Gotta love 'em.* Since it was Steve's fiftieth birthday, he and six others continued on and went coast to coast, four thousand miles, ending up in San Francisco. The pack included John Beck, Paul Marshall, Jerry Morgan, Steve Baucco, and Rex Boatright who hit a flying chicken while traveling one hundred miles an hour. Thankfully, Rex didn't wreck, but the wayward fowl was vaporized—leaving only a few swirling feathers like something out of a Looney Tunes cartoon.

That year we began our first store line-dancing competition. More than two hundred line-dancing teams competed. At first they vied for local crowns, then went to our national finals. Talk about a jolt of energy and enthusiasm—not to mention some mighty fine heel, toe, do-si-do. We've been doing the contest annually ever since. If you've ever been to one of our restaurants, you know that our folks line-dance once an hour, contributing to several key things that make Texas Roadhouse so special. I'm not telling the first of these, and the second I can't remember. Hey, I'm not going to tell *all* of our secrets.

For the first time ever, that year we sold $50 million in gift cards between Thanksgiving and Christmas. For years we had run contests between states, as well as within stores, promoting gift cards for the holiday season. But this was the first year that the concept really took off—we averaged more than $100,000 per store—and we were pretty darn excited. Our store managers can win trips, and store employees can win TVs and other cool stuff by selling the cards.

# MADE-FROM-SCRATCH SIDES
# (WHAT I LEARNED):

- To develop your mission and values, moderate open and honest discussions with groups around your company. Your people will tell you what ideas are already in place and what they are striving to achieve. Take a stand and keep these statements simple and meaningful—don't try to include everything.
- If everyone who works for you can't recite your mission and values, it's your fault as a leader, not theirs. Throw it out and start again. Keep it simple.
- Don't underestimate the importance of physical and mental wellness in the workplace, or the desire of your people to participate in humanitarian efforts and give back to those in need.
- Choose influential employees to serve as Culture Coaches, assisting new hires in understanding your culture and guiding them through their early months. To retain new employees and keep them engaged, you've got to offer a lot of TLC and mentoring.
- Aggressive growth can be both a blessing and a curse. Well-trained people, properly acclimated to your culture, should rule over Wall Street or banker directives.

## CHAPTER 15

# FIFTEEN WAYS TO KEEP YOUR LEGACY

In 2008, we would open an additional twenty-nine restaurants, and we had our first closure in twelve years, in Hartford, Connecticut. Closing a store is a little like losing a family member. Not your wife or father, but maybe a favorite pet. It stings a bit, you shed a few, and then you have to move on. I was still spending about forty-five days a year visiting potential sites with our now three real estate guys. We would typically visit three to five potential locations each day on the road, with me usually approving two or three. About that time, I began to notice many retail brands shifting away from traditional malls to upscale, outdoor shopping areas called power centers or lifestyle centers. In the past, we had chosen a lot of our sites on mall out-lots (the land on the outskirts of mall developments), but around this time we started shifting more to Walmart lots and power center out-lots. We weren't seeing the full power of Amazon yet—or its brutal impact on retail brick-and-mortar locations—but it was coming. What Netflix, Redbox, and other video streaming services did to Blockbuster and Hollywood Video, Amazon was just beginning to do to large and small retail brands.

Our main competitors for these prime parcels were the drugstore brands, which were gobbling up sites (and overpaying), only to then shutter many of their stores a decade later.

Keeping an eye on changing traffic patterns in towns around the country was becoming a bit tricky, as we had to anticipate changes that might happen a decade or more out. Thankfully, people still want to leave the house and shop for groceries and visit Walmart, and they do enjoy eating out. Visibility, access, and adequate parking spaces still rule the day when considering locations. Site selection in the future will be even more difficult because a store location must work for a minimum of fifteen years to recoup its investment.

On February 17, 2008, we celebrated fifteen years in business, our crystal anniversary, appropriate given the delicate state of the economy. We had hit the three-hundred-store inflection point, and I knew that many concepts before had achieved that only to falter soon after— usually through self-inflicted wounds. We had harvested many of our talented folks from two of those doomed brands: Chi-Chi's and Bennigan's. Those concepts had been highfliers for a time, the hot new thing, the literal definition of the flavor of the month, then just as quickly were not. In many cases, with concepts that weakened, the founders and many long-term employees had left and "professional management" had taken over. These folks arrive with MBAs, statistical analyses, charts, graphs, and a bunch of numbers people who, for the most part, have no clue how a restaurant works or how to empower and motivate a staff. The main thing—that thing that made the concept so successful in the first place— no longer remains the main thing, and self-destruction is the result.

One of those that suffered this fate in 2008 was my old alma mater, Bennigan's, which shuttered all 150 corporate locations after its parent company declared bankruptcy. Since the chain had given me my start, and there were still people there I liked, I didn't gloat. Instead I wanted to do something to help. Knowing that customers of Bennigan's still held gift cards to the chain, we decided to honor them at Texas Roadhouse restaurants. We knew we might lose thousands but thought the goodwill would be worth the expense. So, if a Bennigan's customer came in with a twenty- or fifty-dollar gift card, we'd take it like it was our own. The guest got that much off their meal—no questions asked, no stipulations. Yes, we are saints. (Well, not really, just made our ex–Bennigan's folks chuckle.)

The decline of Bennigan's was another wake-up call to keep our standards sky-high and not slip into corporate-think. Thankfully, our company is run by people who have grown up in actual restaurant operations and many were eyewitnesses to either Chi-Chi's or Bennigan's' demise. We have and definitely need professionals in legal, accounting, finance, marketing, HR, and other roles. Yet, in our company, all of us in support roles know who we serve—the Roadies who feed guests in our stores. We at the restaurant Support Center embrace our roles in a relaxed, support-oriented culture. If someone gets a big head, they quickly find the exit.

Most of our operations leaders have grown up in the restaurant business either in our system or other restaurant groups or chains. Our culture takes time to become ingrained and we've found that people who rise from our hourly ranks tend to be our best performers. Quite a few people who today lead the company started in hourly roles.

About this time, I was asked to give a speech about my take on such things to the MBA students at the University of Kentucky. About two weeks before, I was discussing the event's logistics with a school staff member. I mentioned that I had flunked out of UK's MBA program years before. Funnily enough, a week later I was informed—due to an unfortunate scheduling conflict—that my speech had been canceled. *Huh*.

We celebrated our fifteen-year anniversary at our conference that year, and I passed on to our folks a few words of advice I'd received in 2004 from Herb Kelleher, cofounder of Southwest Airlines. He had told me, "Don't tip your gate agent." But after that, he said something even more relevant and to the point: "Follow that old Texas maxim 'Dance with those who brung you.' " Actually, now that I remember, he didn't say it to me, he wrote it to me. I have proof. In other words, he wanted us to always remain true to our company's strengths and core values. As such, I rolled out a list of fifteen things we should not change, throw away, or screw up over the next decade—the values that had brung us this far. They were:

1.  Legendary Food, Legendary Service, always.
2.  Managing partners, center of our focus.
3.  Love your people, kitchen eagles, service heroes.
4.  Hand-cut steaks, legendary meat cutters.
5.  Fall-off-the-bone ribs, no shortcuts.
6.  Made-from-scratch fresh-baked bread.
7.  Made-from-scratch sides.
8.  Ice-cold beer, legendary margaritas.
9.  Peanuts.
10.  Upbeat country music.
11.  Three-table stations.
12.  Alley rallies.
13.  First-time-guest focus.
14.  Manager in the window.
15.  Fun.

A decade later, in 2018, I whipped that list out of its hermetically sealed safety case (or maybe it was just in my desk, it's fuzzy) and was thrilled to see that all fifteen were still in effect, and our restaurants were averaging a million dollars more in sales per year than in 2008. We could live with that. Herb's advice was solid. Stick with what works.

Our speaker that year at the conference was President George H. W. Bush. Prior to his visit, we worked closely with his speechwriter, as the former president wanted to make sure that his remarks were to our liking. He could not have been nicer and was such a humble man. He flew down early to go fishing with a buddy of his in the Bahamas before speaking to our group and was thrilled to show us a picture of a fish he'd caught. He blew our audience away with his speech and his ability to poke fun at himself.

The president delivered a lively thirty-minute speech, and I realized then and there that I preferred giving or listening to speeches that lasted half an hour. Our people are action-oriented, and I find our attention span seems to last about thirty minutes if we are just sitting there. So from that point forward—*so let it be written, so let it be done*—half an hour became our standard maximum time frame for talks from the podium. If only politicians could follow that advice. Probably not.

While the former president was giving his speech, I couldn't help but be a little distracted as I noticed one of the Secret Service agents eyeballin' me. He kept edging closer, whispering into his sleeve now and then. If he was about to take me down, I had zero plans to resist. But I was like, damn, why am I getting nervous?

Finally, the guy was behind me. He tapped me on the shoulder and slipped me a note. It read: "I remember you from Ballard H.S. and wanted to say hi."

Geez. What the bleep? Coronary averted.

Another humble leader whom I admire greatly attended our conference for the first time (and he came back several years after) was Pete Coors. Pete arrived by himself with no posse and walked to church before the conference began. He also had a great time walking up to attendees who were drinking a competitor's beer and asking politely, could he give them a fresh one? He would then replace the beer with a Coors or Coors Light. I am not sure who enjoyed the whole experience more, Pete or our attendees! Pete even got up onstage and danced during one of the concerts. I have always admired leaders who do not take themselves too seriously, as I think they can always relate better to their employees and they have a better sense of the pulse of the business.

As for me, I would much rather go incognito in order to get to know what our people are really thinking. Some say that I am the original undercover boss. As a leader, I've always believed you have to get your ass out of the office and go visit the people in the stores, or wherever you have your business. And when you see a great idea, you write the person who thought it up a note and thank them. I send out many notes every month.

I believe so much in actively seeking feedback from our stores, especially from those working directly with customers, that some Sunday nights (after the weekend rush) I'll call stores at random and ask to talk to half a dozen servers and ask if guests like or dislike new menu items, what guests are complaining about, what they are raving about, and so on. Also, when I visit a restaurant, my first stop is always with the servers; then I make my way to the meat room, then the kitchen line, and finally to the managing partner. By the time I get to the manager, I know if he or she is full of crap because I've already talked to the other people. Then it's dinner, a couple of beers, maybe a margarita; yeah, baby.

I took a much deeper dive into the world of country music at that conference in 2008, when we invited some of Nashville's most prolific songwriters to attend. Growing up, I was never a fan of what was back then called country and western music. I was more into to rock 'n' roll. And in college in my day, you were either a Rolling Stones fan or a Beatles fan. I chose the Stones and have continued that loyalty for the past forty years, attending more than seventy concerts. However, there was one type of country music that I was attracted to. It's called outlaw country, and includes artists such as Merle Haggard, David Allan Coe, and Willie Nelson. I guess I liked that these musicians, like me and my track buddies, were outside the mainstream and not afraid to go against the grain. Who knew that some thirty years later I would become friends with one of those outlaws.

The Nashville songwriters we invited to the conference included legends in the industry Bob DiPiero, Candy Coburn, Kendell Marvel, and Tim James, and they participated in a songwriter-in-the-round where each told the story behind a particular (often number one) song and then sang it. It was so cool to hear how these tunes, which are always associated with some of the industry's biggest stars, came about. Most folks take the songwriting process for granted and the writers never get much credit. We made the point to our attendees that it's like that in the restaurant industry. Nobody gives enough appreciation to the meat cutter or the Roadie working the grill or the baker who made the perfect yeast rolls—and yet Legendary Food, Legendary Service, doesn't happen without them.

After the conference, I struck up a friendship with Kendell and Tim and we discussed writing a Roadhouse song to use on our phone system when guests called in. We agreed to meet in Nashville and booked a recording studio. Being from Kentucky, I took along a bottle of creativity juice: Maker's Mark bourbon. I figured after a few sips, the lyrics would begin to flow like the Ohio River. I contributed a little more than the bourbon, as I got to add a few lines to the song. Today you can still call Texas Roadhouse and hear a few seconds of the song.

I was so inspired by this whole process that I became a licensed songwriter myself and later wrote a song I am very proud of called "River of My Life." Like I did with my ideas for a restaurant all those years ago, I have shopped it to some folks; I haven't found the right fit, but I will keep on trying!

Later, I unwittingly contributed to another country song. The songwriters had made such an impression on us that we partnered with BMI (which protects musicians' rights) to sponsor a few of their songwriter conferences in Florida, Colorado, and Hawaii. In 2016, while attending the Key West event, I was walking along Duvall Street and noticed some plastic tumblers with funny sayings on them. Never one to pass up an irreverent T-shirt, bumper sticker, or cup, I purchased a few of the drinking glasses. Later, I was downing some creativity juice from one of those cups while listening to songwriters perform poolside at one of the events. Not sure why, but as I was leaving I gave my cup to a random girl who was leaving with some other artists. I believe I said, "You look like you could use this cup." Well, the next year at the kickoff event for the songwriter conference in Crested Butte, Colorado (which raises money for cancer research), Storme Warren of SiriusXM introduced the third performer of the night, Julia Cole. I did not know her name, but she looked familiar. I did not recognize her first couple of songs, but when she started the third song, a light bulb went on. She said the inspiration for the song "#GetAwesome" came about when she attended the Key

West songwriters' conference and a random guy gave her a cup with the phrase I'M NOT DRUNK, I'M AWESOME on it. Julia said that the cup had sat on a shelf in her apartment and it later inspired her to write the song. I found her after the show and joked with her that I should own half the song! Storme interviewed us both about the connection for his radio show, and the next year we invited Julia to attend our conference so she could tell the story and perform the song for our attendees.

That September, we were a finalist for the National Restaurant Association's Good Neighbor Award for Community Outreach or, as you might know it, the NRAGNACO. Someone was finally figuring out what our focus was beyond advertising. I've always believed in doing a ton for our communities and spending any marketing money locally, never nationally. For instance, in 2008, the PGA brought the Ryder Cup to Louisville. Since it was in our HQ hometown, we were hit up to do a big sponsorship, like put our name on a hole, a tent, or the PGA Village. All of these ideas were just too expensive for us and did not fit our strategy. We felt slapping our logo on a corporate tent on the course would not really create any buzz or drive any guests to our restaurants. Besides, we had another idea that was right up (way up) our alley. Turns out when the PGA comes to a golf course, it owns all the space. Every inch where someone could put a sign is controlled. Everything, that is, except the airspace. So my PR guy Travis Doster had an idea. He hired a small plane and flew a huge banner—about four stories tall and four stories wide— back and forth above the course.

I was in a tent on the ninth hole, a guest of one of our vendors, and it did not take PGA officials long to find me and demand that we stop flying the plane. They said it was a distraction, but when I pointed out that a sponsor's blimp flying around seemed okay, they backed off. Minutes later, they came back and said that some golfers had complained about the noise of the little plane, but when pressed, they could not name any specific golfer. Funny how they were okay with a sponsor's blimp, which paid them a couple of million bucks, but our little plane was deemed a distraction. I said if noise was the problem, then we could take it up a little higher; of course, since this was Travis' idea, I had no clue who was flying the plane.

In the end, we received a ton of press for our plane stunt and lots of buzz (no pun intended). Just about everyone thought it was a smart way to market. We spent $3,000 but gained a ton of attention, and even today I'll hear someone speak on a local talk radio show about the plane and how we found a creative way to get attention. I bet no one remembers who sponsored Hole 4.

With 2008 winding down, we began construction on my latest idea: Aspen Creek. It would be the restaurant that I'd hoped Buckhead would have evolved into. The menu was basic American fare, well done, with a Colorado theme.

The year 2009 began, as we all can fondly recall, with the economy down the poop chute, our stock price at an all-time low, and the mood of the country pissy at best. We cut our growth projections in half from

thirty to fifteen new locations, but, other than that, kept on as usual. We did not change our offerings, kept our compensation model the same, and laid no one off. We even held our conference as usual—this time in San Francisco—even though other companies were canceling events left and right. We thumbed our collective noses at the economy. That attracted some interest from the media—*Why now? Why when things are down?*—and we told them: "Because this is when our people need a lift the most."

In fact, one of the riskier things we did was invite CNBC to our conference to broadcast live. Some argued that we'd be letting the fox in the henhouse, as the coverage was sure to be negative, and they wondered how investors would react to our company zigging when others were zagging. Why were we going ahead and spending money on a company conference during the Great Recession? Instead of playing defense, we decided to play offense. It would either be a crazy strategy or a brilliant one. As it turned out, CNBC treated us very well. Sure, they covered the downsides and mentioned that other companies were cutting costs, but they were more than fair to our side of the story and how important these events were to company morale and our people's continuing education. The anchor Mark Haines concluded the story with the statement "These are my kind of people."

We were later presented with a number of awards from the travel industry for helping out their people when things were hard.

Our conference theme mirrored the Summer of Love from the Bay Area scene during the late sixties (minus the marijuana). We did not allow the negativity in the country at this time to distract us from reconnecting, celebrating, and thinking positive thoughts. Cindy Perkins, from Terre Haute, Indiana, was our Managing Partner of the Year, while Debbie Hayden, our leader in purchasing and one of our Chi-Chi's alumni, won our Legends award.

Steve Ortiz and his team delivered some great information to the group. They had divided their message into four baskets: (1) quality of operations, (2) people, (3) culture, and (4) financials. Of the many businesses that have succeeded over time, those four areas, in balance, seem to matter the most—in good times and bad. Yet in tough economic times, it is easy for CEOs (pressured by boards and large shareholders) to cut quality or people, and lose their culture in an effort to preserve their precious quarterly bottom line. The long-term damage to their brands for this short-term thinking usually becomes clear a few years later when these executives are shown the door. *Buh-bye, take care*. At those times, I can't help but chuckle reading their BS public statements: They wanted more time with their families; they will be pursuing "other opportunities"; or they will be retiring early.

Our first Aspen Creek in Louisville opened to good crowds, but our next two didn't fare as well. And we found they'd started taking sales from nearby Texas Roadhouse locations. Since we didn't want to compete with the mother ship, we converted one restaurant to a Bubba's 33 (a new concept we would introduce), and the other two were sold to one of our franchisees, with restrictions on how close they could be located in relation to a Texas Roadhouse in the future. Just like in poker, according to Kenny Rogers, you got to know when to hold 'em, know when to fold 'em.

In September of 2009, we opened our much-anticipated Texas Roadhouse location in Logan, Utah, of which 95 percent of the profits would go to our Andy's Outreach Fund, for the benefit of Roadies in need.

> **TRAVIS DOSTER, president of Andy's Outreach, VP of communications**
> Over the years, it has become a cliché for some companies to talk about "taking care of employees." The campaign to build Andy's Restaurant and donate the profits to help employees in times of crisis validates that Texas Roadhouse truly is a people-first company. As of January 2021, Andy's Outreach has granted $17.4 million in assistance to 12,521 Roadies!

In 2009, Julie Juvera, one of our HR Roadies, was on a Southwest Airlines flight when she met a flight attendant with a big smile, a welcoming spirit, and a small button that read I ♥ MY JOB. The flight attendant hadn't received the button from her company but said that her husband had given it to her since she was always gushing in her praise for her beloved Southwest. She proudly wore the button every day.

Julie ran the I Love My Job idea by Mark Simpson, our head of HR, and they had some bumper stickers made up. At our conference that year, during the general session, Julie tossed out a few T-shirts that featured the slogan to the crowd of Roadies. Our folks went back to their restaurants and started reprinting the shirts for their team members, and the idea spread fast. Quickly we had to approve the new shirt, as most of our employees preferred it to the current model. They actually loved their jobs! How cool. According to a 2017 Gallup study of the American workplace, from 55 to 80 percent of people say their work is something to be endured rather than enjoyed. Ask one of our employees when they stop line-dancing about that report.

While our outlook for 2008 and 2009 remained bullish, investors took note. *Forbes* named us one of the top ten fastest-growing retailers in 2010. *Nation's Restaurant News* ranked us number two in a consumer survey of favorite casual and family restaurant chains, and we received the USO Service Award for volunteerism for our humanitarian efforts at our annual conference that year in New York City. Awards were flying in; Scott Colosi, our CFO, was named CFO of the year in Louisville; and we were chosen as *Business First*'s Louisville Large Company of the Year.

When you get that much notice, I always say it's the perfect time to ease up on the gas, rest on your laurels, and pat yourself on the back. Yeah, right. Life sometimes isn't much more complicated than the gears on an automobile. While my car has three gears—drive, neutral, and reverse—we humans have only two. There is no reverse on the road of life. You have to just keep moving forward, and every now and then you try to catch a little neutral.

I knew we'd need a new challenge to keep our folks focused and driving ahead. And then, just like that, poof! Wish granted.

G.J. was getting some positive press individually, and I could sense his desire to run his own show. Many of our board members sensed the same and felt that G.J.'s time was coming to a close. G.J. and I had a pow-wow, and I told him I was years away from retiring. He said he would check out the scene at other places as his desire was to be number one. That was his end goal. No problem, baby. I'll give you all the references you need, I told him. As one of our board members said, I guess it's tough to be Peyton Manning's or Tom Brady's backup (he was referring to me being the star quarterback, I guess, and G.J. the backup). If we had to go with that analogy, I was kind of thinking I was more John Elway (as a longtime Denver Broncos fan). C'mon, man.

G.J. had done a fine job organizing our support center and bringing on quite a few support people. At the same time, he was going through a divorce with his wife, Juli, and she was still working for us. Awkward. I remember having to be deposed in the split. I told the attorneys from both sides that it would be a waste of time interviewing me. Any information I would give in the deposition would have no impact on the final dollars to be split up, and they certainly didn't need multiple attorneys there to listen when the thing was being recorded.

Juli later confirmed that no information from my deposition was used in the divorce—big surprise.

Thus, my advice to others in a similar situation: Have your attorney send you a bill weekly, with no rounding up. As to phone calls between attorneys, tell them you'll pay for one lawyer on the call, and it should last no more than fifteen minutes. In order to keep the meter running, most (not all) divorce lawyers will play up the distrust and anger of the moment to delay the entire process so they can bill additional hours. Another shocker, I know.

Anyway, back to the story, got carried away. Sorry.

# MADE-FROM-SCRATCH SIDES (WHAT I LEARNED):

- Searching for the best retail locations is a process that must evolve year over year. What worked for us in the past (mall out-lots) changed to power centers and Walmart out-lots with the emergence of Amazon and online shopping.
- Businesses that are successful often are sunk when professional management comes in and are clueless as to how to empower and motivate a staff. The "thing" that made the concept so successful in the first place no longer remains the main thing.
- Professionals in legal, accounting, finance, marketing, HR, and other roles must know whom they support—those working with guests.
- Only if something stops working should you change it (if it ain't broke . . . ), otherwise stay true to the values that "brung you to the dance." Thank you, Herb Kelleher.
- Of the many successful businesses that have succeeded over time, we believe they focus on (1) quality of operations, (2) people, (3) culture, and, last, (4) the financials. Yet in tough economic times, it is easy for CEOs to cut quality, people, and lose their culture in an effort to preserve the quarterly bottom line. To be clear, this is what we call a mistake.
- When a positive idea takes hold in your company—like our I ♥ MY JOB T-shirts—embrace it. The best cultures can turn on a dime.

## CHAPTER 16

# GOING INTERNATIONAL

The year 2011 would see Texas Roadhouse, and the economy, scurrying out of the recession like a horned toad from a cowboy's boot. Our sales were heading in the right direction. Early that year, we made the move to start paying dividends to our shareholders. We had been getting pressure from many of our large investors, such as Greg Wendt from Capital Group, who visited with our board to describe how shareholders viewed a stock's performance to include appreciation as well as dividends paid. Many public companies face these discussions when they reach the size we had reached. Growth inevitably slows and investors usually want company leaders to (1) borrow funds to buy back stock, (2) add a dividend, or (3) accelerate growth. At these times, some companies also choose to shed costs and employees to keep Wall Street happy, with resulting lower morale, worse service, and deteriorating food quality, all of which leads to a sales decline.

This *will* be on tomorrow's quiz. You have been warned.

As our sales were still kicking derrière, adding debt to buy back stock was not going to fly with me. I saw that as a short-term solution. I also didn't want to accelerate growth beyond what we could handle, hire too many people too fast, and shortcut training to please a handful of shareholders with a short-term perspective. So, adding a dividend seemed to fit. Greg had given us solid advice, and new investors started giving us a look.

G.J. was interviewing with other companies, hoping to find a number-one spot. That summer he took a position with California Pizza Kitchen, owned by Golden Gate Capital. With his Texas Roadhouse experience over the past ten years, he had convinced them that he had the knowledge and skill to advance their same-store sales and profitability to higher levels than they had seen before.

With G.J. gone, I moved back into the CEO slot, promoting Scott Colosi, our CFO, to be our president. Price Cooper, our lead finance guy, became Scott's replacement as CFO. Later that year, Scott told me that being president wasn't exactly the fun gig he thought it would be. He loved working with numbers and the Wall Street cats, but he didn't care for the people issues that were coming his way. I told him that's why he was getting paid the big bucks, to deal with the stuff that would distract me from pushing the company forward.

Being the figurehead again, I had to attend things like the CEO summit in DC. At one of those events, while I was waiting in the lobby of a Marriott for our team to come down, I decided to catch a few winks. I was tired from an international trip and slumped in a chair, wearing my usual jeans and boots, a cowboy hat pulled over my eyes. Suddenly I felt someone kick my foot. Startled, I lifted my hat to see a security officer staring down at me. "Hey, buddy, there's no sleeping in the lobby. Move on." I tried to tell him I was waiting for my colleague, but he was having none of it. He knew a homeless person when he saw one. When I told him I was a guest of the hotel, he snorted. "Yeah, right, you aren't the first guy to pick up a room key and feed me that line." He told me to beat it. Our company had spent more than a million dollars that year alone with Marriott (with our conference and other business), and I was getting kicked out of the lobby.

I waited out in the cold for Travis, our PR guy, to come down, and he hooted about what had happened all day long. It's okay, though. I've always liked to fly under the radar and look the part of a poor country cousin (which I was for at least forty-five of my years on earth). Dressing down helps me go incognito into many of our stores—as I said before, I was the original undercover boss. That show *Undercover Boss* has actually approached me a couple of times, but I told the producers I wasn't interested. I was already doing it, and it was working great. I'd sneak into a store in a costume, pay with cash, and then call the managing partner to let them know what I'd seen. I'm also convinced that dressing down has helped us get better real estate deals. Landowners don't know me from Adam when I show up and start negotiating, and we usually can get a killer deal before the owner clues in to the fact that I'm representing a multibillion-dollar enterprise. I even keep my phone unlisted for that very reason; when I call a potential land deal, the name is "Unknown Caller."

Our conference that year was in Naples, Florida, where one of my faves, Chris Blythe, won Managing Partner of the Year, and another fave, Gina Tobin, our new market partner in Florida, won our Legends award. That fall, several of our senior directors were promoted to vice president, including Debbie Hayden, Mike Keaton, Chris Jacobsen, Mark Simpson, and Juanita Coleman.

We also had our first international restaurant opening in the Dubai Mall in the UAE. We could have opened a year before, but I wanted to wait for a location on the first floor, which had the most foot traffic. We landed a choice spot near the parking-lot entrance by the main escalator. Even in faraway lands, traffic flow matters—whether cars or people.

Designing the layout for the international restaurants is an interesting process. Each country has its own customs and traits. Privacy, view lines, peanuts vs. no peanuts, table size, and menu offerings differ from country to country. Line-dancing is okay in some places but forbidden in others. The debate over what's okay to put on a mural in one country as opposed to another can drive you crazy.

The freedom of choice we have in America is too often taken for

granted, as I have experienced some bizarre and, in a few instances, scary stuff around the world. A few times, innocent questions posed to potential franchise partners—trying to understand the customs or politics of the areas—would not be answered. They often feared that our rooms were bugged, our driver might be recording us, or a government lip reader could be at a nearby table. Crazy, huh?

I closed out 2011 with a remarkable opportunity. As a young man, I would never have dreamed I would be walking through the gates of the White House, but I had a chance late that fall to attend a country concert on the grounds. The tickets had come through a local congressman and the only requirement I was given was that I was not to wear jeans—I guess that would embarrass my local representative. Our internal PR folks followed up and called Leslie to make sure that I dressed up, even suggesting a bit of a compromise in having me wear a black suit and cowboy hat. I felt the whole jeans things had been more of a "suggestion," and figured no self-respecting country music fan would wear a suit to a country-music concert. I figured the vast majority of attendees would be wearing western attire. Was I ever wrong. I was the only guest to pass through those famous wrought-iron gates wearing jeans and boots. I should have been embarrassed, but I have never minded flying solo. I think too many people get hung up on what others think about them or how they judge them. I don't have that gene. I mostly care about results. And something cool came out of that night. I ran into Darius Rucker (then a solo country artist who had gained fame as the lead singer of Hootie & the Blowfish). Rucker was the only other human on the premises also wearing jeans. We spotted each other and had an instant connection over our Wranglers and Ariats. We had a great conversation. I made a commitment to bring him back to play at our conference two years later, and as usual, he put on an amazing concert. He would play again for us in 2019.

The biggest bummer of the night was their refusal to let us take pictures of the event. That might not seem like a big deal, but it ticked me off. Since college, I had been the "picture guy." I have always been very visual, so being the photographer was a good fit for me. Back in school, some guys were happy to make beer runs, others were good at recruiting girls for the party, but me, I ended up in charge of making sure to capture those Kodak moments. (Google it if you do not know what that means.) I estimate I've taken more than twenty thousand pictures since college and am still going strong. Photography has come in very handy in detailing wild adventures with my buddies and in detailing the history of Texas Roadhouse. Plus, if you are the one taking the photos, there are fewer pictures of you!

The role of picture guy became a blessing over the years. I'm now able to look back and cherish the memories I made with my family. These pictures allow me to reflect on the past and remind me that I was present for many important events.

In 2012, we ramped development back up and saw system-wide sales pass $1.5 billion. Our conference that year included country duo Big & Rich and rock band 3 Doors Down, two very fun acts. Our late-night party was nicknamed "the Rock Star Lounge," where our people's partying would have made Keith Richards proud. Longtime high-performer Mitch Hauber won Managing Partner of the Year, representing Wichita, Kansas.

Since our international growth was not moving as fast as I'd have liked, I decided we needed someone to head it up who knew what they were doing. I interviewed candidates in various odd places—the Atlanta airport, a bazaar in Istanbul, and finally a coffee shop in Moscow, where I met Hugh Carroll. He was operating a restaurant company in Russia and had experience with TGIF, running restaurants in Asia as well as South America. Within weeks we made him an offer and Hugh said, "*Sí. Da. Hai.*" Hugh partnered with Greg Moore who was the international liaison on our board, and one of our up-and-comers, Chris Colson, who came to work for Roadhouse several years earlier after working with my outside lawyer Bill on our IPO (Chris was later called on to head up our legal team as VP in 2019). Having the right person and team dedicated to international has made a huge difference in our growth into ten countries outside of the United States.

In September of that year, we were voted the number one steakhouse in America by *Nation's Restaurant News*. Of course, *Consumer Reports* also named us the Noisiest Restaurant in America. All press is good press, I guess. Being the politically correct person that I am, we printed up a bunch of PROUD TO BE LOUD T-shirts, cranked our jukeboxes even higher, and celebrated with our usual decorum (not).

I have often thought of our restaurants as either throwing a party every night or possibly a play coming alive in this cool-looking theater. Think dinner playhouse. Hopefully, the curtains pull back with a well-lit building; a nice-looking, well-kept landscape; and plenty of available parking. But wait, that's only the beginning. Inside, everything from the bathrooms to the bar needs to impress; there's hot, timely food served at our guest-friendly prices. Thanks to our awesome kitchen folks and our legendary in-house meat cutters, our food should taste yummy. The final stars of our play include our amazing front-of-the-house folks, the actors and actresses who—with big smiles, energy, and enthusiasm—guide you through your dining experience. Entertainment, or should I say "eatertainment," and hospitality should rule. Our goal is to be the friendliest place in town, baby.

In 2013, our twentieth year, we were on a tear, opening thirty-four new restaurants, including our first on a military base. The army had taken a poll of its soldiers, asking which full-service restaurant brand was their favorite. Guess who was first? You got it. We won.

We also opened our first new restaurant concept since Aspen Creek. It's called Bubba's 33, a sports bar featuring pizza, burgers, and beer. A couple of years earlier, I had attended a restaurant CEOs' meeting, which G.J. typically had attended. With him gone now, I went in his stead. I received the cold shoulder from the heads of Outback and Applebee's—no surprise there—but I got the same from the head of Buffalo Wild Wings. Since Texas Roadhouse was competing with the first two, I understood, but why would the head of a sports-bar franchise dis me? So I decided to take a shot at competing with them. Why not? That night, pencil in hand, after a few beers, I started sketching the building face, designing the kitchen layout floor plan, and writing up a preliminary menu. Four hours later, at about three a.m., I was done. To this day, our menu selection is about 85 percent the same as that night.

The first few Bubba's 33s had two bars, which we later changed to one, increasing the dining area and making the place more welcoming to families. It had taken me ten stores and three years to nail the Texas Roadhouse prototype. And true to form, it took three trips around the sun and store number ten before we finally had the prototype nailed for Bubba's. Apparently, it takes me a while to figure stuff out.

Our bar areas have garage doors, so on pleasant weather days we can open up to the fresh air, and in most locations, we have an outdoor patio. And all Bubba's have both sports and music videos playing on the TVs. We've found most people don't go out to dinner hoping to catch a glimpse of Rachael Ray or Lester Holt on the boob tube. They prefer upbeat music action or sports with their cold frosty beer, award-winning cheeseburgers, and made-from-scratch pizzas. (This is not an advertisement because remember, we don't advertise.)

At our conference celebrating our twentieth anniversary, in Maui, Hawaii, we had leadership expert Chester Elton throwing out carrots (less collateral damage than hurling coconuts). Mike Schmidt (not *that* one) was named Managing Partner of the Year. He had started in 2000—at age seventeen—as a service assistant in store number five in Clearwater, Florida, and had worked his way up to assistant kitchen manager, kitchen manager, and managing partner. He is now a regional market partner, running more than one hundred restaurants in Texas and Oklahoma. Many of our management leaders at Texas Roadhouse have followed a similar path. And that, my friends, is ultracool.

> **MIKE SCHMIDT, regional market partner**
>
> Even as a busboy, I always dreamed of achieving something big. I was lucky to join a restaurant that loves to make big dreams happen for those who work hard. I like to say that Texas Roadhouse is a vehicle to success. It goes very fast and has lots of available seats. But it's up to you to choose to get on board.

My biggest thrill that year was landing both Glenn Frey and Joe Walsh, of the rock band Eagles fame, to play for us. They rocked for the two thousand–plus folks we had assembled, plus another thousand or so locals who had turned up when they found out a couple of living legends were playing. They filled up the public beach area and we were happy to entertain them; we welcomed the freeloaders and just asked them to visit one of our stores when they were back in the continental forty-eight.

It had been my dream to get the Eagles back together at our conference, but one of our booking agents had told me the various members of the band didn't necessarily all get along and they would not play together, so I needed to stop asking. In 2012, I had attended a screening of the Eagles documentary at the Sundance Film Festival in Park City, Utah.

We had already booked Glenn Frey to play our conference. I spotted Joe Walsh and Glenn Frey a few rows in front of me. After the film was over, I scooted over to them. I mentioned to Joe that we had booked Glenn in Maui and would love for him to join us. He shrugged and said, "Sure, sounds fun." So much for the idea they would never play together. You've got to ask.

Glenn, a consummate gentleman, also agreed, and we were able to land two Eagles legends onstage.

That was cool, but the coolest thing that happened that year was the birth of my first grandchild, Lila. Before folks have their first grandkid, there's always a debate about the child's name and how much input you'll get as a grandparent. I didn't bother to give my daughter my opinion since kids will inevitably go another way if you do give it. However, I was set on what name I wanted my grandkids to call me. I gave my daughter three options: Chief, Boss, or F'n Chief. Pick one. She selected Chief, what I'd wanted to be called all along. She didn't want her kids (now three daughters) calling their grandfather the "boss."

So, for all of you out there really wanting Pops, Grammie, Papaw, or the like, know that there are ways to steer your kids in the right direction. Of course, you might end up being called Geezer or Grand-Dude, so be careful what you put on your list of options.

# MADE-FROM-SCRATCH SIDES
# (WHAT I LEARNED):

- Decisiveness, action, and accountability reduce the amount of crap a leader has to shovel. In the absence of those leadership qualities, team members get consumed by petty quarreling.
- When making decisions, get the facts, involve the right people, and make a decision. Too many companies and leaders over-analyze decisions, take too long, and eventually become flat squirrels—those who can't make a decision and become roadkill. We even have an original menu item called roadkill (fresh and tasty).
- There are so many subtleties and nuances to doing business in new parts of the world. Having an experienced person and team dedicated to international makes a huge difference in your growth.
- Don't expect perfection on your first retail location. It took me three years and ten tries before we got the prototypes right for Texas Roadhouse and Bubba's 33.

## CHAPTER 17

# A TARGET ON OUR BACK

We opened another thirty Texas Roadhouse restaurants in 2014, including our first store in Asia—in Taipei, Taiwan. That year, we were also named one of the 100 Most Trustworthy Companies by *Forbes* (honestly!) and our payroll department won the Prism award from the American Payroll Association.

I've often wondered who votes in these awards. I was especially glad to make the *Forbes* list since we don't advertise in magazines. We just keep our heads down and do our work.

I also found that as we grew as a corporation, it was hinted that the size of political donations might also bring us status, appreciation, and power within a particular party. How do I know? Because I've been approached countless times by politicians on both sides of the aisle buttering me up like carnival corn on the cob. My answer: "No thanks, not interested. Guessing a root canal might be a better option." Funny, when I was poor, I never got a single call.

As to politics, I've always found it best for leaders to keep their opinions to themselves. We have seventy thousand employees, which means we have seventy thousand differing opinions on political issues. Who am I to say I represent all those voices just because I'm the CEO? And as to

Texas Roadhouse, it can't have an opinion. As much as we love this place, it's not a living, breathing entity; it's an idea that was built on serving everyone like they are family. When was the last time you agreed with your uncle Stu or cousin Bernice? Even if you disagree, you know to love 'em, treat 'em fairly, and feed 'em well.

During 2014, we decided to transition our training managers (those in charge of getting our new managers and employees up to speed) into the newly created role of Service Coaches. This would require a significant investment, as we would have more than twice the number of service coaches as training managers. Consistent with how we operate with our product coaches—who work with our stores to ensure legendary meat cutting and food that is recipe right—our service coaches would work hand in hand with our market partners to deliver a higher level of hospitality. In addition, new-store training would still be part of the plan for these folks.

While our competitors might be increasing their ad spend (which would likely guarantee their winning the Best Use of Bathroom Tile award), we doubled down on improving the guest experience with a laser focus on food and service quality. Yes, this added expenses that would take time to earn a return on, but we knew, based on the results seen with our product coaches, that it was worth giving it a shot. The numbers people were not totally on board—surprise, surprise—but in our company, operations rules. It wouldn't be long before we surpassed $100,000 per week per store in sales, double our volumes fifteen years before.

Our conference in 2014 was in Amelia Island, Florida, where Scott Schraeger from Toledo won Managing Partner of the Year. Jerry Morgan, father of our manager-in-the-window idea, won the Legends award. We also country-rocked to the music of Darius Rucker and Little Big Town.

In October, we opened the Taipei restaurant. Whether Texas Roadhouse is in the Middle East, Asia, or the Americas, we find a way to succeed. I believe our focus on hospitality, fun, and energy within the restaurant are just as important as our food and service. And you don't have to be young to exude energy. My mom is in her eighties and has more get-up-and-go than folks half her age. And yet about this time, a few people at the U.S. Equal Employment Opportunity Commission felt that we had too many young people working for us—so we must be discriminating against people over forty (like me, who by this point was pushing sixty).

So without a single complaint ever filed against us, the EEOC filed suit. I'll go over this all in more detail in the next chapter, but the long and the short of it was that the suit cost us and the government tens of millions of dollars and accomplished little to nothing. We, like almost all casual-dining restaurants, have many young folks working our dining rooms. According to the government's own statistics, while the average age of a U.S. worker is forty-two, the average age in food service industry-wide is twenty-nine—it's typically even lower when you consider just front-of-house. We have many older workers front-of-house, and they are fantastic and love their jobs and we love them.

This founder, realizing I'd never told anyone to hire based on age, was more than ready to fight, and that gave the EEOC the window they wanted. I believe the agency's objective wasn't getting older folks jobs, but about creating law. Since a company founder is more likely to fight rather than settle, and they anticipated taking us to court and that we might be found guilty by a jury, that would open the door to creating a legal precedent and they could sue other companies without a complaint. As more fuel to my theory, the EEOC filed suit in Boston (a city with typically more anti–big business juries, according to our attorneys).

Four long years of providing documents and e-mails, as well as in-person depositions, were to follow. I remember showing up to my deposition in sandals, shorts, a Willie Nelson HAVE A WILLIE NICE DAY T-shirt, and being asked the same question over and over in positive and then negative ways, with constant questions as to why I don't e-mail people in the company about everything. My answer: I use a phone and call people like a decent human being because direct communication creates action, results, and accountability (something apparently these government folks found hard to process).

A few weeks after getting grilled by the EEOC, I turned off the negativity and attended the *Nation's Restaurant News*'s conference in Dallas, Texas, where I was honored, along with the CEOs of Cracker Barrel, Taco Bell, 7-Eleven, and Potbelly Sandwich Shop, as a Golden Chain award nominee, which many consider the highest honor you can receive in the restaurant business. Very cool and totally legit. I was voted the 2014 Restaurant Operator of the Year on the final night, the big award that is voted on by restaurant operators nationwide. Totally cool.

Earlier that year, I decided to try doing a fast-food restaurant we call Jaggers. The goal was to create a place that would have better burgers than Five Guys, and serve chicken tenders and sandwiches that could compete with Raising Cane's and Chick-fil-A. Leo Martinez, John Beck, a few others, and I spent six months working on developing made-from-scratch burgers, buns, fries, tenders, and chicken sandwiches. The subtle differences in meat-to-fat ratios, hamburger grind sizes, marinades, and bun specifics were an ordeal in trial and error. The design of the building, kitchen, drive-through, along with spec'ing lighting, walls, flooring, ceiling, and seating took some time as well. Finally, on December 9, 2014, we opened our first prototype in Noblesville, Indiana. Sales were decent, though the numbers were a far cry from those of Chick-fil-A or Raising Cane's, but ahead of Five Guys. It would take a couple of years of fine-tuning and another restaurant opening to finally match the sales of the big dogs.

In January of 2015, after fourteen years as our COO, Steve Ortiz announced his retirement at age fifty-six. I reacted to the announcement with grace and decorum. Yeah, right. I gave him a hard time. I had selected him to be my replacement as CEO and was considering doing that at our conference in San Diego in 2018, which would be our twenty-fifth year. Steve said he knew of my plan and decided to retire before I could promote him. Crap.

---

**STEVE ORTIZ**

I had thought this move through for quite a long time. Kent and I were traveling together when I shared my plan. He questioned me a couple of times and asked if there was any chance I would change my mind. I let him know there wasn't. It was a very difficult decision because of how much I identified myself with being a big part of Texas Roadhouse, a big part of the word *Legendary*. Leaving Texas Roadhouse was leaving a piece of me behind. With that said, I also discussed with Kent opening a few franchise restaurants on the West Coast. He agreed, and it made me feel good that I would still be connected to the (Texas Roadhouse) brand.

---

Doug Thompson, a Roadhouse veteran, took Steve's place, first as vice president of operations and later as COO, with Texas Roadhouse legend Jerry Morgan taking his role as West Regional. Before making those moves, I had had discussions with our fifty-some market partners and many managing partners about who should replace Steve. Doug received the most votes, with Jerry Morgan getting the second most, even though he was not a regional partner at the time. Don't feel bad for Jerry, I later named him president in 2020. I always ask the opinions of those who will work for a new leader, as well as peers and others who will interact with a person. I feel that having direct, confidential discussions—feeling the confidence and passion in people's voices—works much better on promotions than hearing from just a few voices and getting board approval. I think general ass-kissing, office politics, and cronyism fall by the wayside when you do that, and that those who vote for the final choice are now bought into that person's success.

Our conference in 2015 was in Phoenix, Arizona, where longtime MP Pat Ryan, from Thornton, Colorado, won Managing Partner of the Year, and Mike Keaton, VP of real estate, received the Legends award. We were entertained by Dierks Bentley and Foreigner blasting out "Juke Box Hero." Dierks was especially moved by the conference's humanitarian efforts in his hometown of Phoenix.

On November 11, Veterans Day, we proudly served a free lunch to more than 250,000 armed-services veterans and active-duty personnel around the country. Veterans Day is my favorite day of the year to visit multiple stores, shake hands with our military folks, and let them know how much we appreciate their service. In turn, it's great to see how they welcome our efforts to serve them.

My dad's experience in the army created in me a sense of pride and appreciation for the men and women who protect our country. As a kid, I swelled with pride when I told others that my dad was a lieutenant and I was born on an army base. Over the years, a statistic has stuck with me: Our nation counts on 1 percent of the population to protect the other 99 percent. That should be a wake-up call for all of us who live in a free country: The few protect the many. And that's why I have always felt it was so important to support our troops in many ways, including giving away hundreds of thousands of free meals to retired and active-duty military service members each Veterans Day.

As is the case with most Roadhouse initiatives, our Veterans Day celebration wasn't my idea. It began with a few stores in Indiana and Michigan in 2002, and I grabbed on to it and embraced it. It became nationwide in 2010. On Veterans Day, we open for lunch and serve only veterans, active military, and their families. I am very proud of our team for the service they provide to our military heroes and their loved ones. I believe we are the only restaurant company that provides a full meal, drink included, at no cost. In my visits to stores that day, I love to see veterans sitting together, sharing their experiences, and reconnecting with one another.

**PAUL MARSHALL, market partner, state of Texas**

Back in the early 2000s, I was a managing partner of a store in Killeen, Texas, where Fort Hood is [located]. It was Veterans Day and my phone rings. It's Kent. He said, "Here's my personal credit card." It wasn't the company card. He wanted me to buy dinner for everyone in the restaurant who was a veteran or on active duty. My service manager and I started walking around, thanking people for their service. It was such an emotional night. The servers were in tears, I got teared up. What made it all the more special was we didn't have a ton of money back then to do that sort of thing, but Kent wanted to take care of the people who take care of us. He ended up spending about $5,000 of his own money. He did the same thing the next year, and a few years later we started doing it company-wide.

Our support for our troops does not stop with a free meal. We were one of the original supporters of Homes For Our Troops, which builds specially adapted homes for post-9/11 veterans. HFOT has built more than three hundred homes since its founding, and I am proud to serve on its board. Lots of organizations talk about helping, but HFOT is doing hands-on work every day to build homes for veterans and their families. That's work that has a real impact, one that can be measured in the hearts and lives of the recipients.

One of our more unusual efforts to support the military involved the USS *Texas*, which is a class-two nuclear submarine. One of our team members read in a Texas newspaper that the sailors referred to their galley (kitchen) as the USS *Texas Roadhouse*. We were honored and reached out to the captain to see if we could "adopt" his ship. It took a while to connect, as the sailors were out on maneuvers and received limited messages. Once the sub returned to port in Connecticut, we held a huge celebration for the sailors and their families. In addition to serving Roadhouse food, we outfitted the boat's galley with Roadhouse gear, including aprons, coffee mugs, cactuses to decorate, and a cool USS *Texas* neon sign. Recognition is such a huge part of our company culture and success, and when you can recognize and thank people alongside their families, I think it means even more. That's why we encourage the spouses of our employees to attend our annual conference, and we pay their expenses. It's important for family members to experience our culture and realize how much we appreciate their sacrifices.

The USS *Texas* was later transferred to Pearl Harbor and the captain invited me to visit Hawaii, take a ride on another submarine, the USS *Badfish*, and see the crew in action underwater. That I was not about to miss. It turned out to be one of the most amazing experiences in my life. When I went aboard, my first impression was that Hollywood makes submarines look much larger than they really are. It takes a special person to be cooped up with 134 other sailors in what amounts to fifteen hundred square feet of living space. These sailors were laser-focused on their jobs, not on the setting. Not one of them complained about the confined space; instead they went about their tasks with a practiced efficiency. I can't help but think of that experience every time someone complains that their office is too small or they need more space for their department.

Our support of the troops has been been recognized several times over the years, including Coca-Cola's award twice; and the USO awarded us the Rita Alt award for volunteerism.

The year 2016 would see us cross the five-hundred-restaurant mark and debut on the *Forbes* list of America's Best Employers, as well as being named as the number one full-service restaurant in the nation by *Restaurant Business Magazine*. Those accolades are pretty cool, but in a way they can be distracting. I always like chasing someone ahead of us, playing the underdog and fighting to outperform another company that has more market share or better recognition among consumers. Now that we were ranked number one, we couldn't be the scrappy underdog anymore. We had a target on our back and other restaurant companies were chasing after our success, trying to poach our people, and aiming to knock us off the podium. So our focus became improving our performance by targeting specific areas, measuring these, and holding people accountable to higher levels of performance than ever. I wanted to strive to be even better, never satisfied, discovering potential obstacles and creating solutions.

When you think about it, that's how Michael Jordan played basketball. A fellow UNC alum (*Go 'Heels!*), Jordan was known for outworking and out-training everyone, and for demanding the most of himself and his teammates. He never asked more of others than he was willing to give himself. He had a complete focus on getting better every day. He seemed to savor the hard work, and as we all know, he never let up—like scoring thirty-eight points despite battling the flu in Utah in game five of the 1997 Finals.

As MJ once said: "I can accept failure, everyone fails at something. But I can't accept not trying. I've always believed that if you put in the work, the results will come."

Tim Grover, who was a speaker at one of our events, was MJ's personal trainer in the 1990s and the author of *Relentless*, in which he classified NBA players as Coolers, Closers, or Cleaners: the good, the great, and the unstoppable. Grover describes Coolers as careful, watching what others are doing and then following. The Closers can handle the pressure, but they seek recognition and attention, and are very aware of what others think of them: They love media hype, rewards, and the perks associated with fame, and care about the bling and showy lifestyle.

On the other hand, Cleaners could not care less about how they are perceived by others. MJ, Larry Bird, and Kobe Bryant were the ultimate Cleaners. These people are usually motivated by results, not by the attention. They're usually self-made, never in it for the money. "Love what you do and the money will follow" is their motto. It's not about talent, brains, or wealth, it's about the relentless, instinctive drive to do whatever it takes to get to the top of where you want to be and stay there.

Our conference that year was in Miami, at the Fontainebleau hotel, a favorite hangout back in the day for Frank Sinatra, Dean Martin, Sammy Davis Jr., and the rest of the Rat Pack. Frank did it his way, and we did it ours—with Jake Owen and Flo Rida playing. Our speaker was Dick Vitale, *bay-beee*, the iconic ESPN basketball commentator. He "prepared" for his speech in a most unusual way, by hanging out by the pool with his wife the day before, chatting up our folks. And yet, when he hit the stage, we noted that he had adapted his remarks in order to be more relevant to our experience, and our folks loved it.

**DICK VITALE, legendary ESPN sportscaster**
My wife, Lorraine, and I had a fantastic time when I was the keynote speaker at the annual Texas Roadhouse Managing Partner Conference, which pays tribute to their restaurant management teams. I was so impressed with the terrific spirit, energy, and passion that Roadhouse has created. The enthusiasm was off the charts, and you could feel the joy in their hearts. Yes, I would simply state [that] it was a memorable event due to their number one guy, Kent Taylor. The chemistry that he develops with his people leads to maximum production. Kent impressed me so much that if I was talking about him on ESPN, I would say he is AWESOME, BABY, with a capital *A*!

We added Manila, the Philippines, to our list of international Texas Roadhouse locations in 2016. The design for that store differed slightly from Taiwan as well as others we'd done. Before we put shovel to ground in any country, I spend time visiting restaurants, food courts, and even retail stores. I want to see the type of seating people are attracted to, lighting, music (selection and volume), along with sight lines, elevations, and the materials used, which always vary by culture. For some people, the vibe, energy, and buzz in the room might differ only slightly in a new country, but for the keen observer there's much to learn. No matter what country you're in, interactions between people, facial gestures, smiles (or no smiles), and movement within a room give clues as to the success or potential failure of any given restaurant.

# MADE-FROM-SCRATCH SIDES
# (WHAT I LEARNED):

- Transitioning from training managers to service coaches required a significant investment, but we knew this would help us deliver a higher level of hospitality. While competitors might up their ad spend, we double down on improving the guest experience and let operations rule.

- Ask opinions of those who will work for a new leader, as well as peers and others who will interact with them. Having direct, confidential discussions works much better on promotions than hearing from just a few voices. Those who get a vote in the final choice are now bought into that person's success.

- We give free meals on Veterans Day to hundreds of thousands of armed-services veterans and active-duty personnel. Find a way to use your products and services to give back to a cause you care about.

- At some point you are no longer the underdog fighting to outperform another company that has more market share or better recognition by consumers. When the target is on your back and other companies are coming after your success and poaching your people, improve your performance by targeting specific areas, measuring those, and holding people accountable to higher levels of performance than ever. Be relentless and strive to be even better, never satisfied, then find potential obstacles and create better solutions.

## CHAPTER 18

# GUILTY UNTIL PROVEN INNOCENT

In 2017, we finally closed an ugly decade-long chapter in the history of Texas Roadhouse, settling our age-discrimination lawsuit with the EEOC. I am still blown away by how big of a sucker I was in taking the bait to fight a government agency—thinking that since we were in the right, we would prevail. Ha! I realize now that I was being used to create a precedent for an agency that would allow the government to sue anyone they wanted, at any time.

Yet in all the years leading up to the final court battle with the government agency, I had remained convinced that right would win out over might. After all, Texas Roadhouse just doesn't attract that many older workers as we are mostly a dinner-only concept. I thought that in the court of public opinion, if average people heard about this injustice, they'd be on our side.

But I needed help.

It just so happened that I'd read a book by an attorney named Lanny Davis, who had been special counsel to President Clinton, and he knew DC. He was also a partner in a law firm that had represented Hooters in a similar case with the EEOC, so they knew the restaurant business. We got in touch with Lanny and he helped us make our pitch at the Capitol. The plan was to meet with the right lawmakers, who would then put pressure on the EEOC to dismiss this frivolous case. That was the plan.

We spent eighteen months traveling to and from DC, and we met with lawmakers on both sides of the aisle. My team jokingly called the trips "Mr. Taylor Goes to Washington." We'd walk as a team through the hallowed halls of the Capitol building, and the others said I was hard to miss: a tall guy in cowboy boots and a Stetson hat. Even more attention grabbing were the Willie Braids we'd hand out to the politicians. One day we even grabbed a snapshot with John McCain wearing a pair of our Willie Braids on the Capitol floor. The senator and I connected right away and he thought the braids were a hoot.

For eighteen long months we wore a path to DC. Name a politician— from Chuck Schumer on the Left to Rand Paul on the Right—and we met with him or her. They were respectful and attentive; some agreed to argue our case in front of the committees they served on. At the same time we attended dozens of hearings, with politicians speaking up on our behalf. Our case was even taken up in front of the powerful Ways and Means Committee, some of whose members were so incensed that they promised decisive action on our behalf. We heard later that our story had indeed made an impact on the committee, the government's budget arm, and they cut the EEOC's budget request for the following year! That's right, the EEOC would only be getting a 10 percent increase in their budget.

Ten. Per. Cent. Only in government can a department be penalized with a double-digit budget increase!

It takes me a while sometimes to catch on, yet I began to slowly realize that you can't fight city hall. As a case in point, one day we walked into a representative's office and stopped dead. Every single person in the place was smoking. It was like an episode of *Mad Men*. I was brazen enough to ask these folks how they could puff away inside when it was illegal in every other building in the country. Their response was basically: We make the law. Thus we are exempt from the law. Wow.

Finally, we got a meeting with one of the most influential figures on the Hill, Mitch McConnell. He listened carefully, commiserated with our plight, and was the first person to really tell us the truth; we appreciated his wisdom. He said the money and time we were spending on fuel flying up to DC were ill spent. He explained that since the case was already in the legal process, no politician on earth could do anything about it. No matter how righteous our cause, we had to give up expecting legislated relief.

With lawyers, lobbyists, and the like, the whole process of getting ready to go to court cost us ten years and millions of dollars (the equivalent of four federally purchased leaf blowers). The only good that came out of it was that we did improve our ability to reach out and attract older front-of-the-house employees. Of course, since we are reasonable human beings and always want to do the right thing, that could have been accomplished with an hour-long meeting over tuna sandwiches and Fanta if someone at the EEOC had bothered to visit, call, or even send a letter.

Here's what *should* have happened:

**EEOC:** Hi, I'm Agent Tugnutt from the EEOC, and this is my colleague Edna. [*Edna nods.*] We are concerned about an issue. We think you need to hire more people over the age of forty in front-of-house jobs.

**US:** Oh. No problem. We'd love to do that. How do you think we could attract and retain more older workers in these jobs? See, we don't typically get many applicants of that age to be servers or hosts.

**EEOC:** Here are some ideas we've seen used by other companies.

**MONTAGE:** *EEOC and TXRH people work together, sleeves rolled up. At the end everyone high-fives and then goes to lunch.*

**US:** [*Back in the conference room*]: Wow, Agent Tugnutt and Edna, your ideas were tremendously helpful! It's great to see our government at work helping businesses succeed. [*Edna nods.*]

EEOC:  Naturally. We believe in giving corporations a chance to improve. We'll check back in a few months to see how your efforts are going.

  US:  Thank you. We will welcome you back at any time to check on our progress.

**CURTAIN**

Of course, that is not what happened. Not at all. What we went through was a ten-year witch hunt that cost us and the government (so, us again) more than $50 million combined. Was it worth the time and trouble? You be the judge. Did we find that certain people in government get a kick out of trying to ruin people's lives and bring down family businesses for the sake of their careers? Again, you be the judge.

**NORA FITZGERALD MELDRUM, in-house litigation counsel at the time**

We were accused by the EEOC of violating the Age Discrimination in Employment Act (ADEA), which protects workers ages forty and older from workplace discrimination based on age. The EEOC said we rebuffed older workers for front-of-the-house positions, such as server, host, and bartender.

A typical employment discrimination case follows a formula: An individual has something bad happen to them (they don't get a job or they get a job and something goes wrong), then they go to a lawyer or the Equal Employment Opportunity Commission, claim that there's a link between whatever happened to them and their protected status such as age, gender, religion, race, etc., and they file a lawsuit (at the time the EEOC went after us, the agency had a backlog of seventy thousand real Americans with cases they had not addressed).

What happens next in a typical case is the sides try to negotiate an early resolution. Why? Because, even when you "win," you often lose anyway. Attorney costs are almost always in the millions of dollars, the cases create negative headlines that make a company look guilty even when they aren't, and it's typically much cheaper to settle and move forward.

The only ones who really benefit in these cases are the lawyers (pick up a Grisham novel and open to any page). Our law schools teach their students how to keep both sides angry at each other in legal cases, divorces, litigation, etc., so they can bill more hours. Speed and decisiveness give way to indecision, inaction, and long deliberation, i.e., higher fees. Many of these same attorneys, trained for inaction, eventually enter politics, creating laws to allow for more lawsuits, bleeding the economy, or figure out how to blame the "other side" for their inaction, leaving us, the taxpayers, to deal with inaction, discord, and general government, media, and social media negativity. I'm exhausted just writing about it.

If the two sides can't agree to an early resolution, they then dig in and fight it out. Many cases get dismissed on legal grounds at some point along the way, others get settled before trial, and only a very few go to a courtroom. In the overwhelming majority of cases (like, 99.99 percent), they get settled or kicked out before then. And, in every single case before *EEOC v. TXRH*, you had an actual person who believed they were wronged, separate from the lawyer or agency who is representing them.

So back to our case with the EEOC. It didn't follow the usual course. Nothing about the government's case against Texas Roadhouse was typical. First of all, there was no plaintiff. Not one person had complained about our hiring practices. No one had a beef with us. Instead, the EEOC decided to look into our hiring practices themselves instead of investigating these other seventy thousand claims that have been filed by actual American citizens.

**NORA FITZGERALD MELDRUM**
The process started with an innocent-looking letter from the Boston office of the EEOC, announcing that it would do an "audit" of our compliance with the ADEA, and asking for documents about the ages of support center employees as well as the ages of employees in a handful of restaurants. We didn't think much

about it and complied. The EEOC never, in the entire ten-year history of the lawsuit, told us why they picked our company for an audit. In fact, they fought off all attempts to answer this basic question. When the judge during one hearing said, "Why don't you just tell them [Texas Roadhouse] why you picked them?" Mark Penzel, the EEOC's lead attorney, responded, "Your Honor, we don't have to tell them, so we won't tell them." In other words, "It's our ball, and we don't have to share." They never did fess up.

Rumors emerged throughout the case about why they picked us. One was that an EEOC investigator had visited a Boston-area Texas Roadhouse and was rebuffed after hitting on the bartender. He then launched the investigation. Who knows. Another theory was that the Boston EEOC office was slated to be closed and this case helped it avoid that. Again, no idea if this was true. A third theory had something to do with a dart, a map, and a blindfold. The mystery as to *why us* remains.

The EEOC spent two years, and however much money that cost, "auditing" before they shared what they claimed we had done wrong. After looking at support center age data and store age data (including front- and back-of-house positions), they microscoped in on four positions: host, server, bartender, and busser. Based on data alone, they believed that Texas Roadhouse had a nationwide, top-down systemic plan to exclude people over the age of forty from being hired in those spots, and they sought more than $240 million in damages. Since they didn't have anyone who claimed that they'd been harmed, we had no idea who would get any money if they won.

Discovery proved difficult for the EEOC because they could find no smoking gun. There was, of course, no policy of hiring discrimination. It was ludicrous. We had no "plan." They looked for years. They pored over hundreds of thousands of e-mails, internal documents, and conducted thousands of hours of depositions of managing partners, market partners, people department staff members, and former employees. They tried to press in depositions—Perry Mason style—in order to get our people to "fess up" to age discrimination that none of them had ever even considered.

Several years into litigation, the EEOC found a few claimants. Every single person they brought forward had been first approached by the EEOC, who told them, essentially: "We think you have been discriminated against. Want to join our lawsuit?" Duh. Who wouldn't enter that lottery with the federal government? *Why don't you run some "class action" ads on late-night TV during reruns of* Golden Girls, *while you're at it?* This put us in a new position of trying to track down the specific reason why a particular person might not have been hired years earlier. It felt like an expensive game of Whac-A-Mole.

Throughout the case, we did what any responsible business would do: try to figure out if there was a path to settle and stop paying our small army of attorneys and experts, not to mention stop the untold number of hours our people were putting in providing discovery instead of doing their work. Because the EEOC did not have any real evidence, they took a scorched-earth approach—wanting depositions from all leaders, hundreds of thousands of e-mails and documents, even records of every time I had traveled. We made good-faith efforts to settle five times, and each time found ourselves trying to negotiate with the same group of attorneys—those who had come up with the idea of suing us in the first place. They had been crisscrossing the country trying to dig up dirt on us, and they had staked their professional reputations on this lawsuit. In their counters to our settlement offers, they insisted on us paying an astronomical amount of money.

In the fall of 2016, as our trial date was approaching, we made one last-ditch effort to negotiate a deal, and we flew to an EEOC office in Chicago. In eighteen hours of debate that stretched over two days, we offered a large cash settlement (that would go to *someone, somewhere*) and repeatedly offered up creative ideas to hire more older workers. The government rejected each one and stood firm with a demand for an outrageous amount of money. About midway through the second day, I shared what we thought was a generous proposal and said to our mediator, "They need to understand that this is it. If they come back to us still insisting on the other stuff they want, I'm leaving." About two hours later, the mediator came back and said, "They like your proposal and want all of that, and also all of the things they wanted from before." Again, there was no give or take.

Our lawyers immediately started thinking about a counterproposal, but I quietly folded up my papers and pushed away from the table. With no fanfare, no table pounding, I walked out. Members of our defense team—a roomful of highly paid lawyers—were talking all over each other, not paying attention, but I was already jabbing at the elevator button. It was all my folks could do to catch up and not be left behind in Illinois.

It was game on for trial.

Our day in court started in Boston in January 2017. The government had told us that it wanted six full weeks to try its case but was done in two. They didn't have that much: just statistics and a few negative Post-it Notes written by our managers who said things about an applicant like "not a good fit" or "no energy." They also had some circumstantial evidence: plaintiffs who became involved in the case after the EEOC called to kindly inform them that they must have been the victims of an alleged discriminatory scheme perpetrated by Texas Roadhouse.

Our attorneys had warned us that facing the government in court is always hard. Most jurors assume that you—a big company—would not be getting sued unless you had done something wrong. And by the time our case was on trial, the government had done all it could to bias any prospective jury pools. They featured the case prominently on their website and in press releases and did numerous media interviews. A *Boston Globe* reporter wrote a negative and factually incorrect article about the case without asking anyone at Texas Roadhouse for a comment, and the EEOC's head attorney tweeted it out. It cost our Boston-area stores business and affected a lot of our employees' tips and take-home pay—a hard time for those folks.

During the trial, my son, Max, was studying at the University of Colorado, and his roommate was taking a law class. One day, the roommate's class had a visit from an attorney at the EEOC. He turned on a recorder and caught what she was saying, knowing Max and his dad would be interested. It did fill in some gaps explaining why the EEOC was so eager to go to trial.

Here's a brief part of what the EEOC lawyer said to the class:

**EEOC:** There is this thing called settling, that is why this Texas Roadhouse case becomes so crucial, because if there is a complaining party, there is not much we can do about it. If we get the authority to sue without complaining parties, no one can settle, that's what makes this case so important. So if there's no charging party, there's no one to settle the case with us so we can keep going. Right now we are seeking plaintiffs, and those plaintiffs can't settle without our approval, so it changes the whole landscape.

**STUDENT:** So if you win the Texas Roadhouse case, you can sue companies without a private-party plaintiff.

**EEOC:** Yes, for everything. Once the barn door is open, the horse will run free.

**STUDENT:** And you won't have to settle.

**EEOC:** We can keep going. Yes, that's a big deal for us.

**STUDENT:** So you can make law.

**EEOC:** We love to make law; we live to make law. We got to court on our own, we went and found the plaintiffs, and we filed the lawsuit, that's why the Texas Roadhouse [case] is so significant.

The tape wasn't admissible, but it was finally clear *why* we were at trial (not why *us*, but why the trial). The EEOC attorneys didn't want to settle, they wanted to create law. If they had a precedent, they could sue anyone they wanted, without pesky plaintiffs who wanted to settle. The EEOC must have known the only way to get to trial was to go after a company that was operated by a founder, a person who would be willing to fight it all the way through to a jury decision because he felt he was in the right.

It was sobering. We had a sliver of hope that there were people behind them at the EEOC who were trying to do the right thing for American citizens. We had hoped the agency was truly mission driven at its core and had the right motives, even if their aim was off. The tape removed any last vestiges of that hope.

The trial wore on and I could see how hard it was on our people. The EEOC called numerous employees and grilled them on the stand. But it was also clear that they were trying to line me up as the bogeyman behind the case. It was clear I had to testify. There's nothing easier than pointing a finger at a rich defendant whom the jury hasn't met. He's an easy target.

The day before I was to take the stand, I was suffering from the flu and was sick as a dog, blowing my nose every five minutes and downing cold medicine by the glass. I was drained and weak and miserable. I woke up on the day I was scheduled to be in court and felt no better. I made it to the courthouse in Boston at nine a.m. and slumped into a waiting room chair. I wasn't sure if I would be able to do it. I half listened as my lawyers explained that they would ask me questions for about half an hour, and the EEOC would probably take one and a half to two hours. I'd be done in no time. I wasn't sure if I could get into the courtroom under my own steam, let alone survive two and a half hours of grilling. I felt like Jordan in that Finals game five, flu and all.

At about nine thirty a bailiff came out to let me know I had been called to the courtroom. I pushed myself to my feet, feeling as miserable as I ever had, and paused for just a moment on the threshold to the court-room, leaning against the doorjamb, and the strangest thing happened. My flu-riddled body became instantly energized. In about two seconds my sinuses drained, my aches disappeared. I was ready to roll.

I felt like I was back on the track at UNC, waiting for the gun to go off, and the world around me was calm. I was set.

All eyes were on me when I walked in—jurors, judge, our attorneys and theirs, the crowd, the press, a couple of our board members, and the EEOC big shots. Some probably expected me to look like a melodrama villain, wearing a black hat and a handlebar mustache, but I smiled and nodded at everyone. This was just another steeplechase race. It was gonna hurt, but it would be over before I knew it, and I'd be up in the stands sipping a cold one.

After a warm-up, forty-five-minute exchange with our lead attorney, the EEOC had their shot to try to piss me off. By then I was in my second lap and had hit my stride. They did all they could to make Texas Roadhouse—which does such cool things for its people and communities—sound like the most vile company on the planet. I kept my cool.

Their attorney must have been practicing for his chance at me for months, and he fed me a steady diet of lawyer sandwiches (nice part, bad part, nice part), trick questions, and a few queries that were repeated three or four times in slightly different ways. I noticed that if I did not answer the same way each time, he would do an "aha" kind of thing, accusing me of BS. *Nope, just trying to find a different way to say things so you'll stop asking the same question.*

Still. Cool.

Finally, three and a half hours later, their guy was done cross-examining me. He didn't get what the EEOC wanted, but I didn't really care by that point. All I wanted to do was haul ass to the bathroom. The water I'd been drinking to stay hydrated with the flu had to come out. When I finally leaned over the urinal in extreme relief, I jumped to find a reporter had moseyed up beside me with a tape recorder (at least it wasn't a tape measure). He asked for a comment. "You got to be kidding, right?" From then on, I had one of our attorneys accompany me into the restroom so I could pee in peace.

**NORA FITZGERALD MELDRUM**
We'd had a big debate about what Kent would wear to trial; should he wear jeans and a cowboy hat or a suit? We had a very traditional judge who ran a very

formal courtroom. Kent agreed that he would wear a suit as a sign of respect for her and for her courtroom. It was definitely the right call. But when Kent showed up to testify that morning he did not look well, at all. I was less concerned about what he was wearing and more concerned about this health. Kent sounded like death and was loudly blowing his nose every few minutes.

There was a special energy in the courtroom. After hearing from mind-numbingly boring statistics experts, the jury was excited to hear from "Mr. Taylor," the man that the EEOC kept suggesting was the mastermind of this alleged scheme. In walked Kent, smiling and ready to go. It was like his cold had instantly vanished. I've never seen anyone turn around so quickly. Kent did a great job answering our team's questions and held up well under the EEOC's cross-examination, at one point accusing the EEOC's lawyers of serving up a "lawyer sandwich" of words. The jury and some of the EEOC crew laughed, and sure enough, that comment landed in an online news article the next day.

After my testimony, we could tell the jury was growing bored, and we wrapped up our defense quickly—taking just a week in total. Dragging things out was not going to benefit us. In federal court, the verdict has to be unanimous, with all nine jurors agreeing (we were down to eight jurors by the end because one had to drop out a few days before the case was over). The jury received the case and started deliberations on a Monday morning. Around noon, we had a message from the clerk that they had asked for a calculator. My heart sank. They were probably calculating damages. At this point, we had spent so much money, had dragged our Roadies through a contentious war for a decade, had personally asked them to sacrifice so much time away from their families, only to lose within hours of closing arguments. It was demoralizing, to say the least.

But we found out the calculator wasn't for damages; the jury was trying to calculate its own statistics (and maybe figure out how much to tip the pizza kid). Monday stretched into Tuesday and Tuesday into

Wednesday. There was still no verdict. On Thursday, the jury returned. We held our breath, waiting, but they said they were deadlocked and couldn't agree. The judge sent them back. This happened twice more, which I worried might not lead to a fair verdict. I figured: *It's Boston, it's Super Bowl weekend, New England is playing, these folks might compromise and rule for the government just to get out of here*. But Friday came and the jury was still stuck. Our lawyers filed a motion for a mistrial, and it was granted by the judge. It was over.

Except it was not.

The cure for a mistrial, when you have unlimited resources like a federal government, is to ask for a new trial, with a new jury. We were about to go through the entire drill again, repeated from scratch, just a few months later. The judge did order a new trial date for May, but she quickly told us all to get together and work out a deal before then. And she put the case in the hands of a no-nonsense magistrate judge who would rule over us like a referee, calling shots, and forcing the contentious battle to end. The magistrate quickly saw that the government was rejecting all reasonable proposals and stalling. Their lawyers were so unhappy that they had been denied their trial verdict and had, in my opinion, long lost sight of their mission: to advance equal opportunity for all in the workplace. The mediator ordered that their boss, and their boss's boss, be present for negotiations. That got stuff done.

### NORA FITZGERALD MELDRUM

Our goal at this point was to stop fighting and move toward peace. And we achieved it. We knew the EEOC wasn't going away without saving some face. The Consent Decree we negotiated was (at $12 million) a fraction of any offer the EEOC had been willing to consent to pretrial. We did not admit any wrongdoing and did agree to all of the meaningful steps that we had previously offered (outreach, training, and so on). In our final round of negotiations, we flew back to Boston to meet face-to-face with our trial judge, who pulled Kent aside to talk directly about various terms. The EEOC failed to show her the same courtesy, sending the lawyers as their proxy with the bigwigs calling in by phone from their offices in DC and New York. We emerged with robust, EEO-compliant hiring practices, but we did so in a way that was authentic to Texas Roadhouse.

I look back on a few lessons. For instance, did we think that reaching out to politicians on both sides of the aisle would benefit us in our battle? Damn right. We believed someone in an elected office would be able to help. Do we believe that now? Not in the least. It was a complete waste of time since our case was already in the courts. We should have sought their help sooner.

What I took away from the ten-year battle was to let things go. I learned to decompress during this period by getting back to basics. So my suggestion: Go plant a garden, talk to your kids, read a book, play a board game, or go for a bike ride, pet a llama, run, or walk. You have the power to embrace a full and positive life, on your own terms. We are merely a speck in the universe and only alive for a limited time, so why not make each day your masterpiece?

Okay, enough of my BS.

Let's get back to the year 2017, which would see us hit our stride with Bubba's 33 being named one of the year's "Hot Concepts" by *Nation's Restaurant News*. Our award was handed out to us by Gene Simmons, of Kiss fame. He was quite an interesting cat and really wanted to learn about us. He apparently has an astute business mind.

I was also asked that year to throw out the first pitch at a Cincinnati Reds game. We sell our peanuts at the stadium, so I thought it would be a good chance to check out our sales efforts and what people thought of our product. And since the team was playing the Cubs—one of the Reds' rivals—I knew the stadium would be packed with prospective guests.

While it would have been a nice little honor to toss out the ball, I realized absolutely no one in the ballpark would care that some sixty-year-old guy with a fancy title was on the mound, so I came up with an idea that I thought would garner much better publicity for the stores.

I showed up thirty minutes before showtime and told the organizers I had a back injury (all's fair in love and baseball). I explained that there was no way I could throw six feet let alone sixty, and I suggested a replacement pitcher: our mascot, Andy the Armadillo. I could catch for him. The Reds' PR team freaked out. They didn't allow mascots to throw out pitches. Everyone knows they can't get their puffy little arms to toss a regulation baseball the required distance. One of the PR team took off to find the VP of sales, who returned wearing a stunned expression. It was as if I was suggesting we switch out the game ball with a pineapple.

Mascots can't throw, he reiterated. It was physically impossible.

I kept arguing for them to give it a go. The Reds' VP finally relented—a little—saying that Andy would have to prove that he could pitch the ball sixty feet. The guy was dead serious. Andy would have three tries to throw the ball, under the stadium, and if he miffed all of them, then the deal was off.

Deal.

A big problem, however, was that the young and spry intern who was supposed to play Andy had been a no-show. That just left either our VP of communications, Travis Doster, or me to pull on the suit. Travis drew the short straw (this was a PR event, after all). He wasn't exactly psyched to make a fool of himself in front of tens of thousands of fans, but I knew he'd played sports in high school, so I appealed to his ego: "Well, if you don't think you can throw it that far, I guess you don't have to." That's some fancy reverse psychology at work there, folks. Travis took the bait. He pulled on the suit and I stepped off sixty feet and squatted down to catch.

Despite the puffy padding and hands as big as Mickey Mouse, Andy the Armadillo proceeded to toss three balls in a perfect arc, all in the tunnel, and all connected with my catcher's mitt. I was as shocked as the Reds' VP of sales, but a deal's a deal, so the bigwig nodded and we headed out to the field. After the PA announcer informed the crowd that Texas Roadhouse's Andy the Armadillo mascot would be tossing out the opening pitch, people perked up and began to pay attention. The stands were indeed full, and this was definitely something the crowd had never seen before.

I went behind the plate and started heckling Andy. For his part, Travis got into character. He theatrically shook off a few fake signs, did an elaborate windup, then tossed the ball as hard as he could.

We both watched as it sailed about eight feet over my head!

I think everyone in the ballpark got a kick out of the moment, but no one more than the three Reds mascots—who must have felt liberated now that the ban on mascots pitching was over—and they rushed the mound and celebrated with Andy as if they'd just won the World Series.

The crowd cheered, the players came out of the dugout to watch. It was a great moment.

Using Andy to toss out the pitch, I believe, was an example of our kind of marketing. First, you don't take yourself too seriously, and second, you put brand over individual. Who would the crowd—especially the kids—rather see: some random business guy or a seven-foot-tall armadillo wearing a huge cowboy hat who could very likely fall off the mound and make a fool of himself?

Amazingly, by the way, the minute Andy threw that ball my back felt much better.

Our conference that year featured another astute guy, Jim Koch, founder of Boston Beer Company, which makes Sam Adams and Angry Orchard. He was a colorful speaker, really adapting to our mostly crazy, relaxed vibe. After his speech, as we walked off the stage together, we

started joking about who used more colorful words in his talk—him or me—not realizing Jim's microphone was still live. Our folks found the discussion most amusing.

John Calipari, legendary UK basketball coach, was our other color-ful speaker, and was introduced by my dad, a Wildcat fan for more than eighty years, who ribbed John about one NCAA game that had gotten away from him. I had to quickly grab the mic before Dad said whatever was coming next. My dad is a huge fan of John's, and I was not sure our crowd wanted to hear their usual, fun back-and-forth bantering.

I've watched a few of Calipari's practices over the years, and he not only coaches his players on how to play the game at a high level, but he also teaches them how to be a positive influence in life in general, which I've always admired.

Our entertainment was super cool with Jason Derulo and the band Train performing. We try to keep our conference entertainment secret until they step onstage, though that's not always possible. For instance, that year we had forged a partnership with Kenny Chesney to sell his Blue Chair Bay Rum and we'd been making a big deal out of it. When I walked out onstage with Kenny, absolutely no one was surprised, though everyone did welcome him with typical Roadhouse wildness. I challenged Kenny to return and play for free if we sold over a million Kenny's Cool-ers over that year. He looked over his guys, who signaled "no way pos-sible," and he said, "Okay." Sure enough, we did sell over a million, and Kenny—a man of his word—played for us the following year, too.

At that conference, I decided to take up golf for the first time. I'd always enjoyed grabbing a golf cart and some adult beverages during the conference golf tournament and riding around the course distracting those who were taking the game a little too seriously. I'd crank up the music, grab my megaphone, and make wisecracks. Mark Twain once said that a game of golf was a good walk spoiled. For a former competitive runner and now avid skier and cyclist like me, golf seems a bit slow. But my attitude changed that year. My primary goal was to spend more time with my dad, who loves the game. I am so proud that at age eighty-nine he has shot less than his age more than 130 times, and he has the score-cards to prove it. I think playing golf has kept him young and connected to his friends. As for me, the sport is still frustrating, but the opportuni-ties to be with my dad are well worth a spoiled walk, especially since my golf bag may or may not have a built-in cooler. Bet you didn't see that coming.

The year 2018 would see us rock in many ways. We expanded our re-gional team, adding Steve Melillo, Bobby Wiejaczka, and one of my big-gest crazies, Neal Niklaus, who started running one store back in 1995. Gina Tobin, who ran our first prototype store back in 1996, assumed the role of VP of training, and one of our early staff accountants was named CFO. That's Tonya Robinson, a twenty-year Roadie. We expanded our board, adding Curtis Warfield and our Legends award winners included Chris Jacobsen (Chief Marketing Officer) and longtime Roadie fave Rosie Drury.

Unlike other companies that have a revolving door of top executives with MBAs and impressive résumés, we tend to favor long-term folks who have earned their role and title and totally understand and contrib-ute to our culture. And speaking of culture, Dave Eubanks of Mesquite, Nevada, won our Managing Partner of the Year award and, if we had an award called Party Animal, he would definitely have been in the running for that as well.

Since it was our twenty-fifth anniversary, we went big with our speaker and entertainment. I know you have to be wondering what big looks like to us. Well, it means famous and tall. Our speaker was Bill Walton, of UCLA and Boston Celtics fame; our entertainers were tall guys Florida Georgia Line and a surprisingly tall Snoop Dogg. And for you folks that like cats not so tall, we also had Bob Weir (of the Grateful Dead), Nile Rodgers (disco-era legend), and one of my favorites, Steven Tyler of Aerosmith, who told us his first job was as a pot scrubber—as he called it. That was quite fitting, as we had brought three of our original employees to the conference who still worked at our Clarksville, Indiana, store number one: Dish Daddy Robert Mattingly, Prep Guru Dan Cannon, and Broil Stud Mike Richardson, and Steven Tyler gave them a big shout-out. *Yee-haw!*

If you haven't read Bill Walton's book *Back from the Dead*, you need to check it out. An amazing story. And Bill's wife, Lori, is an equally amazing person with a huge heart. She and Bill give so much back to their community of San Diego.

I say that jet planes don't have rearview mirrors for a reason. There's no need: They only go forward, and they do it fast. Just like entrepreneurs. But sometimes life makes us stop and look back. The passing of one of our board members, Jim Parker, in 2019 was one of those events. Jim was a kindred spirit for me in many ways. First, he was a former CEO

of Southwest Airlines, a company that we admire and modeled much of our culture on. Secondly, he had worked with a crazy, outside-the-box CEO (Herb Kelleher), so I always felt like he understood my thinking and did not get caught up in BS. Third, he was a lawyer, so he was able to provide guidance and reassurance, especially during the EEOC trial and my deposition preparation. With his calmness and vast business knowledge, he was a valued member of our board. I could go into a meeting venting about this or that, and he would calmly say in his Texas twang, "Well, Kent, let's talk about that for a second," which immediately defused the tension. He would garner all the facts, push me if I didn't know them all, then would provide seasoned advice. All leaders should have a counselor with whom they can blow off some steam. The key is to find someone who is quick to listen and then offers sound advice. We all need a sounding board, not an echo chamber; someone who will let you rant but then put the issue in a proper context and not overreact.

The year 2019 rolled on and would see us attain the goal of six hundred restaurants between Texas Roadhouse, Bubba's 33, and Jaggers, and set us on a path to do amazing things in the next decade. Heck, I even skydived at age sixty-three into our conference that year before my speech, and then we heard some cool tunes from a reunited Hootie & the Blowfish and Toby Keith (who may have remembered an episode on Willie's bus with yours truly, but maybe we can't remember).

We were ready for 2020. What could go wrong?

As we all know, crap was about to hit the fan.

## CHAPTER 19

# SERVICE WITH HEART, SIX FEET APART

Throughout the spring of 2020 I would have flashbacks to the early days of Texas Roadhouse and the persistent panic that prevailed: that holy-crap, waking-at-three-a.m.-in-a-cold-sweat, not-sure-how-I'll-pay-my-employees-or-suppliers kind of terror. It was back, all right, with a vengeance.

As the coronavirus pandemic had been spreading, I had been out of the loop on an annual two-week vacation with a group of friends, which stretched through the last week of February and the first week of March. We were skiing in Austria and had little idea what was going on. The local television channels were all in German. I spent my time reading an interesting book cover to cover: *American Icon*, by Bryce Hoffman, about Alan Mulally and his fight to save the Ford Motor Company through the financial crisis of 2008–09. I had met Alan at a gathering of the Marshall Goldsmith 100 in January that I'd been invited to by two authors—Adrian Gostick and Chester Elton—who have helped me edit this book. Alan spoke for a few hours and was an interesting cat, and the book chronicled his nine years at the helm of Ford and was all about crisis management, the very thing I was about to be thrust into.

On Monday, March 9, I arrived at my office rested and still pretty much in the dark. As the situation was explained to me, I knew on the food side we were in pretty good shape. Our managers have always followed strict standards and guidelines on food prep, sanitation, and steps of service—so I knew we could operate in whatever climate of safety the new world was about to demand. I'd always encouraged our folks to keep an entrepreneurial spirit alive in their stores—where it was okay to try new things, spend money on fun, and engage in their communities in their own unique ways. I often call the most creative, if not roguish, of our store managers and ask their opinions on new and innovative ways to operate our restaurants. I call this group my crazies. I had little idea then how many completely mad, certifiable, batshit wacky ideas we were going to need to survive what was to come.

## WEEK 1: SHOCK AND AWE

That Monday, March 9, 2020, I found our crisis people in action. They were watching events state by state and brainstorming next steps. They told me our restaurants in the Northeast were going to be forced to close their dining rooms before too long—moving from sit-down sales to one hundred percent to-go.

Before this, we'd been having a record year. Throughout our system, stores had been averaging more than $105,000 per week in sales—with most doing dinner-only service Monday through Friday and adding lunch on the weekends. Overall, we'd been up 4.5 percent over the previous year. As for to-go orders, they averaged just $7,000 to $8,000 a store. Curbside had never been a large part of our business, and we hadn't really tried to push it. We were built to have a party every night in our dining rooms—providing what we hoped would be Legendary Food, Legendary Service. But from what was happening in the Northeast, it seemed that this could change throughout our system.

By Thursday, our sales were down 9 percent compared to the prior year; by Friday, we were down 15 percent; Saturday by 20 percent. Our stores in New York State alone had lost 43 percent of their revenue.

Like most of America, on Thursday I went to the grocery store and stocked up on two weeks' worth of food. Then I texted my grown kids to do the same. By Friday, shelves were pretty much empty, and an inexplicable global hoarding of toilet paper and pet food sent our collective IQ to a pre-caveman low.

With the expectation that the pandemic was going to hit the economy and our company hard, we debated as a management team if we should draw down on $200 million of our existing line of credit with JPMorgan. We had kept a line open in case we ever made an acquisition. We were otherwise debt-free, and I liked it that way. I still remembered owing money to a lot of people in the early days, and never wanted to be back in that situation.

We discussed things as a group, and the consensus was to keep mulling the question over. If we took the loan, we would have to report it to the Street, and some worried how that would be perceived. Would we look like we were on the brink of disaster? We decided to chill for the weekend and reassess. I headed home but hardly slept that night. It was Friday the thirteenth, after all. Worst-case scenarios kept playing out in my mind—all of our restaurants closed, all our people out of work, the potential burn rate as we lost our cash reserves hand over fist. We needed that loan to survive. If our sales dried up, the money could keep us limping along for eight or nine months, enable us to provide some relief to our frontline people, and keep our managers and support center folks employed. If our upper management was willing to take a pay cut—and I was willing to forgo my salary—we could make it through.

When I woke up Saturday morning, I went for a bike ride to clear my mind. When I returned, I left a message on the cell phone of Paul Costel, president of the JPMorgan Kentucky market, that we needed to talk. I was pissed off with myself that I hadn't pulled the trigger on the loan on Friday. Twenty minutes later, I called Paul at his house. Then I texted him. Then I called his home again another twenty minutes later. *Stalk much, Kent?* Paul finally called back. "We're pulling down on our line. Can you please call your guys on their cell phones and start the paperwork so we can hit the ground running Monday?"

He agreed.

I called our CFO and VP of legal and said, "It's time, game on. Action rules, and action needs to be quick."

In retrospect, getting everyone involved in a discussion the day before had been the right thing to do, but putting the decision on hold was not an option for me. From that day forward, I committed myself to the view that all issues would be raised with the group, discussed and debated, and then acted upon—generally within twenty-four hours or less.

After a sobering weekend, we would come back Monday to find a lot of our restaurants in the Northeast had indeed been forced to shutter their dining rooms. Within about a week, the rest of the country would follow suit.

**WEEK 1 RESULTS:**

| | |
|---|---|
| TXRH Sales Week: | $44.7 million (down $16.7 million from prior week) |
| Store Average: | $86,000 (down $32,000 from prior week) |
| Inside Sales: | 80% |
| To-go Sales: | 20% |

## WEEK 2: LEARNING TO PIVOT

Since we had stores in Taiwan, the Philippines, and Korea that had already been affected, I reached out to Hugh Carroll, our head of international, to learn how the coronavirus had been pretty well contained in those countries. Taiwan, for instance, is just 110 miles from the Chinese mainland. They have twenty-four million people (more than the entire New York City metropolitan area) crammed into an island barely larger than an IKEA store, yet they had just five hundred Covid-19 cases and only seven deaths during the spring of 2020. Amazing.

Having learned lessons from the SARS outbreak of 2003, Taiwan had responded quickly to minimize cases, something quite different from what was happening at the time in China and Italy. Early on, Taiwan put in place travel restrictions, did aggressive testing and screening, quarantined the affected, and demanded strict social distancing and personal protective equipment from citizens. The question was, what could we learn from their example in our restaurants?

We decided to order massive amounts of gloves, masks, and temperature monitors for our people. That would not be a popular decision. "You'll freak out our guests if we wear gloves and masks," was a frequent pushback. I didn't mind swimming upstream and was prepared to require our people to wear the stuff, as I believed that soon we'd be freaking out many of our guests if we weren't wearing safety gear.

**HUGH CARROLL, president of Texas Roadhouse international**
The second week of March I was asked to discuss Taiwan's and South Korea's response to the pandemic with our Roadhouse leaders. We addressed masks, gloves, safety glasses, thermometers, temperature logs, and so on. Not all of the voices in the room were completely accepting of those ideas.

Kent listened to everyone debate, made up his mind, wasn't afraid to go against others' wishes, trusted his gut, and got us set up with PPE and thermometers as quick as possible.

Equally pressing to the care of our Roadies and guests was figuring out how to move our operations from inside dining to to-go. How could we move the party to our parking lots? Doubling or even tripling our curbside business to about $20,000 a week per store would be a monumental task, and I didn't have the answers. I made a note to call more of my crazies that evening, as I knew many would be figuring things out and we needed to learn from them.

The early years of Texas Roadhouse had been mostly about survival. Back then, I was stressed out and a total mess most days, as we barely covered payroll—with me accumulating my paychecks in a drawer since there wasn't enough money in our account to cover them. With this crisis I was stressed, yes, but I'd been through so much that I was now firm with my hunches. I needed to be quick and decisive about charging forward.

We had always said we were a "people company that just happened to sell steaks." Well, I was going to live that maxim now. Priority one was going to be figuring out a way to pay our people and keep them working (selling steaks). Then, with so little food left in grocery stores, priority two was going to be feeding America (steaks). We'd also throw in some salads, potatoes, and a side of love.

That Saturday, our leadership team held the first of many weekend crisis conference calls. Knowing that you-know-what was about to hit the fan, I sent out a note that all stores should send people out that very Saturday afternoon to their local restaurant supply store and buy up all the to-go supplies they could get their hands on. Everything they had. I'd have been okay if they hit up back-alley, black-market Styrofoam peddlers if it came to it (joke, people; chill). By Monday all the to-go supplies would be gone. I was guessing that by the following weekend inside dining would not exist in the United States.

It was obvious that some thought the boss was overreacting. Most of our stores were still open, after all. But that wouldn't last. Within seven days, all but a handful of our restaurants were closed to inside sales, and after another week we were one hundred percent curbside. When that happened, *Nation's Restaurant News* predicted that dining rooms were going to be shut down for two weeks. *Yeah, right.*

That evening I cruised around Louisville, visited a few grocery stores, and saw what was happening to America. It was nuts. There were absolutely no paper products. There was no pet food, no meat. Forget about hand sanitizer or Clorox wipes.

Another idea began to brew, but I let it percolate as it seemed too crazy, even for the crazies.

Based on what had already gone down in Asia and Europe, I felt two weeks of citizen lockdown was not going to cut it. We'd be looking at a minimum of six. And, frankly, since most of us Americans get freaked out about wearing gloves, masks, and safety glasses in public—and no one in government would try that hard to enforce the new rules—I figured it would be closer to two to three months before we got through this. Why politicians from either party can't learn from other countries' successes and failures is beyond me; I've spent my whole career learning from others' successes and mistakes.

Monday, March 16, we set up in a larger control room for social distancing—at least six feet apart—with about twelve of us coordinating efforts. Using bullhorns and signal flags to communicate with each other (it felt like), we set about the monumental task of moving from 93 percent inside dining to nothing but curbside. And yet, to complicate matters, a few states had a transition period where we could do 50 percent inside occupancy for a while. In those stores, we were trying to ramp up curbside sales, but had nowhere to locate the expanded to-go operations inside the restaurant.

In the control room, the various cable news channels blared the latest updates while we created to-go iPads for outside orders, designed to-go banners and flyers, found more to-go supplies and gloves. We then calculated how to sell dispensed iced tea and brainstormed how to get the word out via social media about our various new promotions (as you may recall, we don't do major media advertising). A debate raged for some time on whether to ditch our famous peanuts or put them in a bag (the bag won).

I drew up a diagram for a double drive-through, which worked for a few days as volume spiked. Eventually most of our stores ran with a curbside to-go model.

After a few calls with market partners, it was clear that our to-go sales were being hampered by kitchen constraints and other logistics issues. Our stores just weren't designed to cook, package, and sell to people driving up in their cars. I removed myself from our control room and its many distractions—especially the constant media barrage, hysteria, and drone of talking heads—and locked myself in my office to dial up my crazies.

One of my favorite crazies is Greg Beckel, our market partner in North Carolina. His market partners had been selling Family Packs for some time—a collection of four steaks/chicken/ribs, two sides, and rolls for a kick-ass price. I called Greg, listened, and asked him to flip his fifteen-store market right away to to-go and family packs and then be prepared to show the rest of us how it should be done. He was all in.

### GREG BECKEL, market partner

I had worked for Bennigan's for seven years prior to Texas Roadhouse and it was miserable going to work every day. Whenever you asked for anything, the answer was always, "It's not in our budget." With Roadhouse, the answer is, "Yes. What's the question?"

When the virus started, it was the most depressing thing I've been through. I literally had a store do $18,000 that first week, 80 percent negative sales. Kent called and we talked about how we could adapt. He asked, "What do you think about this or that?" He wants to learn but he also wants to influence.

We'd had success with Family Packs in the past, so we created six of them starting at $19.99 to feed a family of four. Kent always wants to provide this incredible meal that you take home because there's a crazy amount of food. The next big deal he wanted me to try was this ready-to-grill thing. He says, "Let's sell raw steaks." We argued about price; it was lower than I wanted to charge, and we agreed somewhere in the middle. He wanted me to call two of my crazies and give it a shot that weekend. We marketed it just with social media, and hell if those two stores didn't make more selling refrigerated raw steaks in one day than my other stores did all week. The next thing you know, my whole market was doing ready-to-grill. Those are the kinds of things he encourages, outside-the-box thinking in the most difficult times. And the crazier the idea, the more excited he gets.

Next I called Steve Miller, a market partner in Denver, because I knew he'd be "flying like an eagle." He was selling drive-up five-dollar sliders in an adjacent parking lot. Steve was doing decent sales. "Amen, brother," I said. I filled him in on Greg's Family Pack idea and asked him to give that a shot, too.

Next up was Neal Niklaus, one of our five regional market partners, who oversees more than 125 restaurants. I said, "What's up? What kinda crazy shit are your folks up to?" Don't let the formal, professional tone throw you, I'm typically much more casual than that. Neal told me the out-there stuff his folks were doing, and I told him about the things I'd been hearing from the other crazies. He agreed to incorporate them. "We're on it," he said.

**NEAL NIKLAUS, regional market partner**

I had a couple of stores start selling ready-to-grill steaks out the door. I put a halt to it and came back to Kent and told him we'd made a mistake. He said, "Who says we can't?" He saw that grocery stores were going to get empty and we could be like a grocery store to America. We then had a couple of stores doing a whole farmers market outside–selling groceries along with our food–and it changed the whole way we did things.

Every morning I was communicating on a briefing call with my stores. We'd all give our best practices. If one store was trying a party-pack with this item and that, and they were having success, we shared those things. One store was able to get with Meals on Wheels. Now we are trying to do that nationally. Everyone learns and everyone benefits.

From the time I was a rogue managing partner running one restaurant in Ashland, Kentucky, Kent has constantly been wanting me to try new, often crazy ideas. And he has always kept me protected from those not comfortable with my aggressive, out-of-the-box ideas.

With our management team focused on bank financing, messaging, procuring to-go supplies, developing capacity plans, sanitizing stores, and worrying about how to equitably reduce hours for our workforce, I felt it was important for me to communicate my thoughts at the moment to our Roadies. The world was changing fast and what I said one week might be obsolete the next, but they still needed to hear regular messages of hope.

On Wednesday, Travis Doster, our VP of communications, started working the politicians. He sent out pictures I'd taken of empty grocery shelves to every local official, state officials, and a few senators and congressmen we knew to let them know that we were here, staffed up, stocked up with supplies, and ready to feed America safely. We wanted them to give us a chance to help, and not shut down our to-go, curbside business.

That day I also sent a plane we rented to North Carolina to fetch home a group of our Bubba's 33 trainers who had been stranded in

Gastonia, North Carolina, training staff at a new location. Flying commercial was beginning to freak people out, and our trainers, their parents, and our headquarters staff had been trying to figure out how to get them safely back to their homes in Texas and Colorado. The picture of relief they sent me when they landed was worth a thousand words.

What normally would have been a three-month to six-month test for a new store became a three-day cram session, but hey: Crisis times call for crisis training.

The weekend coming would be a full-on push to let family meals fly.

Late on the night of Thursday, March 19, I sent out a motivational video to all our folks and included the song "America" by Lee Greenwood. My group of secret rule breakers got a message with Prince's "Let's Go Crazy."

By the weekend, new crazies were signing up. As Neal mentioned, a farmers market that sprang up in the parking lot at one of our stores crushed it. The fresh meat ready-to-grill idea for his area had come from Hilliard, Ohio, thanks to new crazy rising star, managing partner Tonya Bosher.

**TONYA BOSHER, managing partner, Hilliard, Ohio**

One of the things that makes Roadhouse so amazing is that you're encouraged to do what is best for your local community. I did a farmers market on a Saturday and Sunday and had a ton of support from the company. My market leader was there as well as my regional partner, Neal Niklaus. I had meat cutters from multiple stores cutting ready-to-grill steaks. It was a huge team event and hands down the most successful day in my career as a restaurant manager. Sunday morning, I got a phone call as I'm standing out in the parking lot giving an alley rally, the preshift meeting, with about thirty people standing in a circle all appropriately socially distanced. I'm hollering and trying to get everybody fired up and my assistant manager whispers, "Kent Taylor's on the phone." And I was like, "Shut up. That's not funny." She said, no, for real, you're going to want to take this. He was calling to say he was proud of me. He gave me his cell-phone number and asked if he could call later because he wanted to learn from me. I was floored.

When I called back, I learned some of the other innovative ideas Tonya had implemented in her store—from Taco Saturdays to the Golden Roadie awards—which were, I quickly realized, reasons her people stepped up for her in such a big way during the pandemic.

Other crazies joining the group included Randy Boss (market partner in West Virginia) and Jeff Augustus (market partner in Pennsylvania). Phillip Dunn from Bubba's 33 in Waco, Texas, played drive-in movies on the side of his building with his carhops serving food, with vehicles spaced ten feet apart for social distancing. Our folks were taking free food to hospitals, first responders, and even the mayor of Louisville's crisis team.

That week I sat in on a call with many of the major restaurant chains' CEOs. The bulk of the discussion was about putting together a request for the federal government to set aside a portion of the upcoming business-loan package to assist chain restaurants in staying afloat during the crisis and provide assistance to employees. When they asked, I told them how many employees we had, but that I wasn't interested in taking taxpayer money. We were already working on our own employee stimulus package that would roll out the following week for our hourly folks—many of whom weren't working as many hours as they had before the pandemic. That slowdown in hours wouldn't last too long, but it was affecting them in the pocketbook right now and we needed to help our own.

By March 22, we locked down our financing from JPMorgan and prepared to roll out millions in extra bonus money to our frontline employees.

We were two weeks into the crisis, and there were glimmers of good news: Our people were going to get some more money in the bank, we were geared up to sell to-go and Family Packs, and crazies all around the system were trying anything and everything to find a way to save this company they loved.

**TONYA ROBINSON, chief financial officer**
I started out at Roadhouse as a store staff accountant and here I am, twenty-two years later, as CFO. What a great ride.

During the first couple of weeks of the crisis, Kent, as usual, was a collector of ideas. He keeps a finger in everything, so he quickly got up to speed, kept everyone thinking, and was open to all ideas. However, once he made his decision, everyone stepped up and worked together, and everyone was empowered to act. He kept us focused, kept it light, and everyone was engaged, energetic, and the pace was fast. Financial security, caring for our people (with [physical] safety and in financial terms), along with feeding America, became our mantras early on.

**WEEK 2 RESULTS:**

| | |
|---|---|
| TXRH Sales Week: | $15.3 million |
| Store Average: | $29,800 |
| Inside Sales: | 0% |

# WEEK 3: LET'S GO CRAZY

My crazies were reporting early success selling ready-to-grill steaks (think uncooked, chilled, beautiful USDA choice cuts—kinda makes you wanna fire up the Weber, doesn't it?). Speed was critical in taking this across the system. Still, as the new world of curbside service ramped up, we were facing the challenge of getting people to come in to work. Some employees had locked themselves up at home out of fear of the virus; others had taken unemployment compensation as the number of hours we'd offered the first two weeks of the crisis were down an average of 60 percent. Still others had decided to cut back their hours since they had other jobs, had family members at high risk and wanted to quarantine with them, or didn't need the money as much and wanted to give shifts to those who needed them (bless their hearts).

We put the finishing touches on our own stimulus package for workers, which was set to be about $9 million and was designed to benefit those in hourly roles who were still working. I would donate my pay for the rest of the year and threw another $5 million of my savings into our Andy's Outreach Fund, which, you may recall, was designed to help Roadies in need.

We needed to conserve every dollar we had if we were going to make it over the long haul, so we had decided to pay only those employees who were working shifts and not those who had taken themselves out of the schedule voluntarily. And yet, knowing that most of our Roadies would have worked if they could—and that Covid-19 had been thrust upon them and the world by an uncaring Chinese government—how could we not include everyone? The decision became clear. We would spend an extra $2 million and base the bonus on hours worked previously. If anyone disagreed, they could kiss *my* stimulus package, if you catch my drift.

Next, our entire leadership team and board took pay cuts, with Doug Thompson, our COO, following my lead and dropping his salary and bonus. So, with those savings, we also decided to allow employees who were still working to take a week of paid vacation that they had not yet earned to help them out financially. Doug also did an amazing job communicating with our stores with a daily video message.

Next, with lessons from the crazies, we reselected our options for the family packs and debated their pricing. My crazies had already tested which performed better—cheaper or more expensive—and no shock to anyone, the cheaper prices were winning. Not only did we move more product, but people told their friends and neighbors about the great deals. Many of our typical customers were hurting and needed a break.

As a company, we are used to our cost of food equaling about 30 percent of our retail price. I argued that 40 or even 50 percent was fine given the circumstances (many grocery shelves were bare). If we could break even when adding up our food costs, labor, rent, and other expenses, then who cared if we didn't make a profit for a while. If we could provide a service to people in need, keep more Roadies employed, and Feed America, then we were staying true to our values. Not only that, but it would make my momma proud. #feedamericastaytruetovaluesandmakemommaweepwithpride.

After we figured out pricing, we rolled the idea of Family Packs to the entire country in just three days. We then began tinkering with butcher shops in the parking lot. With the knowledge we'd gained from our Taiwan and South Korea franchises, our focus continued to be getting everything we needed to make our people as safe as possible and begin to change our habits. My idea about the thermometers and masks was still not being gleefully received. Did it bother me? Hell no. Sometimes you fly in the face of the wind and wait for the pack to figure stuff out. But as my favorite band, the Rolling Stones, sang, "Time waits for no one." And besides, I'm generally not that patient.

### CHRIS COLSON, General Counsel and Corporate Secretary

There's a pattern to how Kent operates. Whether [it's] supplies, inventory, or whatever, he wants debate. With Family Packs, he said early that people's paychecks were going to get smaller as their hours got cut. He said we needed to come up with a value pack. Kent shares his vision, then he creates a feedback loop where he starts listening and takes learning from the field and recycles and shares best practices.

One thing about Kent, he's good at bringing together teams with diverse views and personalities and complementary skills. You end up with a healthy dynamic tension. You have people with very creative ideas, and some who are more letter-of-the-law. We may debate things, but at the end of the day we commit and move forward. That's why we are able to move so fast.

With the previous week of average sales as low as I could remember at just over $29,000 per store, we needed something big to change the vibe of our company and, hopefully, move things in a positive direction. Financial love had gone out to our employees, our Andy's Outreach Fund now had enough money to help those Roadies who needed an extra boost, my crazies were still brainstorming creative ways to make sales in the parking lot, and we were getting some positive social media attention as employees were chatting online about what we were doing.

We were building up an inventory of aged steaks, however, and within four to six weeks we would have an issue. As one of my heroes, Herb Kelleher, Southwest Airlines founder, would have probably done, I pulled a little corporate deception. I told our folks in the field that our meat was going to go bad in two weeks (as opposed to the four to six it really had) and we auto-shipped large boxes of steaks and ribs to the restaurants. I figured that if meat was stacked floor to ceiling in our coolers and our people knew the clock was ticking, they would get creative. They did.

On Wednesday, March 25, our legal and finance people had to file a release about our borrowing the $200 million. They were also required to disclose any changes to my compensation. I would rather have said nothing, and I expected a yawn from the public on both counts, but was surprised when my pay deal generated a ton of positive social media comments. Lots and lots of free press, likes, smiley faces, hearts, and thumbs-up.

Then, when our people got their Texas Roadhouse stimulus checks the next day and posted their thanks, stuff got crazy. We ended the day as one of the most talked-about stories on social media, and we got *really* busy. That night a Roadie from St. Louis sent me a picture from his restaurant that showed vehicles lined up for half a mile, with many of the guests telling him they heard the CEO was doing the right thing and they wanted to support us. More likely, the reason we were so busy was that grocery-store shelves were bare, and people had had enough of Chef Boyardee.

Store sales spiked 45 percent in one week. Yee-effing-haw.

Not only did we sell almost all of the meat we'd shipped to the stores by end-of-day Friday, we had to call Greg Keller and Mike Green, presidents of sister companies SYGMA and Sysco, who agreed to open their warehouses for four hours that Saturday, something hardly ever done. Thanks to our suppliers' responsiveness, were able to resupply. Otherwise most stores would have had to close by Sunday since we would have run out of food.

We try to be fair with our suppliers about price, payment terms, and the way we've treated them—we even invite our suppliers to our annual MP conferences to learn a lot with us and party a little, too! Too many companies of our size act like jerks and make unfair demands of their suppliers. A solid relationship makes for good endings to stories that might not have concluded so well. Debbie Hayden, Jordan Trout, and Peter Rosenberg, our supply chain superheroes, had built such positive relationships with our suppliers that it showed, once again, that Love Rules.

**GREG KELLER, senior vice-president of sales and chief customer officer, Sysco**
The Sysco and Texas Roadhouse partnership extends more than twenty-five years. Via Sysco and SYGMA, we have worked together to enable Texas Roadhouse's prolific growth and incredible success. Calendar year 2020 certainly presented some unforeseen and unprecedented headwinds in our country, our communities, and in our partnership. In typical fashion, Texas Roadhouse swiftly and decisively responded to the operating environment with a focus on their associates, their guests, and their suppliers. Texas Roadhouse had to pivot their traditional model and challenged us to pivot along with them. Congratulations to the entire Texas Roadhouse team for the incredible results. Your performance is a testament to the amazing culture that you continue to foster and the Legendary Food and service that you provide to your guests. As your business partner, we continue to be inspired and motivated to enable your mission. The motivation stems from our shared passion for success, but more importantly, we are motivated because of how much you value our role as your business partner. Your willingness and focus on taking care of our drivers and associates and recognition for the role that they play is unprecedented and so appreciated. With everything going on, I received a handwritten, personal thank-you note from Kent for SYGMA and Sysco's support. We continue to be motivated and inspired to be a part of the Texas Roadhouse family—thank you for the opportunity!

## DEBBIE HAYDEN

One of our big suppliers of beef and pork told me of the nasty calls he was getting from some of their customers. He was like, "They are acting like we caused this pandemic." He told me how refreshing it was to work with us. Our vendors aren't just our suppliers, they're part of our culture, they are friends. I know the names of their children, their spouses, their parents. And friends don't let other friends down.

Very early on, Kent asked if it was okay if he sent a letter to our vendor partners to let them know how much we appreciate what they've done and what they're going to be doing for us. I gave him addresses [of] various people high up on our distribution side. He did it that day, wrote them personal notes. Then he said, "Are you okay with doing something for our SYGMA drivers who are delivering to our stores every day?" And I was like, "Kent, I love you."

Trust me, Debbie doesn't love me every day. There are times when she admits she's ready to throttle me, but we support each other and her team does exceptional work—something that was never more evident than during the crisis. So, during a week when our competitors were closing stores, making massive layoffs, and some were anticipating bankruptcy, we were taking care of our people, Feeding America, and benefiting from beautiful partnerships with our vendors (and making Momma proud).

What was to come the following week?

How about a music video shout-out from American legend Willie Nelson to tie in with a great video shout-out from our buddy Toby Keith (another great American). We were also about to roll out a Pandora Texas Roadhouse channel called Jukebox Jams. Travis Doster's team worked a miracle on that one—getting it up and running within a month—after I had the idea one night for a country music video jukebox channel. Another after-midnight idea; go figure.

**WEEK 3 RESULTS:**
TXRH Sales Week:  $21.4 million
Store Average:        $42,000

# WEEK 4: SAFETY RULES

On Tuesday of week four we had another nice bump in sales with the nationwide "Great American Takeout Tuesday," where everyone in the country was encouraged to support restaurants by eating at least one delivery or pickup meal. Fantastic idea if you ask me. That week we were also finally able to secure enough safety equipment for all our Roadies to be geared up properly. We had masks and protective eyewear for most, even though in the parking lots many Roadies had to wear their shades until we had more eyewear. We were paying anywhere from 45 cents to a dollar a mask, so price gouging was real (we now pay about 7.5 cents per mask).

As to-go containers and safety gear were getting harder to locate, we recruited additional folks in the support center to help. It pretty much looked like the string of texts printed below, in which I informed Peter Rosenberg, director of operations support, that he had a new team member, and then told Jenn Taylor (no relation) that she had a new assignment.

**ME (TO PETER):**
JENN TAYLOR NOW PART OF UR TEAM. SHE WILL BE IN CHARGE OF HOW TO GET PPE SUPPLIES TO STORES IN 1 VS 5 DAYS. SPEED RULES.

**PETER:**
AWESOME!

**ME (TO PETER):**
THANKS FOR ALL YOU'RE DOING. YOUR TEAM = KICKING ASS.

**ME (TO JENN):**
CONGRATS. YOU'RE NOW PART OF PETER ROSENBERG'S TEAM.

**JENN:**
WHO IS THIS?

With crazy ideas raining from heaven, we began looking at starting a new company that would sell frozen steaks on the internet. I mean, if they can do it in Omaha . . . We threw together a team of folks from marketing, IT, product coaches, and operations to look into the concept.

Insane? Maybe. But no more insane than selling ready-to-grill steaks out in our parking lots.

As we were getting better at to-go, Family Packs, and ready-to-grill, sales kept moving up and we were approaching an average of $50,000 per store per week—increasing our revenue 2.5 times in one month. While the sales were encouraging, my big push was to ensure one hundred percent compliance on gloves, masks, and eyewear for our employees. There was some pushback, but I would have none of it. I even had Gina Tobin, our head of training, create a safety-themed T-shirt that I was planning on wearing during an appearance on cable news scheduled for Friday, and we created a safety poster, KENT'S TOP 10, to educate our employees on safe practices at work and off the job. Many of our employees are young and live with roommates, so we taught them concepts such as: Do not share towels, disinfect doorknobs and refrigerator handles, and wear gloves at the gas pump. Thermometers were finally in every store, and we took all employees' temperatures before they started their shifts.

We also broke Roadies into smaller teams—kitchen, packers, and runners—and kept employee interaction among the groups to a minimum. Kitchen staff would leave food for the packers and then step back. The packers boxed everything up in the dining room and took it to the front. They'd leave the food and step back, then runners would get it out to guests' vehicles and take payment. If a member of a runner team, for instance, came down with the virus—which did happen a few times, mostly in the Northeast—then we only had to have five or six people removed (with pay) from the store for a quarantine period rather than losing the entire shift. By wearing masks and gloves, and encouraging our people to be safe at home, we were able to keep such incidents to a minimum.

We considered grabbing another $100 million in funding to make sure we could ride out a full year of downturn if it came to it, but the banks had already switched to a tight credit mentality. Every lending institution we spoke with wanted a ton of information and promises, and interest rates had doubled since we'd gotten the $200 million just two weeks before. I told Tonya, our CFO, to let them know we were good and

# KENT'S Top 10+ FOR SAFETY

## TXRH SAFETY (MANDATORY)

1. Wash Hands
2. Glove Up
3. Mask, Bandanna, Or T-Shirt
4. Eyewear, Safety Goggles, Sunglasses – Be Creative
5. Service With Heart 6-Feet Apart

ROADIES,

THANKS FOR THE AWESOME JOB YOU ARE DOING.

WORK SAFE - BE SAFE

LOVE YALL'S ENERGY, CREATIVITY, AND EFFORT.

STAY SAFE!

*Kent*

## PERSONAL SAFETY

1. Home Kitchen
   - Disposable Towels, No Reusable Towels
   - Eliminate Clutter So It's Easier To Clean
   - Disinfect Knobs, Sink Handle, Refrigerator Handle Often
2. Home Bathroom
   - Don't Share Towels
   - Disinfect Knobs, Toilet Handle After Each Use
3. Grocery/Drugstore – Wear Protective Gear (Gloves, Mask, Eyewear)
4. Gas Pump Handle/Keypad – Bad Germs Exist On Both
5. After Going Anywhere
   - Dispose Gloves
   - Before Entering Car, Sanitize Hands, Door Handles, Steering Wheel, Keys, And Knobs
6. Vaping And Smoking Increase Risk Of Sickness

If You're Living With Roommates, Think Social Distancing In Your Home.
BE SAFE - LIVE SAFE

needed no additional funds. We had what loan money we were going to get, we weren't waiting on Uncle Sam to bail us out, and there were no rich doctors hanging around in our bars to hit up for funding. We were going to have to let store sales get us out of this.

On Friday, I appeared on Fox News wearing my freshly made safety

T-shirt, a mask, and gloves. I was set to answer questions about how we were leading the way in helping America be safe, but the first salvo was about me giving up my salary. I scrambled to come up with a coherent answer. Then the anchor, Martha MacCallum, wanted to know our plan for getting our dining rooms back open. Geez, I don't know, pixie dust? In-store dining had been closed for just three weeks and exactly no one was thinking we'd be open anytime soon. Instead, I talked about our scrappy Roadies selling Family Packs and ready-to-grill steaks in our parking lots.

The last question: What was my message to other CEOs? That was easier. "Let your people think on their own, and they'll figure it out." And that's exactly what our folks were doing. That very weekend more restaurants in Florida and Texas started testing the farmers market idea, and they sold ready-to-grill steaks and partnered with our produce suppliers to sell bags of fresh vegetables. Cars lined up and they sold out in two hours.

As with everything, we had early adopters and those who seemed afraid to try something new. Some of this hesitation may be timidity, but most of the time they are capable and smart leaders who just don't know yet how to make things work in their stores. We had leaders who had been burning it up curbside and with these new ideas. I called them our Big Dogs. And we had some managing partners who couldn't seem to get off the porch, whom we affectionately termed our Puppies. By now, we had paired Big Dogs with the Puppies, and the Puppies started venturing off their porches, having fun, and making sales.

**STEVE MELILLO, regional partner, Northeast**

With Covid-19 being very active in the Northeast, we were committed to employee and guest safety in our parking lots. Our process, our systems, along with our third-party health provider, worked quite well for us.

Our people in the field were carrying our company on their shoulders. Their love for Roadhouse showed through. We are a great place to be in good times, but an even better place to be in tough times.

Toward the end the week, we were touched when Willie Nelson and his sons Lukas and Micah sent us a beautiful video containing an acoustic version of "On the Road Again." They expressed heartfelt thanks to our Roadies for Feeding America safely and for taking care of first responders with free food. Willie's video went out after the Fox News broadcast and bounced around social media, creating a cheerful buzz to start the weekend, which turned out to be a very busy few days thanks to Willie's message to America (he is, you may recall, a partner in two Texas Roadhouse stores in Austin, Texas).

**WEEK 4 RESULTS:**
TXRH Sales Week:  $25.3 million
Store Average:        $49,000

## WEEK 5: APRIL LOVE

It was a somber start to week five as word spread that our regional facilities director in the Northeast had lost his son, who was in his thirties, to the virus. I had spoken to him over the weekend and could only imagine the pain he and his family were going through. With my own two daughters in their thirties, and my son in his twenties, the reality of deaths among young folks hit me hard. I vowed to double down on the safety of our people as a top priority in the weeks ahead.

Easter weekend was coming, and we brainstormed affordable Easter to-go packages. Normally, Easter is a slow time for us, but we expected a rush with everyone spending the holiday at home.

We also started thinking about the future, especially about what our operations would look like in one or two months. Could we operate at 50 percent occupancy? What would that look like, and could we even keep the doors open at those levels? If so, what kind of staffing would we need? I argued that some guests would be nervous about going back inside, so we'd need tents, picnic tables, heaters, power, lighting, and still more to-go containers so people could eat in the fresh air if they wished.

We wanted to create a "safe party in the parking lot," to keep curbside sales and Family Packs rolling, and start ramping up for a vision I had of dining under an outside tent that I lovingly called the Texas Roadhouse Trailer Park.

We also spent time finalizing a partnership with Loop TV to send country music videos to Texas Roadhouse restaurants, as live sports content was almost nonexistent. Our music channel on Spotify was gaining traction, so why not do the same with music videos?

We landed a vendor for our frozen steak business idea and started planning for a fall launch. The motto: "From our kitchen to your home." There were rumors that beef plants might close (a pork plant had already been shuttered) and that was a concern. Yet it was even more of a reason to launch quickly, as frozen steaks might provide a backup supply in a time of need. We'd never used frozen meat in the United States, but we had to do so with our stores in Saudi Arabia, as customs time frames were unreliable in the Middle East.

That week, appreciating that our employees were working incredibly hard in an uncertain world, we sent out another round of stimulus bonuses to our frontline workers. We called it April Love, and included sincere gratitude for their service. We also put together something nice for our food delivery drivers who worked for SYGMA. They deserved April Love as well. After all, if food doesn't get to our stores in the right condition, at the right temperature, and on time, we can't take care of our guests. We gave the drivers food and gift cards.

Who recognizes their delivery drivers? We do, that's who.

**JAMES LAFOE, vice-president and general manager, SYGMA Network**
All across our nation, the onset of Covid-19 proved an especially difficult challenge for essential workers, a group that includes not only frontline health-care workers but food-service delivery drivers. The partnership of Texas Roadhouse

provided a tremendous positive boost for the SYGMA driving staff. They went out of their way to recognize those drivers who continued to deliver to their restaurants. Gift baskets, gift cards, and most especially letters of appreciation provided to our drivers during those early moments of the pandemic provided a much-needed boost and uplifting message to our associates. Only during times of great adversity are the true natures of partnerships revealed.

Finally, I had floated the idea of a pizza delivery test for Bubba's 33, and some of our people had jumped on it. A team from operations, legal, IT, and food found a way.

So, there we were in the middle of a major crisis, creating new business models, starting a music channel, delivering pizza (of all things), and paying bonuses to our workers. Who knew what would happen next?

**JEFF PETTY, regional partner, Southeast**

I think the reason we have done so well is that everyone's a partner in the company. They have skin in the game, they own a piece of what they are doing and they are not just here for a paycheck. Our culture embraces entrepreneurship, where everyone has a voice, that's where awesome ideas happen.

**WEEK 5 RESULTS:**

TXRH Sales Week:  $26.7 million
Store Average:      $52,000

## WEEK 6: WHERE'S THE BEEF?

As the week of April 12 opened up, I jumped on a bunch of calls with groups of stores around the country and learned much that I was able to share with the rest of the company, including some creative plans to reopen inside dining at 25 to 50 percent occupancy, and how we could best feed people outside under tents, on picnic tables, or at picnic tables with umbrellas in the parking lot. I found out that many restaurants were doing large catering orders for factories producing items critical to the country (masks, gloves, face shields, etc.). Also, many were continuing to cater for hospitals, firehouses, police stations, and Meals on Wheels. In some places our people were partnering with churches and selling ready-to-grill products in their parking lots. And they weren't spending much at all to promote it; most of the good word was spread online.

Sales were getting stronger, and based on the results of our farmers market test in a few cities, we were excited to gear up for a big weekend. Federal government stimulus checks were arriving in people's mailboxes, and we planned for almost one hundred restaurants to hold farmers markets. At the last minute, however, we had to cut the number down by about half because of a depleted inventory of aged steaks. Strong sales volume during the previous two weeks and a constricting national supply derailed our plans. Several meat plants had been shuttered across the country as workers had become ill. The plants were being cleaned and sanitized and the workers quarantined—as no one was sure who might and might not have the virus—and it was getting hard to find the meat we needed.

In part, we were victims of our own success. We'd sold so much that week that there wasn't much left in our stores. It did end as a super-strong week but could have been even better. We also knew the upcoming weeks might be tough if we didn't find additional supplies of quality meat. We began searching all corners of the country, hoping to secure more before word spread of the slowdown, which would only be a week away.

That Saturday, Milford and Hilliard, Ohio, two normally decent-performing but not top stores, set one-day sales records for Texas Road-house, feeding guests only in our parking lots. I'm often amazed at the power of our people when you give them the freedom to try, to fail, and to try again and succeed. Milford alone did $68,000 in sales in one day. I called the MP on Sunday morning to congratulate him and ask him how he did it.

> **BRIAN KUTCHER, managing partner, Milford, Ohio**
>
> The entrepreneurial spirit of Roadhouse is instilled in the managing partners. It not only encourages but expects you to come up with new ideas that work for your location. They'll never tell you no. Sometimes it's a flop, sometimes it's a hit. But that empowerment that Kent and the company have given us has really paid off.
>
> That weekend we did our farmers markets in the parking lot, where we sold boxes of fresh produce, ready-to-grill steaks, bread, and margarita mix and iced tea. We planned it, executed it, and advertised the heck out of it on social media, and it blew up more than I could ever have imagined. The line to get in our parking lot was three thousand cars long. Seriously, it backed up to the interstate and we had the Milford police wrap our line around the giant theater across the street. Some people waited five hours to get into the parking lot and none of them were mad. I went up on the roof and thought, *You could be giving away free money and I still wouldn't have waited that long.*

That Sunday, I sent out several sheets of my handwritten notes and diagrams to our stores, giving them the ideas I had handpicked from calls with individual stores on what reopening would look like—inside and outside. In addition, I decided that upon reopening, we would need glass or Plexiglas partitions by the end of June, in all six hundred stores. The following week we came up with a plan, created a bit of chaos as usual, and within two months—thanks to our amazing people—all the stores received and installed their partitions.

**DOUG THOMPSON, chief operating officer**

Kent's not much of a talker, but he is a doer. He will listen, will act quickly, respond, and hold people accountable. Education, motivation, and appreciation based on true partnership is how we operate at Texas Roadhouse. Hospitality, showing people a good time, rules. Whether it's inside our buildings or in our parking lots, Legendary Food, Legendary Service is what we strive to deliver.

**WEEK 6 RESULTS**

TXRH Sales Week:  $32.3 million

Store Average:        $63,000

## OPENING BACK UP

As we closed out April and headed into May, reopening our dining rooms at 25, 33, and 50 percent capacity, we continued to learn from our operators, kept our focus on safety, and kept truck'n with out-of-the-box ideas. We added partitions between booths in six hundred stores in six weeks, we improved our to-go efficiencies, and we became better at online and app orders. But most of all, we stayed true to our people.

Many people have an emotional home that they go to in a crisis. This massive pessimism of thought either crushes you or it produces massive opportunities for those creative people to find new breakthrough innovations. At Texas Roadhouse, we once again discovered that our Roadies can think creatively, make tough decisions, and have the faith to act.

As we successfully navigated the summer, we still had our plans in place if things went south. Unfortunately, that happened in November and we had to pivot back in many states to where we had been in late March and April. Once again, our people delivered. While Covid fatigue was increasing for our people, guests, and the general public, thankfully news of a pending vaccine kept us thinking positive and staying safe through the cold winter ahead (thanks to our board member Kathy Widmer of Johnson & Johnson for keeping us in the loop and updated on the vaccine front).

In a way, 2020 was the ultimate symbol of what we have created at Texas Roadhouse. It was a year that showed our people's ingenuity and grit; a year that displayed the best of what our Roadies had to offer. When the country was scared and grocery-store shelves bare, we kept the lights on, America fed, and our Roadies employed. And for that, I am eternally grateful.

# THE MOST POSITIVE PERSON IN THE ROOM

As I end this narrative 2020 has turned into 2021 and that's it for now: my life so far.

I've enjoyed sharing my story, and I hope you've taken away a tidbit or two to help you attain a more positive and fulfilling life for yourself and your family.

Know that you get what you earn. Life will always have ups and downs, and how you view and deal with obstacles and struggles will define who you want to be and can be. After sixty-five years on planet earth—making good and bad decisions and facing my share of challenges—I've realized that each day and each moment gives us a choice. Happiness does not come with fortune or fame; it's a state of being that resides in our hearts and minds. Fear is inevitable, as is pain. I've never met a successful person who did not overcome some personal hurdle or tragedy. But we can make a choice each and every day to either listen to the negative around us and react emotionally, or we can smile and try to be the most positive person in the room.

If I can offer a little advice after my ride, it is to not let others—whether your friends, family, or those you may work for—define who you can become. Turn off outside negative influences (the TV, media, politics, or social media), and find positive books, messages, or podcasts that can free your mind and inspire you to reach your true potential. Excuses are for others, inspiration requires perspiration and a dedication to staying upbeat.

Achieving something positive was my goal in owning my first restaurant (that and I wanted to earn enough money to buy a home, which is also positive). With the restaurant, I wanted to create a fun place to serve food that I was proud of, all at a value price. More importantly, I wanted the people who would represent the restaurant to be full of smiles, friendliness, and hospitality. I hoped that was either who they really were, or it was who they aspired to be. My life's ambition was, and remains, to search out positive folks and quickly exit those who choose negativity. Because of this, our Roadies tend to be more compassionate and generous with their time, giving back to their communities. And to create a positive company, I've found treating your folks right helps encourage them to treat others right. For us at Texas Roadhouse, having a genuine concern for others' well-being and joy happens one meal at a time. I actually think our Roadies are lucky to work at night because they avoid much of the negativity that so often is found on social media and television in the evening hours.

So my counsel is to be the most positive person in the room. Eventually good things will happen. Find something that excites you and embrace it. Find a mentor, then outwork everyone around you. Dreams and wishes require a daily plan, which will only happen as you charge forward to make each day your masterpiece. Most importantly, never give up. My dream took well over a decade just to get started, with many days in between when giving up would have been the easier option. Then, as you've read, it took another seven years of many ups and downs to get to where success was more probable than failure. That's seventeen years to achieve what people defined as "instant success." Funny, ain't it?

I've come to accept that creating positive experiences is what matters most. As we age, our wealth may ascend but our health is going to descend and eventually we'll shuffle off this mortal coil. But that's just one more parting in a life that's full of them. Our teenage years end and we say goodbye to that time. Our twenties end; as do our thirties and forties (which are usually consumed with our kids); then our empty-nester and old-age phases. Along our journey we may say goodbye to a marriage, a loved one, even our health.

In one life, we live multiple times.

If you talk with folks in their eighties and ask them about their regrets, some of the most common are that they wish they'd spent more face time with family and friends, had the courage to live their lives being more true to themselves (not to the expectations of others), worked less (unless their work was their passion, and the joy of working was to help others), and spent less time worrying about stuff they had no control over. Many also wish they could go back and advise their twenty-year-old self to embrace the positivity of each and every day and, finally, to be nicer to others.

Joy, gratitude, social interaction, empathy, and helping others seem an easy choice to me over generating fear, anger, and sadness. The happiest people embrace the positivity of life and have a genuine concern for others. Many rich people I've met seem to be quite unhappy, even though they have lots of material possessions. Let me put it this way: I love ice cream. The first bowl is great; the second is okay but starts to get too filling; and if you make it to a third you'll be bloated and miserable. Obsessing with always getting more is not the answer. Too many view success as tied to money, power, fame, and influence. Success, instead, is about achieving positive experiences and, here at Roadhouse, that means creating one memorable meal at a time.

Looking back now, I get less satisfaction from how many dollars reside in my bank account than I do in expressing gratitude (which I do with personal handwritten notes), helping others grow, and seeing others achieve big things. I strive for genuine connections with my fellow travelers on this planet. Those kinds of true, lasting relationships take trust, and I savor the positive memories with those friends and family members that bring lasting peace.

I hope you take away from these pages a commitment to be a little more positive and curious, to listen more than you talk, to avoid contributing to negativity, and eventually to become an eighty-year-old who has few or no regrets.

All that's left now are a few "bonus" sections. The first includes my thoughts on leadership, where I will show some examples of those who prevailed that will hopefully provide some additional inspiration. The final features the books that have influenced me on my journey.

Rock on!

Kent

PART III

# A LEADER'S TOOL KIT

# ON LEADERSHIP

*Lead•er•ship (noun): the act of leading a
group of people or an organization*

Each year, there are hundreds, if not thousands, of books written on leadership, from heads of companies to business school professors to Navy SEALs to curling coaches. I typically read a dozen or so of these each year, and many have helped me better define my own thinking on what it means to lead a team effectively.

When I think of great leadership, I think of good listening skills, passion, commitment, honesty, positivity, innovation, and effective communication. Other important terms include clear vision, humility, focus, and empathy. Still other terms include drive, persistence, courage, gratitude, standards, expectations, and accountability. This may sound like a lot, but that's what it takes.

As the leader of a decent-size public company, I could stand here and say it's about big words like Vision and Strategy, as well as Results and Shareholder Value. Well, not really, it's mostly about relationships. Other stuff I will talk about in the next several pages is definitely relevant, but relationships rule the day. Relationships with our folks, suppliers, guests, and our communities are why it's so cool that I get to be in the restaurant business. Our Roadies get to throw a party in our buildings every night, proud to serve our family of guests with something yummy-for-your-tummy, an ice-cold beverage, and some delish rolls. How much fun is that?

Anyway, back to the business-writing stuff. If you study any of the most successful entrepreneurs and leaders of the last hundred years, I think you'll be hard-pressed to say that leaders are born. Most are made. I believe the inner spirit to inspire others lies dormant within all of us, locked and loaded, ready to fire. It doesn't matter if you're an extrovert or an introvert; you can count just as many successful people in either camp. There is also a split as to whether a happy home life as a child contributes to a leader's success later in life.

One thing that stands out in the lives of most leaders is that they each had a job at an early age, and at some point had to overcome a struggle. Abraham Lincoln was born into a farming family and had a strained relationship with his father. Because he was needed as a hand in the fields, his formal education ended before the age of ten. He went on to lose more elections than he won, had to deal with years of debilitating depression, and had two children die in their early years. "Struggle had been his birthright, resilience his keystone strength," wrote biographer Doris Kearns Goodwin in *In Turbulent Times*. She recalls Lincoln having periods of doubt and resulting self-assessment after Senate losses in 1855 and 1858.

Theodore "Teddy" Roosevelt grew up a frail and sickly child. At age twenty-six, he lost his mother and his wife within twelve hours of each other. He then moved from New York to the Badlands of North Dakota, where he worked as a cowboy rancher for several years. Healing, growth, and self-transformation emerged from his personal tragedies—not to mention a killer mustache—with his body now stronger and his spirit resurgent.

Franklin Delano Roosevelt awoke one day at age thirty-eight with the sensation that something was wrong. Within forty-eight hours, paralysis had spread to his limbs, thumbs, toes, back, and bladder. Just like Lincoln and Teddy Roosevelt before him, FDR reinvented himself after this terrible ordeal.

Walt Disney worked hard first on the family farm, then delivered papers twice a day for an overbearing father. He grew up a lonely child but found solace with imaginary friends that he would draw.

Sam Walton (founder of Walmart), Bill Gates (Microsoft), Steve Jobs (Apple), Jack Welch (General Electric), Sara Blakely (Spanx), Herb Kelleher (Southwest Airlines), and Phil Knight (Nike) all worked early in life and each overcame early struggles.

For me, track and cross-country were my chances to prove myself in school. I took my ninety-eight-pound body and shaped it through strenuous training, all while working various jobs to earn money. I agree with the quote from Phil Knight in his autobiography, *Shoe Dog*: "The art of competing, I learned from track, was the art of forgetting. You must forget your limits. You must forget your doubts, your pain, your past. You must forget that internal voice, screaming, begging, not one more step."

I found that around age thirty-six, when I was managing a Bennigan's restaurant in Denver, I could train my mind to be more open to positivity and motivation by reading or listening to motivational books on tape. Whether it was the work of Dr. Norman Vincent Peale or Zig Ziglar, Dr. Wayne Dyer or Tony Robbins, I was digesting as much as I could, accepting positivity, and pushing out negativity. It was tough at the time, as I was going through a separation and eventual divorce. Two books by Norman Vincent Peale, *The Power of Positive Thinking* (1952) and *Enthusiasm Makes the Difference* (1967), were my favorites.

Some of the quotes that stuck out from *The Power of Positive Thinking* include:

"Believe in yourself. A peaceful mind generates power, void of outside noise." (Could not be more relevant today.)

"There's genuine magic in believing. If you expect the worst, you get the worst; and if you expect the best, you will get the best." (That's how you survive three of your first five restaurants failing.)

"When you expect the best, you release a magnetic force in your mind by which the law of attraction tends to bring the best to you. But if you expect the worst, you release from your mind the power of repulsion, which tends to force the best from you. It is amazing how a sustained expectation of the best sets in motion forces which cause the best to materialize."

Watching the Michael Jordan documentary *The Last Dance*, I noticed MJ did not believe in or accept defeat. His work ethic and positive approach to life took him to the top place in NBA history. Jordan, as you may recall, did not make his high school basketball team as a sophomore, but didn't give up and worked his way to high school success, winning a scholarship to my alma mater, the University of North Carolina (*Go 'Heels!*).

Some of the most relevant quotes from *Enthusiasm Makes the Difference* are:

"Mental ventilation: Empty your mind by removing dark thoughts, regrets, resentments. Write them down and release them."

In this regard, Phil Jackson, the famous NBA coach, in his last team meeting with the group who had won six championships, had his Chicago Bulls players write down what the team had meant to them and then share their thoughts with each other. He turned off the lights and set fire to the thoughts in a coffee can. It was a powerful symbol of saying goodbye, according to many who participated.

Rewind to when I was thirty-five and working at a KFC in Charlotte, North Carolina. I was experimenting with new menu items I had created and was testing them with customers, with great results. I had permission my from immediate boss, but he had said that if I got busted he would not back me up. Of course, I did get caught. When my regional manager flew in to scold me, he handed me the book 7 *Habits of Highly Successful People* as he kindly informed me that I was probably not the corporate type. With my freethinking, lack of an MBA, and rogue mentality, I was probably never going to get promoted, and it was more likely that I'd be fired. I appreciated his brutal honesty. I read the book and it refired my desire to start my own restaurant—you know, just one.

Stephen Covey's book was an amazing read and I would like to paraphrase the seven habits with respect to the help they gave me to keep desire alive:

## 7 HABITS OF HIGHLY EFFECTIVE PEOPLE BY STEPHEN COVEY (AS PARAPHRASED BY ME):

### 1. BE PROACTIVE.

First, you have to take responsibility for your life (not blaming circumstances, conditions, parents, education, etc.). No matter what's happened to you, you have the ability to control your attitude, emotions, and feelings. It's either act or be acted upon. Are you aware of your circle of concern and influence, or do you waste time thinking about things you will never control? Proactive focus generates positive energy, while reactive focus generates negative energy. That will lead to an unhappy and unfulfilled life.

### 2. BEGIN WITH THE END IN MIND.

All things are created twice. There's the mental or first creation (for me, a visualization, writing it down, and on occasion waking up in the middle of the night and remembering a dream in which my visualization became a reality). Then there's a second creation, physically doing something (like creating a business plan and approaching potential investors, even if it means getting a lot of rejection). Rejection became a game for me. I kept score and each rejection just became a number.

### 3. PUT FIRST THINGS FIRST.

I believe in an independent will to act, hour by hour, day by day, and month by month, activated by practicing effective self-management. I have for years retreated to my office at precisely nine p.m. on Sunday nights to plan and schedule my upcoming week. I settle on personal goals and objectives; and I budget time for business, family, and for individual physical and mental development. I also review my results from the previous week (how did I do?). This can take as little as one hour or as long as two.

## 4. THINK WIN/WIN.

In reading 7 *Habits*, I learned that you have six options when interacting with people in business: (1) win/win, (2) win/lose, (3) lose/win, (4) lose/lose, (5) win, or (6) no deal. We are generally taught, whether it's sports or our corporate lives, that there are winners and losers. In our early days, I was all about chasing Outback, Longhorn, or Lone Star. I was driven to beat them. That's what got me up every morning. At some point I became more driven to improve, be better, and so I focused on us, not them. That's when our business really skyrocketed. Interesting, ain't it?

## 5. SEEK FIRST TO UNDERSTAND, THEN TO BE UNDERSTOOD.

Most people do not listen with the intent to understand. They are either getting their thoughts together to speak, hoping you're in agreement with them, or just catching part of what you are saying. We have two ears, one mouth, and should use them in that ratio.

And the hard reality of this is, if you are not listening to others, guess what? They are not going to listen to you. I found out through two marriages that, generally, my opinion wasn't wanted that often. My significant other just wanted an empathetic ear. Us guys generally suck in this area. We want to fix stuff that our partners don't want us to fix. Just sayin'. A good opener for us might be: "Do you want my evaluation, my advice, or do you want me to find my inner silence, listen, and provide empathy and support?"

## 6. SYNERGIZE.

"I take as my guide the hope of a saint: In crucial things, unity; in important things, diversity; in all things, generosity," George H. W. Bush (first Bush president). Sounds cool, short, direct, well said.

Synergy means the whole is greater than the sum of the various parts. I've always enjoyed creating teams that have different thoughts, backgrounds, opinions, etc. I find that throwing a crazy idea out, sitting back and listening and watching others debate, always opens the door to newer thoughts, better ideas, and new processes. Involving people—allowing them to have a voice and be heard—generally brings us to a group decision that now everyone owns. And if you own it, and if you are an equal part of the team (not caring about who has what title), you are going to do your part and definitely not want to let the team down.

## 7. SHARPEN THE SAW.

In his book, Covey speaks of the four dimensions of individuals: (1) physical (exercise, nutrition, and stress management), (2) spiritual (values, commitment, study, and meditation), (3) mental (reading, visualizing, planning, writing), and (4) social/emotional (service, empathy, synergy, security).

Cardiovascular exercise gives us energy and endurance. The spiritual dimension starts when you're a kid with the values your parents teach you, and maybe a relative, teacher, spouse, partner, or friend later in life. Mental development has become the most challenging objective in today's world. According to various studies, our TVs are on an average of thirty to forty hours a week in most homes in the United States. That number used to be higher, but people are now using other devices (smartphones, tablets, or computers). Reading and writing have increasingly taken a backseat, as have motivation and original and creative thought.

As depressing as that can seem, it's not too late. Collecting phones and turning off the TV for just a few hours each night can become the positive change you and your kids might need in order to live your own unique and positive life. It's your call.

## ON MENTORS AND FAILURE

Finding role models and mentors also seems to be a constant trait among those successful people I talked about early in this section. Abe Lincoln was mentored by a highly successful lawyer named Stephen Logan. Teddy Roosevelt had Henry Cabot Lodge, a Massachusetts congressman and friend, as his mentor. FDR had, in his wife, Eleanor, a strong partner and mentor who helped guide him in the creation of his New Deal. Walt Disney honed his craft with fellow illustrator Ubbe Iwerks (that name is not a typo). Oprah had Maya Angelou. Bill Gates had Paul Allen. Steve Jobs had Steve Wozniak. Herb Kelleher had Rollin King and John Parker. And Phil Knight had a mentor in Oregon track coach Bill Bowerman.

I had several mentors in my life, starting with my parents. My mom's compassion, love of people, energy, and enthusiasm were infectious. I was in awe of my dad's work ethic, drive, and organizational skills. My high school track coach, Richard Bealmear, was a profoundly influential mentor, who never gave up on this frail and skinny kid with no natural talent. Watching Tony Waldrop at North Carolina break the world indoor mile record inspired me, as did viewing from afar the career of John Y. Brown as he grew Kentucky Fried Chicken and then became one of Kentucky's finest governors. And I was very impressed, in my early days at Bennigan's, when I observed one of the restaurant industry's class acts: Norman Brinker, founder of Steak and Ale as well as Bennigan's. Also at Bennigan's, I befriended the other area manager in Denver, Steve Ortiz, whom I unfortunately didn't work for but from whom I solicited advice and shared books and tapes with.

Ask any successful person, and I guarantee they'll tell you that they've had at least one mentor (and probably more) who helped shape their success.

I mentioned earlier in this section that almost all of the most successful leaders/entrepreneurs succeeded only after multiple failures. These people, like myself, started out being very good at failing. But notice how these same folks, when they write their autobiographies, love to talk about their failures—especially about what they learned and how they bounced back—usually against steep odds. Comments often heard are, "I was too dumb to know when to quit," or, "Failure was just a place where I lived, but I was okay with it because it was my choice." Phil Knight once said, "Fear of failure . . . will never be our downfall as a company. Not that any of us thought we wouldn't fail, in fact, we had every expectation that we would. But when we did fail, we had the faith that we'd do it fast, learn from it, and be better for it."

I like what Steve Jobs said about Apple. He believed the company succeeded because it embraced failure. He said, "You've got to be willing to act, and you've got to be willing to fail. You've got to be willing to crash and burn. If you are afraid of failing, you won't get very far." Even the great physicist Albert Einstein said, "A person who never made a mistake never tried anything new." He spent his career revising his early papers as he or other scientists found errors or better ways of thinking about problems, but that never stopped him from innovating. He was unabashed about tossing something out to the academic community and letting others weigh in on its worth, and his willingness to break with the status quo and fail now and then led to revolutions in scientific thinking.

Many people today feel that others are somehow in charge of their destiny. They're full of resentment and are quick to blame others for their circumstances. Some, who benefited from "nicer" upbringings and didn't have to work as hard as their peers, may have been given too much. They rely on constant immediate gratification and believe they are entitled to or owed something by the universe. Unfortunately, neither bitterness nor entitlement will garner any real happiness or success. As Abe Lincoln and other great leaders have shown, change, at whatever age, is possible if one makes the choice, is willing to change their mind-set, and does the work. George Foreman was forty-five when he worked his way back into shape to become the oldest heavyweight champion in boxing history. He retired and entered a new phase in life as a minister and a businessman—making more than $200 million endorsing the fat-reducing grills that helped him get fit again.

In the words of a friend of mine who passed away some twenty-five years ago: "Shut up (I probably talked too much), stop whining (complaining never solved a problem), and get a life (i.e., make a decision, create a plan, and work like hell to get there)." Succinct and not too subtle!

Let's go back to Texas Roadhouse, circa 1993–95. Three of our first five restaurants were failing, money was tight, and change was necessary as disaster was imminent. Fear of failure was a more motivating factor than striving for success at that point. I knew 1996 was going to be a critical year for our survival. That was the year a book called *Nuts* came out. It's about Herb Kelleher and Southwest Airlines, written by Kevin and Jackie Freiberg. It changed how I thought about business, how I was choosing people, training them, and how our culture at Texas Roadhouse needed to evolve.

## ON CULTURE

I have been lucky over the years to have spoken not only with Kelleher about culture, but with Chick-fil-A founder Truett Cathy and Bennigan's founder Norm Brinker. Culture was always a large part of the conversation with these great leaders and what made their companies great. Colleen Barrett, former president of Southwest Airlines (and Kelleher's right hand), said: "The Warrior mentality, the very fight to survive, is truly what created our culture at Southwest."

I also spoke with these great founders about how their companies could keep their culture consistent (or not) when the founder is gone. Some succeed in this (Southwest) and others do not (Bennigan's).

What follows are summaries of my top ten ideas about culture, which I picked up from *Nuts*, and which I believe stand out as must-dos for any business—from a stand-alone store to a multinational company. They are critical in the effort to sustain positive culture.

### KENT'S TOP TEN TAKEAWAYS FROM *NUTS* ABOUT CULTURE:

1. Keep things simple (manage in good times for bad times).
2. Hire for spirit, spunk, and enthusiasm (then train for skill).
3. Do whatever it takes (you'll see very little traffic as you're going the extra mile).
4. Develop a genuine interest in the knowledge of others (ask to learn, listen to learn, watch to learn).
5. Own mistakes, share mistakes, learn from mistakes (and move on).
6. Focus on individuals and capabilities, not titles (deal with people, not positions).
7. Don't let rules, systems, and procedures be your guide.
8. Create a lean organization (one in which it is difficult to hide poor performance and one that continually stamps out bureaucracy).
9. Think like an owner about your job and your life (owners focus on results regardless of who's watching).
10. Make your organizational and personal mission, vision, and values clear (and make sure to recognize others, celebrate, and have fun along the way).

With these thoughts in mind, I started taking action at Texas Roadhouse with an extreme sense of urgency. We measured, rewarded, recognized, and promoted those who got results, those who also embodied our culture. We were focused like a laser on developing our people and promoting our unique "crazy" culture.

With our ramp-up in growth following the infusion of the private money we raised in 1998, all the way through to our IPO in 2004, we managed to bring some very talented people on board and tried our best to maintain standards and not get in our people's way. When our market partners and managing partners were given ownership and lots of autonomy, they created their own subcultures within our overall company culture.

I learned that maintaining a culture takes focus, planning, and a dedicated budget. I also found that as a few people evolve, get promoted, and gain more personal wealth, their focus and intensity can sometimes fall off. Customers (guests) and employees definitely notice, and if you, as the senior-most leader, are not paying attention, these people can gradually take a company down. That's why it is critical to stay connected to your frontline folks, and spot and confront those who lose focus before they screw up.

More knowledge from a book (Really! Last one. Sorry, but not sorry): There is an interesting manual that was used during World War II but has since been declassified. In 1944, the Office of Strategic Services (OSS)—the predecessor of today's CIA—issued the *Simple Sabotage Field Manual*, which detailed sabotage techniques designed to demoralize the enemy. One section focused on eight incredibly subtle, but devastatingly destructive, tactics for sabotaging the decision-making processes of organizations. The manual was written decades ago by intelligence experts in order to bring down enemy organizations through subterfuge, but, perhaps ironically, many of the tactics described in its pages thrive in organizations today. In some cases, they are even encouraged. They are:

1.  Do everything through "channels." (I found this at KFC in 1990 and it's a motivation killer. New ideas from the field? Shortcuts to expedite decisions? *Fuhgeddaboudit.*)
2.  Make "speeches." (If you are in a meeting and the leader is continually monologuing about his views and opinions rather than asking questions and listening, then he/she is most likely in the wrong seat on the bus.)
3.  Form lots of committees. (Large companies usually get nothing accomplished because they always have to refer things to a committee for further study. And those committees are often huge. There's a time and a place for committees, but I have a two-pizza rule. If it takes more than two pizzas to feed the committee, it has too many people to make a smart, quick decision.)
4.  Focus on irrelevant issues. (Too much time and too many resources are spent on issues that some leaders find personally relevant but have

nothing to do with moving a company forward. The leaders themselves have become irrelevant, and when those leaders are removed, the issues magically disappear.)

5. Haggle over wording. (The fewer lawyers involved, the more savings and less time wasted.)

6. Refer back to earlier decisions. (Going back and rehashing old decisions slows organizations down. People's lack of self-confidence in decision-making must be quickly headed off at the pass.)

7. Advocate caution. (In other words, rehash, evaluate, study, slow down, and become a flat squirrel—those people who are incapable of making decisions eventually get run over.)

8. Worry that it's not my call or responsibility. (Someone like that would be called "not promotable.")

Oh, here's a bonus thought that the OSS forgot:

9. Sabotage by cc-ing everyone. (It's called covering your ass and is based on the delusion that people are actually reading your twentieth dissertation this week. This only clogs people's e-mail in-boxes when the truth is that electronic missives are never a substitute for personal dialogue. Pick up the phone or go talk to the person face-to-face.)

Finally: Everyone who writes a book on leadership has their own top three, five, or ten leadership ideas. I figured why not join the club. So, here is my version:

**L** is for Listen (two ears, one mouth, use them in that ratio).

**E** is for Empathize (seek to understand, walk a mile in others' shoes).

**A** is for Authentic (being true to who you are—you define you, don't let others do it).

**D** is for Decisive (decisions are firm, action is required, no flat squirrels—results matter).

**E** is for Energy (quickness, strength, vitality, ability to energize others).

**R** is for Relationships (it's about people, baby).

**S** is for Support (honest feedback, encouragement, continued direction, got
   your back).

**H** is for Humble (modest, not flashy, putting others first, sense of humor).

**I** is for Integrity (truthful, do what you say, make your momma proud).

**P** is for Passion (embracing the positivity of family, work, and life in general).

As you can see, I believe there's a lot of the good, the bad, and the
sometimes ugly involved in moving a group toward a leadership-driven
forward focus. Good judgment comes from experience, and experience
comes from bad judgment. Wisdom consists in knowing the difference.

I'll give the last word to a leadership expert who isn't me:

> A leader is someone who influences others' thoughts, emotions, and
> actions for the greater good. Leaders do what's right, not what's popu-
> lar. They create culture, they don't follow it.
>
> Tony Robbins

And then, finally, as Bob Marley once said, "Love the life you live,
live the life you love."

Hope you enjoyed the ride, peace out.

# BOOKS I DIG

I read *The Power of Positive Thinking* back in the 1980s in an attempt to generate more positivity in my life. Lessons learned: energy, peace of mind, and a life filled with positive thoughts.

Lessons learned from *Enthusiasm Makes the Difference*: Enthusiasm sharpens your mind, creates motivation, and assists in overcoming fear and building self-confidence.

*The 7 Habits of Highly Effective People* is an exceptional book, giving people the fundamentals to balance personal, family, and professional goals to live a more fulfilled life.

*Leadership: In Turbulent Times* features Abraham Lincoln, Teddy Roosevelt, Franklin Roosevelt, and Lyndon Johnson. Four presidents who overcame dramatic reversals and emerged stronger and more resilient.

*Forbes Greatest Business Stories of All Time* profiles great business leaders who, through hard work, self-reliance, courage, and ambition, changed not only their companies but the industries they were in.

American legend Willie Nelson writes about his journey from Abbott, Texas, through local honky-tonks to national stardom in *It's a Long Story*. The singer, songwriter, actor, and author takes the reader through his amazing life.

Sam Walton, of Walmart, tells his story about entrepreneurship, risk, and hard work in *Made in America*. He risked everything to chase his dream. A true American success story based on simple traditional principles that make America the land of opportunity.

Jack Welch, one of the most admired business leaders in the world, blew up the bureaucracy at GE and made the company a respected global giant, as he describes in *Jack: Straight from the Gut*.

*Steve Jobs* is the riveting story of Steve Jobs, a very intense and creative entrepreneur who revolutionized personal computers, music, phones, digital publishing, and animated movies.

Phil Knight, the man who created Nike with Oregon coach Bill Bowerman, takes us through his amazing journey in *Shoe Dog*. Humble, candid, funny, and dynamic, he explains how he defied risks, setbacks, ruthless competitors, and government bullies. Phil is tops in my mind as a true American success story.

*Onward* is the remarkable story of Starbucks's transformation by Howard Schultz, who grew the company to global stardom, only to have to come out of retirement to transform his company again when it had run adrift.

*American Icon* is the story of Alan Mulally, a humble engineer who famously engineered two major turnarounds, at Boeing and then the Ford Motor Company. His ingenuity, grit, and optimism propelled the re-emergence of two struggling companies.

Read the timeless wisdom of legendary basketball coach John Wooden in *Wooden*. He shares his personal philosophy on family, achievement, success, and excellence. Includes personal messages from Kareem Abdul-Jabbar, Denny Crum, and Bill Walton.

*Back from the Dead* is Bill Walton's fascinating journey of resilience, reinvention, and success—both on and off the court. His victory over adversity and his unique positive focus are truly inspirational.

*Built to Last* is the study of visionary companies whose core values, cultural norms, and business strategies made them standout brands that have stood the test of time.

*Leading with Gratitude* is a brilliant book that managers can use as a blueprint to develop more effective people leadership skills. From the thought leaders in building "All In" cultures, Adrian Gostick and Chester Elton.

Motivational guru Tony Robbins shares strategies for mastering emotions, your body, your relationships, your finances, and your life in *Awaken the Giant Within*.

Two of the world's most thoughtful spiritual leaders talk about how we can find joy no matter what we face in life in *The Book of Joy*, by His Holiness the Dalai Lama and Archbishop Desmond Tutu.

# ACKNOWLEDGMENTS

First, thanks to co–book dude Chester Elton, who has spoken to our company several times and written some best-selling business books. He invited me to the 100 Coaches cool-people-get-together, hosted by fellow Louisville cat Marshall Goldsmith in San Diego in January 2020. There we discussed the possibility of me one day writing the story of Texas Roadhouse, somewhat inspired by our speaker that day, Alan Mulally, former CEO of Ford. After reading the book about Alan (*American Icon* by Bryce Hoffman), I became somewhat motivated to tell my own story.

Thanks as well to Adrian Gostick, who became my weekly editor during lockdown. I would handwrite pages, take pictures of each, and text them to him in batches. I think that getting sixty or seventy texted pages on a Sunday night (obviously not the usual e-mail action) may have tripped him out. Still, it was nice that he was cool and didn't let my incorrect use of the English language, strange humor, and bizarre thinking get watered down. And to those English teachers I had in high school and college who gave me mostly C and C– grades, you can respectfully kiss my grits.

And mostly thanks are due to Travis Doster, Texas Roadhouse VP of communications, government relations, and public affairs. Travis was a constant pain in my ass while I was writing this book, noting that my parents, my high school track coach, and early-mentor-then-partner John Y. Brown (former Kentucky governor) were all in their eighties—most of them in their late eighties—and I needed to get on with it. I'm grateful that he persisted. With the 2020 ski season shortened due to the pandemic, I immediately slipped into crisis mode in order to be able to lead our company. Thankfully, I turned off my TV (except for the thirty minutes I allowed myself per day), the screen of which was filled with media types and politicians who couldn't help but fan the flames of despair, panic, and division nonstop. So a special thanks to them folks for annoying me enough to tune them out, become more productive, communicate and listen to our people, pivot, try various solutions weekly, while still having time (usually from seven p.m. until one or two or three in the morning) to listen to music, read at least one book each week, and write the book you are currently holding in your hands.

Finally, to my loving parents, kids, grandkids, family, ex-wives, past pets, current pets (goats mostly), coaches, friends, Roadie family (past and present), Shelly, Karen, and Tamara, thanks for the memories, stories, and assorted other thoughts that have contributed to this book. Lastly, thanks to my good buddy Willie Nelson. Thanks for providing assistance to forget the shit that I can't remember and probably don't want to remember that ain't in the book.

Later.

# AFTERWORD

*Kent Taylor*
*September 27, 1955–March 18, 2021*

When we began the journey to write this book, Kent was concerned that many of the prominent figures in his story were older. He wanted to be sure they would live to see the book published. Never in our wildest dreams did we think it would be Kent who would not live to see the final product in bookstores or in the hands of the people he loved so much.

The former high school and collegiate track champion ended his life in March 2021 after struggling with severe and debilitating tinnitus, a result of contracting Covid-19. Despite many medical efforts, the condition—which affected both ears and worsened considerably over time—was the one hurdle Kent could not overcome.

My last conversation with Kent was about this book, *Made from Scratch*. We talked about the photos, the timeline, and discussed plans for a dinner celebration now that his life story was finally with the publisher and would soon become a reality.

Like everything he did, Kent poured his heart and soul into this project. He left no stone unturned and did so in his typical unconventional way. For example, he wrote the book entirely by hand, on graph paper, with his trademark blue erasable pen. The first few chapters he sent to his longtime assistant, Shelly McGowen, to be typed. Soon after, he decided he couldn't wait until morning to get typed pages so would send the handwritten pages directly to me and our two editors—Adrian

Gostick and Chester Elton. We usually got these texted photos of his pages around midnight or one a.m. The *ding* of incoming texts always let you know that, while you were asleep, Kent was hard at work.

Kent reviewed everything he wrote numerous times after we typed it up, and he'd make changes in pen and then take other photos and text those changes back. While it may not have been the most efficient process, like most things in his life it worked for him.

Kent made edits even down to the last minute, which was also typical. His final concerns also say a lot about this wonderful man. While Kent could be tough and abrupt at times, on his final read he wanted to get rid of any "negativity." Kent never dwelled on negatives in the past and he did not want his autobiography to, either.

By the end of his editing, Kent was proud of his book. *Made from Scratch* has become his goodbye letter to some, a thank-you to others, and for many a playbook for success. He wanted people to know that success is built on failure and to encourage them to keep on trying and working.

Kent often urged Roadies, "Get into my mind and think how I think." Once someone did that, it was glorious for Kent because it cut down on the time it took to explain something, which appealed to his need for speed! It also built trust and allowed him to delegate more. Once you thought like Kent, you never would think the same again. *Made from Scratch* will help many Roadies get in the head of Kent Taylor for decades to come.

I will close with a quote that my friend Kent used in his last communication with employees that sums up his impact and legacy on others.

> Only those who will risk going too far can possibly find out how far one can go.
>
> —T. S. Eliot

Kent not only pushed himself far but pushed everyone around him to go further than ever we thought possible. I hope after you read *Made from Scratch* you are inspired to go even further than you could have imagined . . . that would be Kent's dream for you.

TRAVIS DOSTER
Vice President of Communications for
Texas Roadhouse and friend of Kent Taylor
March 31, 2021

## ABOUT THE AUTHOR

**KENT TAYLOR'S** rise was an eighteen-year overnight success story that was born on a bar napkin.

Kent was the founder and chairman of the board of Texas Roadhouse restaurants. After several stints with ordinary restaurant companies, Kent finally launched his dream of an extraordinary restaurant concept in Clarksville, Indiana, in 1993. His vision was clear: to create an affordable Texas-style restaurant with hearty steaks, killer ribs, and ice-cold beer. But the problem was finding others to believe in that dream.

Kent pitched his idea to anyone who would give him five minutes and many who would not give him the time of day. He was turned down more than eighty times trying to raise money for his idea. He even chased basketball great Larry Bird in an airport trying to sell him on his idea, but Kent was too slow to catch the future Hall of Famer.

Kent finally found a cure for his ailing dream when three Elizabethtown, Kentucky, doctors agreed to provide $300,000 in start-up capital. Using a cocktail napkin, Kent sketched out the design of the first Texas Roadhouse for his new partners.

Kent and his new partners' goal was to have ten restaurants in ten years. This plan hit a snag after three of the first five restaurants failed. But Kent learned some very valuable (and expensive) lessons and vowed not to ever repeat those mistakes. As a result, the next restaurant featured a revamped menu, much-improved recipes, updated decor, and a better-trained staff. The changes would help redefine the brand and help launch its success.

The company currently has more than 620 restaurants in 49 states and ten countries.

A Louisville native, Mr. Taylor attended the University of North Carolina on a track scholarship where he earned a bachelor of science degree. A self-described ski bum, Kent enjoyed the slopes in Colorado and Utah. He was also a lifelong Rolling Stones fan, having attended more than a hundred Rolling Stones concerts.

Mr. Taylor was an active supporter of a number of organizations, including Habitat for Humanity, Special Olympics Kentucky, and the Kentucky Nature Conservancy. He sat on the board for Homes For Our Troops. He had three children and six grandchildren.